The
LAST YEAR
of
the
W A R

Shirley Nelson

NORTHCOTE BOOKS
Wheaton, Illinois

NORTHCOTE BOOKS
Shaw Publishers

ISBN 0-87788-484-6

Library of Congress Cataloging-in-Publication Data
Nelson, Shirley.
      The last year of the war / Shirley Nelson.
          p.   cm.
      ISBN 0-87788-484-6
      I. Title.
  PS3564.E476L37   1989
  813'.54—dc20
                                  89-35349
                                  CIP

99 98 97 96 95 94 93 92 91 90

10 9 8 7 6 5 4 3 2 1

For all my families

❧ ONE

We have a little sister,
and she hath no breasts:
what shall we do for our
sister in the day when
she shall be spoken for?

Song of Solomon 8:8

A dozen students are present around the long white table, four men, eight women. Jo claims she is one of them, the rather scant person, third from the left clockwise—though it is hard to tell. Most of her face is hidden by the glass of milk she is drinking, and the top of her head is sliced off to make room for the caption: "Every meal an occasion." The dark, shoulder-length hair could be anybody's, she admits, but those are her eyebrows. She'd know them anywhere. They hover, straight and a little untidy, just above the rim of her glass. They say nothing.

Examining the picture now, Jo marvels that a camera would expose so little. What was concealed in the living moment should in some way have betrayed itself on film. She wonders why the table is right side up, why the walls are plumb, or why, at the very least, the glass of milk is not exploding in her hand. Yet a person could search the scene forever and discover not the slightest token of turbulence or disorder.

The picture is in *Cornerstone*, yearbook of Calvary Bible Institute. It is lunchtime, a day in midwinter. Outside, snow hangs low in the Chicago sky. Inside, lights blaze across the vast dining room. There are close to a hundred tables, all full, and a thousand voices in conversation sustain a pleasant roar. At Jo's table, one girl holds out a plate of bread (at the photographer's instructions) and two of the boys reach for it, smiling broadly at her generosity.

The bread was stale, Jo remembers that. It usually was, which she considered odd, because often when they stood in the noisy, chatty lines waiting for meals to begin, she thought she smelled rolls baking. But they were always served commercial white bread, a day or two old.

Not that it mattered. A thousand people is a lot to make fresh bread for, and nobody cared. They were too busy and happy. Happiness was a kind of badge at Calvary; it was not only nice to be happy, it was right. It was a sign that things were as they should be on the inside. But while in such an atmosphere *un*happiness was frequently viewed with judgment or shame, it's only fair to add the obvious: A school cannot be held accountable for the inward state of every student. Some things will happen wherever you are, and that is where Jo was, at that school, in that city.

Even so, she is reluctant to insist she ever lived in Chicago at all. In a way she didn't. She scarcely visited the Loop, never shopped at Marshall Field's, never strolled in Lincoln Park, and walked the shores of Lake Michigan only once. Aside from some half-interested peeks in the windows of the imperious stores on North Michigan Avenue, she never saw anything but the worst of the city. The school was pressed in by slums— brown tenements sagged for blocks in every direction.

But there again, she never said to herself, *I live in the slums of Chicago.* She lived at Calvary, the center of which was Van Housen Hall, twelve vigorous stories of new concrete and brick, accessible through heavy oaken doorways. Behind this spread a courtyard, the remains of the old Putney Street cul-de-sac off Chicago Avenue, cobblestoned yet, and crisscrossed brightly with students on their way to the Pastry Shop or the post office. There was not a tree nor a blade of grass in sight on all the campus, but you could hear music at any time of the day. Students sang almost constantly—before every meal and every class, at social functions and any group gathering. Trumpets and pianos rang from the Music Building practice rooms in a tumult of exercises. More than that, in-dividual voices soared up stairwells and floated down halls. The whole inner life of the school, it seemed to Jo, was swept along on currents of spontaneous song.

Calvary made no undue claims for itself, nor does it today. It is neither a college nor a seminary. For the eighty years of its respectable history in the Bible School movement, it has stayed true to its original purpose, which is to train pastors, teachers, missionaries, and church musicians. "Protestant, interdenominational, Christ-centered, evangeli-cal, tuition-free," said Jo's catalogue. "A boot camp of Christian service." Though one must be careful, reading that. The reference was to practical experience, not military order. What to outsiders might have appeared to be a rigid enforcement of control was actually a discipline students had already accepted for themselves before entering the school.

Even that is not phrasing it right. They had simply spurned the world's frenetic search for empty pleasure. They did not smoke or drink or dance or attend the theater or concern themselves unduly with fashions and fads. Girls of the world might pluck their eyebrows into little flying commas and apply bright red nail polish and lipstick. Girls at Cal did not. At most they wore a hint of rouge and powder and touched their eyelashes with Vaseline. Jo liked to think she could always spot a Calvary girl on the street, her face cool and relaxed (if a bit pale) among the strained and the painted, and sometimes she thought she could tell the boys too, by a certain clearness in their eyes.

Oh, she remembers a lot, or thinks she does—though the school is not likely to remember Jo Fuller. There is no reason it should. She stirred no widespread notice and left nothing behind of either spiritual or tangible value—except her red boots and several other small articles, mislaid here and there about the campus. Her experience is untraceable. Even the scenes of it have been remodeled out of existence. Van Housen Hall still stands, mellowing as fine buildings ought to, but the courtyard and the old Music Building are gone entirely, the dining hall has been relocated, and the dormitory where she lived—slept, studied, prayed, washed her hair, and dared at last to die (or so she thought)—is now a parking lot. And Calvary goes on as always, its students still happy—genuinely, lastingly, and infectiously. Anyone may go see.

On the early September day Jo left for school, Nazi forces were retreating from Belgium and France, and things looked good in the Pacific as well. News had spread that the war would be over by the end of the year. As if that were the cause of a sudden juggling of troops around the country, the train from Boston to Chicago was jammed. Scores of servicemen squeezed by one another in the swaying aisles, in a constant parade to the smoking cars and the toilets.

Jo had an end seat that would not recline and was thankful to have a seat at all. She shared it with a sailor who looked too young to be in uniform. Maybe he was, because he fell instantly asleep, like a child, his white hat tilted over his eyes. On and on he slept, across the afternoon and night, all the way to Cleveland. Jo herself did not sleep. She slipped instead into a reverie of motion, the hours ground out in ceaseless iron rhythms. Some of that time the sailor's head was heavy on her shoulder. He became like an old friend, as if they had been here for years in this strange relationship. Once, giving herself to a moment of tenderness, she let her head drop down to his, but the stiff edge of his cap jabbed her in the cheek. So she spent the entire trip upright with this boy sprawled against her, snoring and sweating and taking most of the room. She didn't mind. Sitting straight up that way at the end of the darkened car, she felt like a supervisor, in charge of all these wartime people, helpless in their awkward sleep. So passed the night, poignant with uniforms and responsibility.

More than that kept her awake. It was important to feel herself leaving—going, on the way, a decision completed by action. For a while, crossing New York State, Massachusetts had seemed to stretch along behind them on the tracks, a corner of it caught on the caboose. Then it snapped and flew back into place, getting smaller and smaller as she sped away from it. She imagined Garfield in miniature, tucked between Framingham and Boston, elms, lake, the yellow shoe factory where this summer she had beaten the record for piece work (such a pathetic victory) stitching tongues into G.I. combat boots. On a hill two miles west of town her home hid itself in cedars and juniper, the tiny brown-shingled house where the four of them had merged and overlapped for as long as she could remember. Below it, Cannons' farm settled amply behind its maples, and the gravel road from the old quarry, joining the road to town, rose and fell between the empty fields and the small swamp that had once hissed with her fears. She put herself on the road, hurrying (late again) toward the tall brick high school where she had smothered in boredom along with everybody else—girls who sneaked off to the lavatory to preen with dirty pink combs, and boys doodling submarines on arithmetic paper and sending frantic signals about cigarettes.

That was over. She was not there, she was here, somewhere just south of Lake Erie. It was over and she was terribly relieved, however much she wished she had done better. For there was no question that she had botched the job. The possibilities had seemed enormous for a while, in the first sweep of gladness and certainty at the beginning of her junior year. She had thought she might win the whole town. Staring out the train window now at the dark landscape, she could feel it still, that sense of being ready for anything, every morning.

She had heard of a high school boy in Toronto whose conversion brought such a change in his life that he was allowed to take over the assembly hall and tell everybody the story, and dozens of his friends were saved as a result. She'd have taken an assembly if she'd been offered the chance. Sometimes she had a crazy mental picture of herself flying up to the school roof and shouting down at everybody who went by. But the boy from Canada was a wild kid who had suddenly straightened out. The principal had challenged him—"If you mean this, tell the whole school"— so he had. It was easier for him, in a way. People knew he was different, right at the start, and probably asked him how it had happened.

Nobody asked her that. She had to initiate things herself. Maybe the mistakes lay there, in her impatience. She had considered various bold measures, such as giving an oral book report on the Bible in English class. She was reading it madly, the New Testament, stumbling over the archaic language as if it were a rocky landscape, searching out the streams and springs. She carried her Bible to school on top of her books, wishing it were red or orange instead of black, bowed her head to say grace over her sandwich at noon, and bought supplies at the New England Fellowship Bookstore in Boston, pennant-shaped stickers that said "Christ Died for You," a ring stamped with "Living for Jesus," and a big green campaign button with a yellow question mark on it. She stuck the pennants on her book covers, put the ring on her engagement finger (because that was where it fit), and for a week wore the button on her coat lapel.

"It means: Are you born again?" she answered over and over, praying for boldness and wisdom to explain it right, her heart pounding and her mouth going dry.

That big button disturbed her now. Yet it had seemed completely right at the time, *because* of its wrongness. Tact had appeared as guile, a way to make matters easier for herself and for others. She needed to crack through something, her own self-protection maybe. Was she willing to seem ridiculous? she had asked herself. Embarrass her friends? Humiliate her family? It was worth all that or it was worth nothing.

People thought she was kidding, and when she convinced them she was not they were wary and aloof. Gloria Logan was stunned. All right, yes, she herself had cried when she read *The Robe*, she said, and she had prayed a lot to Somebody, but she did not like the sound of this at all. "It gives me the creeps, that's all. When I'm with you I think, oh my God, Jesus is in her heart! When we talk, I keep thinking He's listening. I don't believe in it at all, not at all, but I have this spooky feeling, and I want you to say it's just a passing thing."

"Oh, but it isn't!" Jo insisted, dismayed that she had not managed to convey that fact above all.

Gloria pressed, this time in a note. They were in study hall. "How can you know for sure? You hear a man preach in Boston and you shake his hand. What's so great about that?" Her question marks were huge, with circles for dots.

"The handshake was not important," wrote Jo. She had explained this before at least twice. It was not allegiance to that man. She could not even remember his name. Sheldon somebody, or Selby maybe—a queer name. What had happened afterwards in her Aunt Yooney's kitchen in Framingham seemed far more important. They were making onion sandwiches, she and Yooney, as they always did on Sunday nights after a day in Boston, while they waited for Daddy to fetch Jo home. Yooney was moving about with her usual breeziness, her right hand confined to her apron pocket like a dull-witted child, where it would not get bumped or cut as she worked. The sandwiches, like hiding dirty dishes under the sink, were Yooney's way of defying the world. They would eat them surreptitiously, following the fiery bites with swallows of cold milk.

Everything was the same as always, except tonight they had not just returned from the Museum of Art or a Chinese restaurant. They had gone to a huge dreary church to hear a speaker named Sheldon or whatever, and Jo had gone down front to accept Christ. On the bus coming back Yooney had alternated between soberness and laughter, squeezing Jo's hand. Now she sliced down through the fat onion with her awesome one-handed skill and said, "He'll turn you inside out, you know. Nothing will be quite the same again."

It was all so new, Jo couldn't think who she meant by "he," and then she saw the word as "He," with a recognition so disturbing and comforting that the force of Yooney's words was like a shade snapped up on a window, and she looked out into an idea that held clearly for only a second: that real life was something else altogether than she had thought, and the world's thermometers and measuring sticks were desperately wrong. She felt wretchedly small and wholly unimportant, all at the same instant. Then it was gone, too much for a human mind to retain.

"I know why I'm alive," she wrote to Gloria, and crossed it out. It came back to her through Gloria's ears, sounding strained and unnatural.

Their dialogue never improved, though it went on for weeks. "You'll get over it, I know you will," Gloria kept saying, as if it were a lingering cold.

But to Jo it was Gloria who was now unwell, or incomplete perhaps. Her future seemed precarious and unhitched. That had never been apparent before, and again Jo said nothing.

She had probably worried too much about how things would sound. Bill Murphy circled her one day after school, riding around her on his bike as she walked home on Prospect Road. "Are you in this for life?" he asked. "I mean, you aren't engaged to God or anything, are you?"

He had laughed, because he laughed at everything anyway. He flunked all his subjects because he couldn't take anything seriously enough to study. To answer his question now seemed totally inappropriate, unless she could make it funny somehow. He gave her a ride home, up the hills as far as Cannons' driveway. "I believe in God," he puffed in her ear. "I just don't like to get technical about it." Then they both laughed, and they never did talk about it again.

As for Gloria, she finally said good-bye, breaking off a six-year friendship. "When you get over it, I'll be around," she said. But Jo knew—Gloria was gone for good, and though she felt terrible, in a sense it was reassuring, the value of her new life proved in its cost.

A surprising number of people said, "You'll get over it." There were other more tactful remarks, like "I'm sure you're very sincere," which was even more disheartening. Corey Byrne, whose father was the Baptist pastor, confronted her as she wore the question mark and told her he admired her guts. But he wouldn't participate. "You haven't got a chance," he said. "This town is ruled by Rome. Seventy-five percent R.C."

He helped her just one time, in a house-to-house campaign, tossing pink and yellow bombs (tracts rolled in cellophane) onto front porches. "No one will read them when they see what they are," he said.

Jo meant to cover the whole town, but Corey went home early and never offered to work with her again. Probably she was just as glad. There was a constriction about him that depressed her. It was as if he had caught something deadly long ago in the damp Sunday school basement of the Baptist Church. At age seventeen he had soured like an old washcloth. His aim wasn't very good either, tossing the bombs. In another year he was gone, off to Bob Jones College in the South, with a 4-D classification to keep him out of the war.

Maybe he was right about the town, because nothing of any significance happened that she could see. They got used to her at school. As her senior year inched along interminably, she was simply "Holy Jo," the kid among them who had a "call."

But at home, even with Loring now enlisted and gone and only three of them there, the house seemed suddenly too small to hold all it had to—not just the bulky furniture, nor the piano in the kitchen and the sounds she herself brought from that, but her father's voice, reasoning, warning ("Go, wallow in the nineteenth century!"), her mother's loaded silences, their disappointment, their anxiety, and at the end their bravery. For in July, in the middle of all the boot tongues and tension, word came about Loring and his picture appeared in the *Framingham News*, his visored cap looking suddenly too big for him, as did—oddly—all the caps of the dead and the missing. It was the same picture he'd had taken when he got his wings, the smile the same for that as for this. If he had come to deliver the news in person, he'd have smiled exactly that way. "Just missing," he'd have said offhandedly, "I'll be back," above all not wanting to make a fuss. Then the smile—flash—there under the cap.

"We must keep going," Daddy said. "Love and lift, that's the ticket." Jo hated their bravery. For her mother it was a garment she sank into, bruised and amazed, while her father donned it fiercely, putting it on each morning the way he did his trousers, with a quick hard thrust of each leg. She was not at all sure why she hated it, and of course they never knew.

"Awfully sorry about your brother," people said, a hundred times that first week. "Thank you," she had answered, so casually you'd think they had paid her a compliment, and instantly she had found herself staring at their feet, wondering how they could have so much as put their shoes on this morning when her brother was missing in action—unless it was to go look for him. Shoes themselves seemed preposterous—eyelets, laces, double knots, fanciful devices to keep people busy and away from the only important fact in the world, which was Loring's danger. All that lasted only a second, then she looked them in the face and smiled.

"I don't think Jo has comprehended it yet," she heard Mrs. Cannon say to Mother.

"Oh, Jo is strong, that's all," answered Mother. "She's always been strong." It was more of an apology than a defense.

Then the summer sank into a stupor. The war crackled on the horizon like a circling storm, making the days heavy. Often it was hard to breathe, and sometimes Jo gasped for air in a panic. Calvary Bible Institute hung cool and waiting around the Labor Day corner. In those slow dead weeks of August she wondered if she would ever, ever get there.

Outside Cleveland, deep into the night, the train braked, then shuddered and swayed as it relinquished speed. Bodies stirred along the car. "Two-thirds there!" someone said with a loud yawn, and the sailor shot to his feet, as if that was exactly what he had been waiting to hear. He left quickly with his duffel bag, and Jo had the whole sweaty seat to herself. She curled up with her head on her fat pocketbook, stuffed full of all the odds and ends she had forgotten to put in her trunk.

Shortly after noon the school received her. At the main building of the campus she paid her board bill, turned in ration coupons, and was given three keys and an escort, a tall girl who led her down a sidewalk full of students and luggage. "This is Jo!" she called to one and another, as if they were expecting her particularly.

"Glad you're with us, Jo," said a boy with a footlocker on his back. He offered his hand, though to do it he had to bend almost horizontal. Flustered at such courtesy, Jo grabbed his hand and pumped too hard, but he didn't seem to notice. He smiled, like all the others, and said he'd see her around.

Two doors led into the narrow stone dormitory, with a paneled foyer between them. "This is Harold Hall," said the escort. What was her name? It had gotten lost in the rush of new names on the sidewalk, and Jo hated to ask again. They were in the elevator now, an ornate bronze cage. Someone had written over the buttons, "Let go and let God." It clanked and moaned as it lifted them slowly upward. Noises from the floors collected in the shaft, girls' voices, a flushed toilet, a clarinet on one careful note, repeated. A smell wafted around them, anciently damp, as if the place had never quite dried out. The girl was saying something, ". . . grand once," indicating all of Harold. "Yes," said Jo. She loved it already, the damp building, this poky old elevator.

They stopped at the fifth floor, the top, and got off into a silent hallway, which they followed to the back of the house and a square room that appeared to have once been a kitchen. Jo's room, number 57, opened off of this. Her third key slipped into the lock.

There was no one else on the floor at the moment. The escort apologized for leaving her alone.

"I'll be fine," said Jo.

She sat down on the nearest bed. Both beds were made—she hadn't expected that—with crisp sheets and a white seersucker counterpane. One bureau with a mirror stood against the far wall, an oak desk and chair before each of the two windows. Ceilings slanted low and the windows sliced into the eaves. There was a coziness to the quarters, another warmth besides the one that banged gratuitously in the monstrous gilt radiator. She pictured her roommate at the other desk, a fiction who would at any moment become a reality and begin a lifelong friendship. As yet, she did not even know her name.

Beside Jo on the bed was a pile of white towels and a cake of soap, and under the soap a booklet telling the story of Jim and Carol Ross. She had heard about them already somewhere. They were Calvary graduates who had been murdered ten years ago while serving as missionaries in the Sudan Interior. They had been caught in the middle of a tribal war and beheaded. It was not a morbid story at all, the way it was told. Their young faces, safely attached to their bodies, smiled from their wedding picture. "To me to live is Christ, and to die is gain," said the caption, a quote from the book of Philippians. The leaflet smelled of soap and the room smelled of clean sheets and towels. A male voice far below them called, "Man on the floor!" and began to sing: "From sinking sand, He lifted me . . . With tender hand . . . ." He vocalized, testing his voice in an echoey hallway. Trunks thumped and banged. Jo thought she would like to stand on the bed and sing too, as loud as she could, and bent to pull off her shoes when the elevator clanked open and shut. A slow uneven step approached down the hall, and a girl (woman?) appeared at the door.

"Hey! Are you Jo?" she asked. "I'm sorry I wasn't here. I was just out mailing a letter. My name is G.U.L."

That's what Jo thought she said. "Did you say G.U.L.?" she asked.

"No. It's G.U.L.," the girl repeated, exactly the same way.

"What does it stand for?" Jo asked.

"What? Oh, I don't know. A diamond, I hope," the girl said, and laughed.

"Oh . . . Jewel?"

"That's right. My full name is Jewel May Thorpe. I'm floor captain this year. I'm God-proud to see you, Jo."

Jo didn't catch that either, and Jewel explained that it was an expression from her part of Kentucky. She seemed to be in her late twenties and wore her hair, which was brown with a little gray in it, in an old-fashioned braid around her head. She was strange-looking in a way Jo could not define instantly. Her shoulders were bony, almost top-heavy, and her flowered cotton dress looked like a hand-me-down from someone younger and smaller. You could see where the hem had been let down to come below her knees. Jo caught herself, just before her eyes slipped all the way to Jewel's feet, where something was definitely wrong. To her dismay, Jewel beamed, as if she was used to seeing people do that sudden reverse action with their eyes and wanted you to know she didn't mind.

"Come on, I'll show you around the dormitory," she said, and took Jo's hand quite firmly and led her out of the room, so Jo was forced to walk beside her at the same broken rhythm. Their clasped hands jerked forward with every step. Jo thought, "Back home I have an aunt with a paralyzed arm," but of course she would not say that. There was no need to say anything. Jewel was in charge.

"You surely are the spindliest little old thing," she said, giving Jo's hand a squeeze.

Then the other girls appeared, and in an atmosphere charged with the shrieks of returning friends, Jo met Louise and Beverly and a large girl called Soup, and Ruth and Ruby, two dark-haired roommates she had trouble telling apart. These girls all greeted her with the same disarming enthusiasm she had been offered on the sidewalk. They were upper-classmen, who seemed to have lived here forever. Even her roommate, Karen Eckstrom, though she was new like Jo, acted as if she were merely stopping at home for the weekend. She arrived last and without haste from Oak Park, swung her suitcase up on the desk, and said, "Whew, it's hot in here. Why don't we open a window?"

"Roommate very nice," Jo included later in her telegram home. It was true, though their efforts to talk that first afternoon faltered and died. Karen was not an effusive person, and all Jo could think of to say were ridiculous things that would never do, like "I've got a new yellow toothbrush."

Her own shyness caught her off guard. It might have been because she was tired, or hungry—she had eaten only a sandwich and an orange since leaving home. But it seemed to be related more to certain aspects of Karen's appearance, her clean rimless glasses, maybe, which gave reflected light one minute and her cool direct gaze the next—or her speech (when she talked), gliding like a good girl's handwriting along a straight blue line. Jo wanted to say, "Tell me your story and spare no detail." It was an old line of her brother's. "I want to feel I've known you always," he would say, even to Mother and Daddy.

The luggage had come. But where to put things seemed more complicated than it ought to. Should her winter coat stay in the trunk, where it would get wrinkled, or hang in the closet, where there was really no room? Should her slippers go under the bed? Jo felt self-conscious making these decisions, pausing to think with her hands full.

The top drawer of the dresser came apart as she pulled it out, and for a second she thought she was actually going to cry, a reaction that was totally unlike her. Then it was merely funny. But when she and Karen both looked up and caught their reflections in the mirror, Jo was smitten with wordlessness again, at nothing less than the difference in how they looked. Karen seemed to be made of other materials altogether. She was not just taller, she was scaled more generously. Her hair was blonder than any Jo had ever seen, and thicker. Even her teeth were larger, perhaps too large, the richness overdone there. Beside her Jo looked cheated, with her narrow bones and sharp face.

Right at that moment Soup appeared, also in the mirror, proving that big and small were relative. She had entered the door behind them. "Welcome to the Tootle Instibibe!" she said, and settled herself on Jo's bed as if she were claiming it.

She was full of questions and information. Her real name was Elizabeth Campbell, she told them. She was from Philadelphia, from the "Church of the Open Sore," and Deo Volente, she expected to go into some kind of work with troubled teens. "Youth's quest for truth," she said. "Say that five times fast." She had brought the orange *Student Handbook* with her and offered them a rundown on Calvary rules, a preview of what they would be getting soon from the proctors.

"This has been called 'The Place of the Skull,'" she said cheerfully, "but that's unwarranted. The rules are much stiffer at other Christian schools. At Prairie Bible Institute in Alberta girls have to wear Ace bandages around their bazooms.... Yes, I heard that!" She rolled one eye at them, like Eddie Cantor, over the top of the book, and smiled with teeth so tiny they seemed surely to be the first set.

Jo giggled a little too hard and her eyes watered, so she went into the closet to find more hangers. She stood there a minute, facing the dark and gathering her composure.

"If you need hangers, I've got a thousand," said Soup. She also offered them laundry soap, Brilliantine, book covers, toilet paper, and a million bobby pins, "real metal, prewar." Her father was a purchasing agent for a chain of drugstores and sent her packages regularly, though he never wrote a line.

"What church are you from?" Jo heard her ask Karen.

"Swedish Covenant. You probably never heard of it," said Karen in her even voice.

"Of course I have," said Soup. "Hey, you in the closet!" she called. "Where are you from?"

"Massachusetts."

"Well, praise the Lord!" cried Soup, though it wasn't clear why. "I meant what denomination are you?"

"I don't belong to any particular church," Jo answered. Were they surprised at that? The mass of hangers in her hand was hopelessly tangled. She shook it, and several clattered to the floor. When she emerged from the closet, Soup was stretched out on the bed on her stomach with the *Handbook* open in front of her.

"Where did you get a boy's name?" she wanted to know.

"My brother named me," Jo answered. "He was three years old."

Soup was swinging one leg in the air. You could see where her stocking was gartered and twisted tightly around her thigh, the seam crooked. One summer pump, chalky with whitener, hung from her toes and there was whitener on her stocking. She smiled again with those teeth. "How did you know the Lord wanted you to come to Calvary Bi?" she asked.

Jo suspected it was a sincere question, but asked by that girl on the bed, a straight answer seemed impossible. She said, "I opened the catalogue and jumped in." Soup liked that. She laughed and said "Praise the Lord" again. And the catalogue, where had that come from? From a field representative who spoke at a church in Boston, Jo said.

Then Soup wanted to know if Jo had ever gone to Tremont Temple Baptist in Boston, or maybe Park Street Congregational. Jo told her she had, many times, and seemed to gain immediate status. Soup said she had Dr. Harold Ockenga's autograph in her Bible, along with Gypsy Smith and Mrs. Billy Sunday. She talked about the evangelists she had heard speak and the summer Bible conferences she had attended, Pinebrook and Sandy Cove. Jo had not heard of them, but Karen had. Then Soup said suddenly, "Well, I hope neither of you has come here to get a man, because the draft has taken most of the good ones." She went on about boys and school romances, and was finally back to the *Handbook*, pretending to read aloud from it.

"Our controls are gentle, you might say. To wit: If a girl's sweater is too revealing, she will be called up to the Dean of Women's offices. For prayer only, first offense. Men too, forsooth, are expected to dress as the gentlemen they truly are, jackets and ties to classes and meals. Women must never wear slacks or shorts except at gym, and must keep their stockings on at all times. On and up, that is! Let's see no knees, girls. Consider your weaker brother. For that matter, let us see no upper arms, and certainly no under!"

"Hi." Louise was there, her pretty face stuck through the door. Jewel had sent her, she said, to tell Jo and Karen there were irons in the basement if they wanted to press things out. She would take them down right now and show them the laundry equipment, if they liked.

"Fiddlesticks, Bonelli," said Soup. "You have been sent to make sure I am not offending these weak new first termers, mere babes in Christ as they are."

"You mustn't mind her," Louise said. "She's a fine girl under the facade."

"Oh!" gasped Soup, covering her ears with her hands. "You Italian Baptists have wicked tongues."

Louise winked and was gone, and Soup stayed on until the dinner bell.

Jo lay awake a good part of that night too. She had thought she and Karen might at last begin to talk, but Karen slept deeply, as if she were the one who had just come a thousand miles on the train, instead of ten miles from the suburbs. Voices seeped from other rooms in soft "phoom-phooms"—roommates talking on and on, while the noise of the city entered through the window in an almost solid sound, a single treble note that rose and fell half a tone. Lights moved and changed against the walls of the room. A siren, far away, lifted out of its sustained note and grew insistently louder. It passed the dormitory with a long frantic cry, as the ceiling stained faintly red, on-off, on-off. Such a lot of wakefulness out there, as if Calvary students were the only people in Chicago who had gone to bed.

Then the city sounds faded and the voices stopped, and Jo's eyes were still wide open, her mind going like a machine, reviewing the events of the evening. At Jewel's summons, about ten o'clock ("lights-out" was at eleven), they had all carried their heavy oak desk chairs to the "kitchen," which was empty except for three bathroom sinks under some old cupboards. This was to be their assembly room. All sorts of directives were taped to the walls—dormitory rules, meal schedules, household cleaning jobs. Jo saw "Bathroom—scrub" beside her own name. A wooden plaque stamped in gold letters hung from a plugged-up gas pipe, "Jesus Christ the Same, Yesterday, Today and Forever." Beside it someone had taped a long piece of paper with "Prayer Requests—Bear ye one another's burdens" written across the top in black crayon.

They had gathered sociably, bumping their chairs into a close, uneven circle. Everyone was dressed for bed. Jo wore the new pink chenille robe her mother had given her, tied around the middle. She felt fat in it, and she was hot. It was too early in the year for chenille, but not to wear it, her mother's gift, seemed disloyal. Actually, everyone looked a little rosy. Dinner had been a noisy, festive affair, and they were still wound up, on the edge of easy laughter. Except Karen, who was cool and in charge of herself. She wore a blue-checked housecoat that matched her pajamas and zipped all the way up. Her Bible zipped too—the covers zipped shut, which seemed very handy. Inside you could keep a handkerchief or notepaper or even a comb.

Jo looked at the other Bibles in the circle, soft and plump from use, or fat-cheeked from misuse. She liked that. Things stuck out of them, tracts and prayer lists and cards with photos of missionaries on them. Verses were underlined in colors and study notes written in the margins. When Jewel opened her Bible to start the meeting, it fell apart. "Oh, la!" she laughed. A clump of pages hung from the binding by threads ("That's Galatians!") and pieces of paper fluttered to the floor. She said she ought to get a new Bible but she didn't think she could find her way around in any other.

Seated as she was in a long robe, her deformed leg was less apparent. Even so, the twist at the ankle showed, and her foot thrust itself out to one side. Not polio, Jo thought. The wasted look was not there as it was in Yooney's arm. In fact, Jewel's leg seemed to have exceeded itself in some way, and shot off at an angle to find a place to go.

If she was giving any thought to the shape of her own leg now, no one would guess it. She had begun reading from a book called *My Utmost for His Highest*. She went from that to various places in the Bible, and they all followed along, quiet now, looking up the verses as she mentioned them, the thin pages whispering. God was constantly working, at the deepest levels of their lives, even when things seemed all wrong, Jewel said. That's all Jo caught. Before she knew it, Jewel was done and they were praying. One after another the girls prayed out loud, easily, as if they were talking to each other with their eyes shut. At the end of each prayer Soup boomed "Amen!" and the others said amen too, but more discreetly, to Jo's relief. She had not yet been able to get herself to lend vocal support to someone else's prayer that way, not even in a whisper. Actually, she was in a panic. She had also never prayed out loud in front of someone else, not even Yooney. Were they all expected to pray right now? She began to plan her words, her heart beating fast, when that part was over too and Jewel was asking for testimonies.

Louise offered to start. She was the prettiest girl in the room, Jo thought. Her long lashes made shadows on her cheeks, and she kept thrusting out her small bosom as she spoke, as if she could hear her mother reminding her to sit up straight. She was from Long Island, New York, she told them, and her family had not been church people at all. When she was twelve, she went with a friend to a Vacation Bible School at an Italian Protestant mission in the neighborhood.

"I accepted the Lord there, and though I was only a child, I knew my life had really begun at that moment. Over the years He has enabled me to win my whole family to him—four brothers! I can't thank Him enough for all He's done for us, and for leading me here to study His matchless Word."

The word "matchless" seemed out of place, but coming from Louise it was not offensive. She also said, "He is my all in all," and it sounded like an original statement, though Jo had heard it several times in testimonies at meetings in Boston, along with a dozen other phrases like it. People might say the Lord had broken every fetter, or set their feet upon a rock, or put a song in their hearts. It was a kind of code language, giving you a way to say things that were hard to word, especially on the spur of the moment and in front of a church full of people. Though there was a danger in that too. If a pastor or evangelist opened a meeting to testimonies, in the uncomfortable silence that sometimes followed a person might stand up and rattle off some of those phrases. "Jesus saves, keeps, and satisfies. He has washed away my sin in the crimson flow and now His peace and joy flood my heart from day to day!"

No one rattled now, though perhaps they sounded too rehearsed, as if they had done this many times. " 'I count all things but loss for the excellency of the knowledge of Christ Jesus my Lord,' " quoted Beverly Johnson, a plump girl who punctuated her sentences with a brief chuckle. She had grown up on the mission field in Kenya, East Africa, she told them, and had "tasted all the world had to offer," two bits of information that to Jo seemed contradictory. And Ruth (or was it Ruby?) cooed too sweetly, drawing out her vowels, saying she owed so much to her parents, who "trooly loved the Loord." Her father was the pastor of a Presbyterian Church in Des Moines. Though she had been raised as a Christian, she was "worldly and selfish," she said, and it was not until she went to Maranatha Bible Conference in Indiana that she gave her life to Him in "full surrender and gained freedom from the bonds of sin."

Ruby (Ruth?) said she also had been taught by Christian parents. They were Plymouth Brethren. "When I was five years old I found the Lord Jesus at my mother's knee," she said. Jo's groggy mind was still struggling with that particular image when Karen began to speak. She could not remember any special time when she became a Christian, she said in her slow voice. She had grown up believing that Christ was her Savior. When she finished at Calvary she expected to enter the Swedish Hospital here in the city for nurse's training, and while she was willing to go anywhere, right now it looked as if she would go to Alaska as a medical missionary. Her denomination had already pledged to support her.

Jo wondered how a person's life could seem so settled. She wanted to hear more, she thought, from everybody. They were skimming along on the surface when there was so much to tell. She hoped she would do better than this herself.

Then it was her turn. Jewel said, "Well, Jo, how about you?"

"Who, me?" she said, genuinely surprised, which made them laugh, and there she was again with a mind that would not produce words. They were waiting for her. In a rush she began to recite the statement of faith she had written as part of her application to Calvary.

"I became a Christian when I was fifteen years old. Until that time I had never heard the Gospel. I heard many family arguments about religion, but I was not interested at all. The occasion of my decision was a day when my aunt took me to hear an evangelist speak in Boston."

It was a stale, stilted composition she had labored over, rewriting and cutting the sentences like a précis, to get it down to a hundred words. She plunged ahead, afraid to make any changes.

"My family has been unhappy about my stand. My father, particularly, who is an agnostic, does not wish me to attend Bible School. But the Lord has gotten me through some difficult times and He will not fail me in the future. 'Therefore have I set my face like a flint, and I know that I shall not be moved.'"

At this point she caught Karen's blue eyes behind the rimless octagonal glasses, and saw a distressing reflection of herself, coming through much too plucky and earnest. "Oh, listen, guys," she wanted to say, "that's not how I meant to tell it."

But Jewel was saying, "Thank you, Jo," reassuringly, and then Soup began to talk. She was sitting on the floor dressed in a pair of men's pajamas with the legs rolled partway up, her head helmeted in tiny flat curls, each held in place by two crossed bobby pins.

"You've all met me before," she began, "even the ones who haven't."

"Oh, boy," inserted Louise. "It's going to be the unabridged edition."

Soup ignored her. "I'm the fat girl who's an only child, with fat discontented parents who spoiled me. I always had friends because I always picked up the tab. Old big-hearted Soup, right up in front, that was me. In the vanguard of promiscuity, you might say. . . . Well, skip that. Here's what happened. There was this drippy girl in my class at high school, kind of a religious nut nobody liked, and one day she invited me to a Youth for Christ meeting at Church of the Open Door in Philly, and I said I'd go. My plan was to bring a bunch of kids and disrupt the meeting in some way. As it turned out, the place was packed. There were hundreds of people there. I was astonished. I didn't know that many kids went to church in the whole country. I thought, they can't all be jerks, they can't all have something the matter with them. I never did know who the speaker was. I just knew he was describing me, my life, and predicting my future, and I knew he was right because I had my parents for models, half soused all the time and fighting over money. I was absolutely crushed and terribly frightened, and when the bloke gave the invitation to accept Christ, I went sailing down the aisle in front of all my friends. Then right away I wished I hadn't. One of the personal workers, a lady, explained the way of salvation and tried to get me to pray. She wanted me to *kneel down!* Mind you, I'd never been to church. The only time I ever knelt was to find my shoes under the bed, and that was a risk. I said, 'Me? On the floor?' She said, 'Why not?' So I knelt, but not a word came out. I didn't even know what to call the Lord. I wanted to run away. Then the lady said, 'Pray after me, sentence by sentence,' and she began. She said, 'Jesus, my Lord,' and

I said, 'Jesus, my Lord.' That's as far as we got, the introductions. The Lord said, 'Well, hello at last, Soup. I know you very well.' I cried and cried, and when I was through there wasn't an ounce of pretense left in me. I gave it all to Him. But remember, I'd been buying love all my life, and it was hard for me to believe God would take me as I am and make me His child. I thought, if something has taken place then He ought to prove it to me. And He did. I reached for my cigarettes—automatically, you know—and I simply knew that I would never smoke again. Nobody had said anything about that. I handed the pack to this lady, and she handed it right back. We did that twice, and then I caught on. I went to the wastebasket and threw them away, and I have never smoked since. I rode home on a wave, to report to my parents. Well, they'd had all they could take from me, and they threw me out. That was three years ago. I owe every inch of happiness I have to Jesus Christ, and someday I hope I'll be able to say, 'His grace which was bestowed on me was not in vain.' "

Soup's voice halted and trembled. Her eyes filled, and she reached up with the hem of her pajama top to wipe them. Jo felt uneasy, but no one else seemed even to notice, and in a minute they were kneeling by their chairs to sing a closing prayer.

"Spirit of the Living God," went the slow chorus, climbing, "fall fresh on me." Some girls sang second and third parts, and someone's voice soared on an obligato. "Take me, melt me, mold me, fill me." They sang it through twice, then rose from their knees, blinking a moment, unself-conscious, all talking at once as they dragged their chairs back to the rooms. Louise gave Jo a little hug. "We're glad you're here," she said.

At the end of Jo's second week at Calvary she met Clyde Mac-Quade. The occasion followed a crazy dream and coincided with the third day of rain.

The rain was a gusty mid-September storm. The dream, though funny, was really a nightmare in which she leaped naked to the wet street from the fifth floor to make it on time for a class. She wasn't hurt. She watched herself from the window as she bustled along the sidewalk, swinging her arms, the other students already where they belonged. Her nakedness was disturbing, yet she was more concerned about her hair. It had come out bent, neither straight nor curly. She had set it in a hurry the night before.

It was not a very subtle dream. For the first two days of that rainy week, she had been splashing around campus getting her feet wet and trying to keep up with her schedule. She had not slept much even yet. If this should have disturbed her, offered any kind of faint alarm, it didn't. She had not been tired at all, not since the first night, only a bit harried.

Energy flowed at the school. One could tap into it. She sensed that on the first day of classes, when at eight o'clock in the morning they had all crowded into Moorehouse Auditorium, gathering to the call of the organ, a piano, and two trumpets. Somebody had said to Jo at breakfast, "Wait until you hear the singing in chapel," but there was no way she could have been prepared. It engulfed her. It broke down out of the ceiling, rang out of the walls and vibrated across the floor, their own voices (a thousand) converging in a single enormous sound. "Crown Him with Many Crowns!" they sang, and "A Mighty Fortress Is Our God," and half a dozen more, as if they had nothing to do but sing for the next two years.

Standing in the middle of all that music, short enough to feel enclosed by shoulders and backs, and unable to hear her own voice though she sang so hard she got dizzy, Jo gave herself up to the force that filled the auditorium. She saw herself lifted by it, above a thousand heads ("Oh, For a Thousand Tongues," they were singing) by two thousand arms.

Then they turned in their books to a number she had never heard before, more like a plaintive love song than a hymn.

The sands of time are sinking.
The dawn of heaven breaks,
The summer morn I've longed for,

25

The fair, sweet morn awakes.
Dark, dark hath been the midnight,
But dayspring is at hand
And glory, glory dwelleth
In Immanuel's land.

So it was dayspring, you might say, for two weeks, all through the rush of welcoming parties and auditions and opening classes. She loved being off in the morning, her heart flying, wearing her red plaid skirt, sharp yellow pencils in one hand and a load of books in the other. At home she had hated lugging books to and from high school. Now she added a couple of extra just because she liked them. They never felt heavy. Here every load of books was topped by a Bible. It was their main text.

She liked everybody—her teachers, the switchboard operator, the janitors, the clerks in the offices. Everywhere you went you heard familiar references to "the Lord," a gracious and accessible presence, as if His offices were just above them, on the twelfth floor. She loved going to the library to sit at the shiny tables next to a row of tall dark books—commentaries by Matthew Henry, Calvin's *Institutes*, Spurgeon's sermons. Hundreds of lives supported her here, Origen, Tertullian, Wycliffe, Augustine, Luther, Knox, Wesley, Moody.

On this third morning of rain (the day she met Clyde) none of that had changed. She simply understood that it was time to settle down and go to work.

She organized her books and papers carefully and brought them to breakfast and Women's Devotions, to avoid a hurried trip back to the dorm. Then she went directly to the classroom to catch up on her reading before first period began. She had hoped it would be empty and it was. She had just gotten settled in her chair, alone in that big room, when this boy came in, breathing hard and imparting moisture into the space around him. From the corner of her eye she saw him remove an Army overcoat and sit down across the aisle from her.

She ignored him, avoiding interruption. But there were no sounds other than the one he was making—an intent, constant rustling—and it was hard to concentrate. Finally she risked a glance. He was ready. He snared her with a flick of his eyes so sudden she jumped.

"I never throw away any portion of the Word of God," he said, as if she had asked. "I'll give these out after they dry."

He had a square, sober face topped by a dark, wispy crewcut. He might be called good-looking if it were not for an excess of cheek. Too much face, Jo thought. Or his mouth was too small. His lips seemed wet, and a drop of water hung from the end of his nose. On the writing arm of the chair lay a handful of crumpled tracts he was smoothing and rubbing with a handkerchief.

"How can you offer anyone a muddy tract like that?" asked Jo, because she had to say something. He wouldn't stop looking at her.

"The power is in the blood, not the mud," he said softly. She could tell from his expression that the rhyme was accidental and he was pleased with it. Something about his diction made her nervous. It was as if his mouth had gotten full of rain out there while he was picking up the tracts and he was now trying to hold it without swallowing. She felt damp just looking at him. He sniffed hard but the drop of water still hung from his nose. That worried her, too. She lowered her eyes to the vicinity of his necktie, searching for a safe place to rest her gaze. "Besides," he went on, "I'm going to iron these later." He meant the tracts. He was going to iron the tracts.

"Oh," said Jo, and ducked down to the columns of Genesis, that being finally the only safe place to look. It wasn't, quite. His brown necktie had fastened itself in her mind and hung against the page of her Bible. There was a tie-clip on it, worn high up on his chest, as an old man would. The clip, like some she had noticed in the school bookstore, had the facsimile of an open Bible on it, stamped with a verse of Scripture too tiny for her to read at this distance.

"I bet you wonder where I got these tracts," he said.

"I'd never ask," said Jo. He would tell her anyhow, that was certain. "Off the sewer grille, at the corner. The storm sewer. You know."

She did. She had seen them there just yesterday, in clumps, wet and matted. Tracts blew daily along the street in front of Van Housen Hall, because students often stood there to give them out to passersby. The trouble was that people who lived near the school had gotten so many. They would accept them from you all right, in a passive, absent-minded way, then let the wind take them from their hands and carry them into the gutter.

"It's a disgrace to the Lord Jesus Christ," the boy went on in his low voice, with that odd way of not moving his mouth. "I can't stand it to see them there like that. When I'm finished, they're as good as new and shouldn't be wasted." His voice dropped close to a whisper. "I know a guy who was saved by *half* a tract."

"Oh, yes?" Jo began reading again, searching for her place. If she kept her eyes on the page the boy might take the hint and stop talking. "And Jacob was alone," she read, "and there wrestled a man with him until the breaking of day." The words were mysterious and moving. She read them again.

"Found it under the seat of a train. It said, 'The wages of sin is death, but—.' Torn off, right at that word. He almost went mad. Definitely under conviction. Finally bought a Bible and read avidly straight through, Genesis to Romans, till he found the verse, whereupon the Holy Spirit met him and he came to the Lord."

Jo raised her head and gave him a brief nod. There were traces of foam at the corners of his mouth. *Can't* he swallow? she wondered, sliding her eyes down again past the necktie to his hands, which were busy separating the wet tracts, and back to her Bible. "And he said unto him, What is thy name?" she read silently. "And he said, Jacob."

"Willing messengers," the boy added. "That's all He asks of us. It's humility that counts most in the Lord's work." He said "*Lords*work," the way some kids said "*born*again." Presented with silence, he continued on.

"Willing to be a fool for Christ's sake, that's the whole secret to successful soulwinning."

He was busy with the tracts for a minute, then added, "We have to *love* the lost, of course." He stopped working and she could tell he was looking at her for a response.

"Just out of high school, aren't you?" he went on. "Used to be you couldn't get into Calvary so young. Now, with the war on, they take anybody who says they're a Christian and some that are questionable. . . . What's your course?"

"Music." She had lost her place again.

"I'm in the Missionary Course myself. I hope to go to Formosa, Lord willing."

Silence, all but the rustling and occasional sniffle. Jo thought he had given up at last. Then he said abruptly, "Over seven million Allied servicemen have died already in this war."

It was a stunning piece of news. The war had lost its edge in these two weeks at school. Now suddenly here it was whole again in this astonishing statistic. Was it accurate? Jo looked up at him, met his dark eyes directly, then looked down again, quickly. But he seemed to have scored a victory. He leaned across the aisle, quite close to her, to see the pages of her Bible.

"Only chapter twenty-two? First time through?"

". . . Yes."

"You're behind already."

"I know it," she answered defensively. She was a slow reader. It was none of his business.

"I've read Genesis through three times since school started and Exodus twice," he offered, moving back to his side of the aisle. "Prior to coming here I'd already read the entire Bible through seven times."

Bully for you, Jo thought. There was a noise in the hall, and it occurred to her they might be breaking rules by being here alone in the classroom. Men and women were not supposed to be together at all

---

socially except at designated times. She did not want to be seen with him anyway. She shut her Bible and began to gather up her things.

"He's a modernist, you know," the boy said.

"What?"

"Dr. Peckham." He had moved slightly toward her again and his eyes had sharpened. "Dr. Peckham," he repeated, back down to a whisper. "A modernist. He does not believe the Bible to be the inerrant Word of God."

"That's silly," Jo answered. She glanced at the platform where Dr. Peckham would soon stand, his funny cross face bobbing over the top of the lecture podium. He had written two books defending the validity of Scripture.

"Listen," said the boy. "It's a very cagey thing. He believes the Bible *contains* the Word of God."

"Has he said that?"

"Of course not. He's much too smart to come right out with it. He'd get booted off the faculty. But I assure you, if you listen carefully you'll see that he does not believe in the plenary-verbal inspiration of this Book. He's a disciple of Barth and Brunner."

"Who?"

"They're modernist theologians. German. I can't prove it yet, but he has made very dangerous statements." He glanced behind him, looking for Peckham maybe.

Jo stood and put on her raincoat. "I'm going to get some air," she said.

"But it's time for class."

The bell did ring then, right at that instant, and several students pushed through the door at the back of the hall. Jo hesitated by her chair.

"I want to give you some advice," said the boy. "Sometime you go right up to Pecky and say, 'Do you believe the Bible to be wholly and verbally inspired, inerrant in the original autograph?' And do you know what he'll do? He won't answer yes or no. Ask him, 'Sir, do you believe in the definite, literal, plenary . . .' "

Jo had started down the aisle, but when she got to the door everyone began to arrive at once. They stamped past her, shaking off the rain and filling the room, men on one side and women on the other, talking noisily. After a minute she went back to her place and sat down, avoiding the boy and feeling a little foolish.

Then the girl seated behind her poked her on the shoulder. "He wants you," she said.

There he was, holding out a tract. "Have you seen this number?" he asked. He wore a smile now, a little one, perhaps as far as he could stretch his mouth. The tract was a token, an excuse to make peace with her. It was a slice of cheap newsprint crowded with tiny words. At the bottom of the page the word "GONE!" leaped out of a crude drawing of two empty shoes. "Will you meet the Lord in the air?" the tract said. " 'For in such a time as ye think not, the Son of Man cometh.' "

"That's a miserable-looking thing," Jo said. She was ashamed of it.

The boy's eyes grew round with disapproval. "You like God's Word on slick paper, do you, with colored illustrations? That's eye service, for men pleasers." He turned the tract over and leaned across to show her the back, "Free while the Lord provides," pointing out each word as if she were just learning to read. "They operate on faith, this outfit," he said.

"What?" asked Jo. She could hardly hear him in the din. He repeated, raising his voice and spraying saliva into the air. Jo felt three pinpricks of cold on her face, one above the right eyebrow, one on her right cheek, and one on her bottom lip. She turned away but he stayed in the same position.

"His Word shall not return unto Him void, right?"

". . . I suppose so."

"I didn't catch you."

"Right!"

"Amen! What's your name?"

He thrust his hand forward, fingers spread, and she took it limply. "Jo Fuller," she murmured.

"I'm Corporal Clyde MacQuade! Honorable discharge, U.S. Army."

The drop fell from his nose and hit Jo on the back of the hand like a wet kiss, sealing them together in some intimate and undesirable alliance.

In the weekend that followed, Jo forgot Clyde MacQuade entirely. She had been given her first assignment on Skid Row.

Each student carried several hours of Practical Christian Work. They provided music at churches and taught classes and visited hospitals or Cook County Jail. Karen ran the junior high department of her own Sunday school in Oak Park this term. She went home on Saturdays to get ready and returned on Sunday evenings. It was a privilege to be chosen for the harder assignments, like outdoor meetings at Bughouse Square, or contacting families in the tenements. Jo felt honored to be part of a Saturday night "group," a Gospel team of twelve students who held services for down-and-outers at the Anchor of Hope Rescue Mission.

They traveled there by streetcar, Chicago Avenue to Halsted, Halsted to West Madison. Off the trolley, they walked in three knots, four each, stepping over broken bottles and puddles of vomit, and thrusting tracts into extended hands that hung in the air like dismantled parts of bodies. The smell alone was unbelievable, not just whiskey and filth, but something else hard to identify, a king of a smell that ruled the sidewalks.

Inside the mission, a storefront with a tin ceiling, the "congregation" sat on yellow kitchen chairs. They coughed and scratched, let loose garbled shouts or huddled behind a wall of stupor. Jo's job was to sing the melody in a girls' trio. She sang as well as she could, consciously reaching into the men's minds with her voice and pronouncing the words very distinctly: "Mar-vel-ous grace of our lov-ing Lord, grace that ex-ceeds our sin and our guilt!" But the harmonies, frail and girlish, got lost among the yellow chairs.

So this was how her weekends were to be, with Saturday gone completely to choir, studio recitals, and trio rehearsals. On Sunday afternoon she wrote letters and stole a nap, and on Sunday morning and evening she went to church (it was expected of students to attend two services), joining the girls on the floor to wherever they were headed. She liked this, her days butted up, every minute with something to do.

On Monday, too, Clyde was no factor. Survey class did not meet. That evening the Social Club put on a "Useless Talent Show" and everybody on the fifth floor of Harold Hall went with Louise to see Charlie Higgins, a boy she liked, stand on his thumbs. He did it, for five seconds. Someone else recited the Gettysburg Address backwards, and a girl who lived in the room directly under Jo and Karen whistled bird calls. They had already heard her, up the radiator pipes.

At the close of the program the auditorium was darkened and colored lights picked up an easel on the platform. On this one of the men students painted with pastels—a swelling green ocean with a big sky and a tiny boat—while a male quartet sang "O Love That Wilt Not Let Me Go." It was all rather sentimental, but the music was lovely—"I give Thee back the life I owe, that in Thine ocean depths its flow may richer, fuller be!" When the overhead lights came on, Jo, who never cried in public, was wiping her eyes in spite of herself, and there was Clyde MacQuade, staring at her from just two rows away.

Nevertheless, on Tuesday morning his presence across the aisle from her in Bible Survey meant nothing, and when she turned her head she was startled to meet his glance again. He saluted her, of all things. A minute later a folded paper landed on her notebook. It was a mistake to open it right then, but she did. Inside was a list of questions.

Things I would like to learn about you, please.

1—How long have you known the Lord?

2—Do you have a definate call to full-time service?

3—Are you willing to give your all for His cause?

4—What is your life verse?

5—What are your views on Eternal Security?

6—Are you a Pre-trib? In case you don't know, that means do you beleive Christ is returning prior to the Great Tribulation?

7—Are you going with anyone?

It was hard to read. Not only was the spelling bad, the handwriting was small and the r's looked like n's. Class was about to begin. Notebooks were opening, and Dr. Peckham's gravelly voice—students cleared their own throats when he began to talk—reached across the room. Jo directed her attention straight ahead, her pencil poised.

What on earth was she to do with these questions? She ought just to hand them back unanswered, but that seemed ruder than necessary. She could write quick answers and get it over with. Number one: "Two years." Number two: "I believe so. (Note spelling, please.)" Number three: "Of course." Number four: . . . She wasn't sure she had what could be called a life verse. She could put "None, as yet," or she could jot down Isaiah 43:1. She had found it last year as she was thumbing through her Bible: "I have called thee by thy name; thou art mine." Her name meant "beloved" in Scotch slang, or so her mother had discovered once in a crossword puzzle, something to do with Robert Burns's poem "John Anderson, My Jo." It had seemed very special, finding Isaiah 43:1 and putting it together with the Scotch "jo," and it had nothing whatever to do with this boy across the aisle.

What right had he to ask her questions at all? Dr. Peckham had pulled a map of Palestine down over the blackboard and was tracing the trade route along the Fertile Crescent—Abraham's journey. Information seemed to pour out of him. Even the clay pots over a campfire bore significance. Jo wrote so furiously the whole hour that her thumb joint ached.

At the end of class Clyde swung out into the aisle behind her, walking close in the press of students. She could smell the wool of his Army overcoat. Was it still damp from the rain? "Miss Fuller—oh, ah, Miss Fuller!" All the way down the aisle her name went on and off like a dim neon light. She pretended not to hear, pushing away from him in the traffic of voices.

He caught up to her in the courtyard. "Do you intend to answer my note?" he asked. He stood directly in front of her, inches away.

"No, I don't think I do," she said. "I really don't have time."

"Then please at least answer the seventh," he said.

"Seventh what?" she asked.

"Question. Seventh question. The last one. You know." People were walking around them and Jo felt embarrassed and cross. "No," she said, scowling. "I'm not going with anyone." Then seeing where that left things, she said sharply, "I'm much too busy to think about it!" and turned her back and headed for the bookstore, though she had no reason to go there at all.

That afternoon as she got settled to practice in her piano room, another folded square of paper fell out of her pocket. "Be vigilant," the note said, "because your adversary, the Devil, walketh about seeking whom he may devour. 1 Peter 5:8. Busy Christians are his easiest pray!" When she opened her music there was another. "Do I assume correctly that you would not go out with me if I asked you? Or would you give it prayerful consideration? Not that I have asked you."

The whole thing was ridiculous. She began to practice, hitting the keys hard in a finger-stretching exercise, both hands opened to an octave (barely—seven notes was her real limit), and leaping up the keyboard together, C to C, F to F, A to A, all the way up and down again, over and over.

In a few minutes she stopped and massaged the little finger of her left hand. Her "pinkies" were weak, Mr. Cooch had said at the last lesson.

She thought it was an odd expression for a grown man to use. A concerto rode in from the next practice room, played by someone with pinkies that were obviously long and strong.

Jo went to the window and stared down at the courtyard. Shallow puddles of water still stood in the hollows of the asphalt. The sun was out. The weather had been crisp since the rain, but the day was balmy now. A dozen students were jumping rope down there with a long clothesline, clowning and shouting something together, a jump-rope chant, no doubt. All Jo could hear was the music from next door, which seemed to be exactly the right beat for jumping. Now there was Karen in a bright dirndl skirt, double-dutching like an expert, her blonde hair flying out from her neck, all in time to the concerto. Jo thought she would like to go down and jump herself, but even watching out the window was a stolen moment.

As a music major she was scheduled for two hours of practice a day and two lessons a week. Her teacher was a composer who had written dozens of hymns and songs. Kids said he had once turned down an invitation to arrange for Fred Waring. Jo hoped he would teach her to improvise hymns, great handfuls of chords. As it turned out, he had given her no hymns at all so far, except for sight-reading purposes. Most of her work was in Hanon and Bach's *Two-Part Inventions*, along with scales and stretching exercises.

"And your name?" Mr. Cooch kept asking at the first lesson. "Fuller . . . Yes, it's on the list. But how did it *get* there? That's the mystery. You signed it. But did you audition? Yes? Then stop trembling and play. . . . Oh, anything. I can tell."

She played the hardest thing she knew, a Hungarian dance by Brahms, while he did a little jig beside the piano. He was a tall man with loose arms and legs.

"Awful!" he cried, when she was finished. "It's either a mistake or a joke. Dear girl, my students are advanced when they *come* to me. Some teachers teach advanced, some beginners, you see? In two years—two short years—a music major gives a formal recital."

"Yes, I know."

"I mean Rachmaninoff's Concerto in D minor, dear girl, and the rest of those big fellows!"

"Yes, I know."

"Yes, you know," he mocked in a high voice. "Then why aren't you leaping off that bench and running out of here like a scared rabbit?"

"Because I want you—." Something caught in her throat, a piece of dust or something, and she had to cough a little and start over. To make it worse, her eyes watered, and she was afraid he would think she was putting on an act. "I want you for a teacher," she said. The word "teacher" came out in a dramatic whisper.

"Oh glory! Gloriosky!" He flopped his beefy hands against his thighs in despair. Those hands must have been ten inches long. He waggled them over his head like slack sails, then he held them together in front of his face, his nostrils caught between his thumbs.

"How long have you been playing?"

"About a year." She said it without hesitation because she knew she had advanced very far in that time. When he looked surprised she thought it was because that was apparent to him too. "I practiced three hours a day sometimes," she explained. He said nothing for a moment. Was he waiting for her to go on? "Do you want me to tell you more?" she asked.

"There's more?" he said, taking his thumbs away from his nose, then putting them back again. "Yes, yes, tell me."

She thought she wouldn't, since he seemed so unreceptive, then she decided she ought to. He deserved to know the facts and she deserved to give them. She skipped the beginning—the terrible slump in spirits at the beginning of her high school senior year, when all she could think about was the day she would leave for Chicago, and in the middle of that valley, whatever it was, the insistent urge to play the piano. It was a strange thing, like a voice singing on and on somewhere at a distance, which you suddenly hear and realize you've been hearing for a long time. But there was no piano in the house and no place to put one. She had said, rather crossly (to herself, or was it really a prayer?), "Well, what on earth do you want me to do about it?" The answer was a knowledge that almost exploded inside her head: "Start with what you have." She knew she was supposed to *act* on faith—go ahead as if she had a promise.

"I had an old John Thompson book for beginners in our bookcase," she said to Mr. Cooch. This was where she began the story. "Then I found a five-foot plank in the shed and drew the keyboard on it. I marked middle C in red, and I taught myself the songs." Soundless kindergarten songs. For three weeks she had been completely absorbed in this marvelous experiment, a mystery of action and belief.

"What are you saying?" asked Mr. Cooch, widening his eyes. "You had no piano?"

"Oh, finally I did." She wondered if she ought to explain to him that she hadn't been entirely without music before this, that she had always picked things out on her mother's mandolin ("Isle of Capri" and "Deep Purple") and that she and Gloria Logan would make up complicated harmonies together in school assemblies. She decided not to say that, after all.

"You had no teacher?"

"Yes, in a while. My teacher was a neighbor. Oh, she used to be a real teacher. She gave me free lessons and found me a free piano." He looked at her dubiously. "Her name was Mrs. Cannon," she added, as if that would help. "The Cannons have a farm near us." Mr. Cooch still made no response, so she tried once more. "I was through book three by February."

Did that sound like a boast? Her father had borrowed a pickup truck and hired three men to help him haul the piano over the quarry road, going to an expense he couldn't afford because he hoped her "religious obsessions" would be diverted. And seeing him work so hard for her, she did determine at least to reward him by doing well. The piano had to sit next to the cook range, where the washstand had been behind its screen. The washstand was moved to a corner in Loring's side of Jo's room, which was all right, since he had enlisted in the Army Air Corps several months before.

"Book three—of John Thompson?" Mr. Cooch asked.

"Yes, and other things."

"And what book are you in now?"

"Still in four." Almost done with four, she should have said. It had gotten slower after the first spurt.

"Only a small plateau," Mrs. Cannon had assured her, pink-cheeked and animated, her barrel body teetering on her thin legs. "Isn't this corking?" she kept saying. "Jo, you are full of latent talent!"

She was a schemer and a planner, Mrs. Cannon was. She wanted Jo to go to Pembroke, her own alma mater. She had it all worked out. She knew people there. She could exert a little influence, get Jo financial aid, and lend her whatever else she needed, to be paid back interest-free someday in the future. Mr. Cannon had agreed. The music courses there at Brown and Pembroke were excellent. "You've got a brain, Jo," she said. "I know you can do well. And they even have a course in Biblical Literature which might fill your needs." It was a generous offer and Jo was sure she had never quite thanked her properly. She said she appreciated it, but Calvary was known the world over for its music course. She was certain that was true, in some circles.

"You mean," Mrs. Cannon said, "that without another thought you are going to turn down a chance to go to Brown University and choose that dreadful Bible School instead? What on earth will you learn at a Bible School? Come now, aren't you just doing this to defy your father?"

"Young lady," Mr. Cooch said, placing his elbows (nose still caught) on top of the piano, "let us have no personal offense. I am saying you should change your course of study, your major, your field of interest, *from* music *to* something you are better at. You can still take lessons, one lesson a week from a student teacher. Do I need to make myself more clear?"

She looked at him but didn't answer, because she hadn't formed an answer, and because she was dejected.

"Ah!" he said. He removed his hands from his face at last and clapped them together. "God is leading you. He has said, 'Study music!'

Right? Such a final argument. Everybody wants to be an evangelistic piano player. *I* want to turn out good musicians—that's what God tells *me* to do. Even a lot of talent needs time. I'll tell you what, Miss Whatcha-macallit, it will take a miracle to make a truly skilled musician out of you in two years. Not that I don't believe in miracles, but let's not waste God's time asking Him for things He never intended. Right? Ha! Whoo!"

He paced the floor and twirled the eraser end of his pencil in the dimple of his chin. "What are you going to be?" he asked. "Church musician? . . . No. Wait. Don't tell me. I can see it in your eyes. Something big. Life threatening! Pioneer missionary. Glory, yes. I bet you know exactly where you're going. Let's see. New Guinea, the interior, where they have no pianos. No? Then where?"

"Afghanistan." It popped out. She had no idea where she was going, or *if* she was. She said it to give him a smart answer and was shocked to realize she had.

"Up there on the top of India?" He was incredulous. "And what are you going to do, push a piano over the Himalayas?"

Was it the Himalayas? She didn't think so. She wished she knew so she could correct his geography maybe. Whatever, she was sure it was possible, if necessary, to get a piano over there. It seemed much harder to get one up the rutted quarry road into her kitchen. Mr. Cooch was laughing and looking down at her as if he expected her to admit her joke. When she didn't, he stopped and smiled, apologetic and teasing.

"I believe you," he said. "Tell me about your call."

Jo stared at the piano keys. She honestly did not know what constituted a call. Students talked a lot about being "called to the foreign field," and some sounded very sure. She had not had any such leading yet. She was not at all drawn by the idea of spending her life in obscurity, but she hoped she was willing. Or willing to be willing.

"Afghanistan is a Moslem country and closed to Christian missionaries," said Mr. Cooch, quietly now. "It is thought to be the hardest country in the world to get into with the Gospel. You are probably aware of that."

She hadn't been, but she didn't say so. The idea of being the one who got into the hardest place did appeal to her. "Someone has to get in sometime, don't they?" she asked. "Maybe music is the way to do it."

Her voice sounded about eight years old. To him, looming above her, she must have looked like some kind of a midget. Her feet rested on the pedals with no leg length to spare. But she knew he was not going to drop her.

He sighed. "Well, you've got nice green eyes, so I'll keep you one term, until Christmas. It's as good a reason as any, under the circumstances. But you'll wish you hadn't. No mercy, no mercy, saith the Lord. Hezekiah 63:100. You know that verse? Now here's what we'll do, Miss Whatsername."

He sat down beside her on the bench and showed her some exercises, singing as he played and periodically squeezing her hands and saying, "Oh, how cold," and "Oh, how little," and repeating under his breath, "Noooo mercy, saith the Lord. No sir."

The concerto next door stopped abruptly, but the jump-roping went on down in the sunlight. Jo watched from the window, her head against the glass. Back home she had filled the house with her exercises, sometimes all afternoon. And here, where she thought there would be more motivation, she had trouble sticking it out for two hours. It was the only unpleasant thing she faced in her schedule. She felt fine as she entered the Music Building. She liked to be with the other music students and to walk up the stairs and down the halls between the practice rooms, caught in a crossfire from either side, volleys of music riddling through you. She was always anxious to begin, full of promise, until she reached her room, where her spirit lagged. She dreaded her own first notes. What she played would not sound anything like what she had just heard.

Still, she had no intention of quitting. It was very clear to her that learning to play the piano, as well and as quickly as she could, was to be part of her training—for Afghanistan or anywhere else. She could do it if she just worked hard enough.

The whole matter with Clyde might have ended immediately if Jo had not decided to answer his last note. On reflection, back in her room that afternoon, her sharpness of the morning bothered her. She thought she should find a way to modify that and at the same time discourage his overtures.

It turned out to be not so simple. An apology in writing blew things all out of proportion. Explanations (why she was so busy) were surely unnecessary. "No, I would not go out with you if you asked me" was the real truth, but she hated to insult him. After dropping four drafts into the wastebasket, she wrote, "I have decided not to go out with any boys at all for a while, even if asked."

Until that moment she had not decided anything of the kind. Now, seeing it in front of her, she felt good about it. She added, "Maybe I will never marry," then crossed that out and put instead, "I would like to keep myself free to concentrate on studying and learning God's will for my life."

She wondered if she was being completely honest. There were several boys she was watching with mild interest. A Robert Somebody did his student employment in the Music Building, pushing a broom and singing opera against the backdrop of sounds. Soup said his life was a mess before he was saved. Once he interrupted Jo's practice to ask if she knew what the middle pedal of the piano was for. He was doing a private survey, he said, especially among the girls. So far no one knew the answer. Did she? She didn't, but to keep him there a minute she made something up. It was like a mute on a trumpet, she said. "Close," he said, "but not quite."

Another boy had a mailbox next to hers in the post office. She had seen him draw a card from a box and present it at the window and walk off with a laundry case. The case was probably full of starched ironed shirts from home, because he always wore a nicely ironed shirt under his brown suede jacket. His hair was slicked back the way Loring used to comb his with water before the kitchen mirror. But she didn't even know who he was, this boy. She only liked the way he looked.

Then there was Roger Honey, an upperclassman who bore the burden of his name with unfailing good humor. He was the artist who did the chalk work at the talent show, where he had been introduced as "the sweetest boy on campus." His art was neither here nor there, though it seemed to be in demand at the Practical Work Department. It was common knowledge that churches requested him all the time for young people's meetings. He could play the trumpet and lead the singing as well as preach and illustrate his talk with the artwork. "The Lord really uses that guy," she heard someone say. It was his easygoing manner that Jo liked, observing him from a distance. If he were to show an interest in her, which was certainly unlikely, she would not brush him off very easily, not if she were twice as busy.

Still, she felt comfortable and unentangled now. She had not had any crushes on boys in two years, and she felt quite sure that was the way it ought to be. She could wait. There was a stickiness that bothered her in some of the Calvary romances, couples logy with desire, smooching in shadowy corners—or girls hanging on boys' arms at free-times, as if they were already weighted down with marriage. Some couples had devotions together on their dates. That might be nice, but something about it made her uneasy. What she had written to Clyde was true and right, she thought, and she had been guided in it after all. "I would like to keep myself free. . . ." She copied it over and gave it to him the next day.

His answer was sticking out of her Bible after lunch. He must have put it there during the meal, while her jacket and books were in the hall outside the dining room.

Dear Miss Fuller! Your words have stirred my heart!! I am in a position to understand perfectly. God has long been speaking to me about this very matter. I am much in prayer about it. Very burdened. A lot of girls around here are making it hard for guys to live close to the Lord. I am glad you are not one of them. Your brother at the foot of the cross. C. MacQuade.

What significance had he drawn from her words? The last thing she had meant to do was stir his heart. But something had been set in motion. In the next few days she was barraged by little notes, in her books and jacket pockets.

If He is not Lord *of* all, He is not Lord *at* all.

In my flesh dwelleth no good thing.

Hate even the garment spotted by the flesh.

Dearly beloved, I beseech you as strangers and pilgrims,
abstain from fleshly lusts.

Jo felt befouled by these notes, as if they were sordid, like the obscene drawings that got passed around in high school. Yet it was nearly all Scripture. "Strangers and pilgrims . . . ." she liked that. What had Clyde done to make it look so silly?

Then, abruptly, the notes ceased. He stopped speaking to her. She thought with relief that the whole thing was over. Yet she saw more of him. At first it seemed merely accidental if he was behind her in the cashier's line in the bookstore, or at the same table in the library, hidden in a newspaper. She would turn in the crowd at the post office when the mail was out at midmorning to find him a couple of feet away, his glance directed over the top of her head, his small serious mouth pursed importantly. He was with her, yet not, like a bodyguard, never speaking or catching her eye.

It made her nervous. She considered wheeling on him with a glare and an icy whisper: "Amscray, Buster!" But that would be admitting she had noticed him, and what was more, she had not yet heard anyone at Cal talk like that to anyone else.

One afternoon, catching a glimpse of him in the courtyard, she darted into the Pastry Shop and hid in a rear booth. The backs of the benches were higher than her head, and there was no way he could spy her through the window. She was the only girl there at the time, and for that reason too she was glad to be unnoticeable. Four men students were having a theological argument in another booth. They were Pastor's Course people. Their books, piled on the floor by their chairs, included Greek grammars and texts for Church History. She envied them. She had glanced through a Greek grammar in the bookstore. The graceful mysterious shapes seemed filled with meaning. Someday she meant to study Greek, and maybe Hebrew.

She had seen these particular boys before. Often when she entered her Personal Evangelism class, the blackboard was full of unerased diagrams from the previous class. Circles and arrows intercepted importantly in a maze of lines that made a journey to nowhere, all of it labeled by words she had never seen before—ontology, soteriology, lapsarianism. The class was always late breaking up. An earnest knot of male students surrounded the instructor, and as Jo's class gathered, the knot would move down the aisle and out the door as a unit, talking all the way.

They debated zestfully now, here in the Pastry Shop, interrupting each other constantly and heaping their words together on the table. Jo, sipping her coffee, strained to follow them. "Decreed will of God," someone said, and "free play for the human will." Predestination. Determinism. If lives were predestined, or even foreknown, how did personal decisions matter a hill of beans? Did you really decide for Christ, or were you chosen to decide? They contended this, voices rising, until one of them (older than the others—at least he was quite bald) cried out in despair, "But what shall I tell the little old ladies at South Podunk Baptist?" The others laughed and patted him on the shoulders. "Both truths, but not in the same sermon," someone answered.

I am from South Podunk, thought Jo. And she had the brains to see that this was no dead-end street. The path led unavoidably on to other disturbing matters. The boys, finished with their laughter, were sprinting on down that path themselves. Four hundred million souls in India, all conditioned to think a certain way, conditioned to find Christ alien, you might say. Even if they heard the Gospel, would they be held responsible for rejecting it? If they heard it badly, offensively, not often enough? Why should they face an eternity of hell?

It seemed to Jo there was no possible solution. The conflict was inherent in both the nature of God and the way He had made man—with a will of his own. But next the boys were quoting a philosopher who said free choice was nothing but a myth anyway, and she could see the truth of that too. A totally free choice would have to be made in a vacuum. For a moment she was frightened. Life was an ignominy, an insult. Yet her fright was only a question. She was sure the answer was out there somewhere waiting for discovery. She had never really doubted in these two years of being a Christian. Except as she saw things through someone else's eyes—her father's, or Loring's. "Picture me in hell," Daddy said once, in the middle of one of those grueling sessions last year. "Go ahead, make yourself see it. Writhing in pain for eternity! Mother, me, Loring? You can't see it, can you?"

"No," Jo had answered, not only because she couldn't, but because she saw how dreadful it would be to him if she could, realizing for that instant (through her father's eyes, or through her own?) the horrible sadism it took to give yourself to the truth of hell.

Yet the boys in the next booth were not really worried, for all their noise and earnestness. Maybe that was how it ought to be. They turned in a unit to God's mercy, repeating the word with assurance. Mercy . . . yes, that's it—mercy. They left the discussion hanging there, as if on a hastily driven nail, and went on to talk about football.

It was at this point that Clyde came in. His presence was an abrupt violation of privacy. Jo felt sure he had seen her as he entered, though he stood with his back to her at the counter. She was angry at this, and provoked with herself for letting it bother her.

She tried to imagine what Karen would do. Karen would catch his eye and be mildly surprised to see him. "Oh, hi, Clyde," she would say, absolutely friendly, discharging the situation of all significance. Jo decided to try it. She gathered her books and left the booth. When Clyde turned, she looked full at him, but before she could speak he cast his eyes in the other direction.

In an hour she had gotten another note, dropped on the table in front of her in the library.

> Watch your eyes. Your eyes are a dead giveaway. I don't want any rumors flying until God has revealed His will for us. Do not lag in prayer. Satan has been raising active opposition at this school lately and the ones he tries hardest to decieve are those who are sold out to Christ. Prayerfully yours, Cpl. MacQuade
>
> P.S. "Zip your lip." Destroy this.

Back in her room, Jo fumed her way through irate answers.

Dear C. Mac! You presume too much. Leave me alone.

Cpl., Sir: I have just receieieived a very silly note from you.

Listen, Mister. What do you mean about my eyes? You had better ask the Lord to . . .

There were noises outside the door, a soft cluck of girls' voices, a little like the sound of dishes in a real kitchen. Karen opened the door and walked in. She looked amiable and breezy, and Jo picked up Clyde's notes to show her, then changed her mind and slipped them into the desk drawer instead.

Karen would never get a note from a boy like Clyde in the first place. Even if one were sent, Jo had a feeling it would never reach her. She seemed protected by something, a manner, a glow, the source of which was unclear. It was her hair, or the tint of her skin, or maybe even a reflection from the carrot sticks she kept in water in a fish bowl on her desk. Often, as Jo buzzed about her duties, she was aware of Karen's face, watching her quietly across the carrot sticks.

An invisible line had drawn itself down the middle of their room. On her side, Karen worked methodically. In the afternoon, her radio turned low on her desk, she rooted softly for the White Sox as she studied. Each night at 10:45 she removed her glasses and slipped a silver retainer on her upper teeth before she got into bed. In the morning she reversed the process.

She had brought things from her own room at home—a braided rug for between their beds, and a bulletin board, one half of which was to be Jo's. On her own half of it Karen had tacked up a picture of Candle, Alaska. Candle was twenty-five miles south of the Arctic Circle. It was a mining town, a handful of shacks, all but buried in the snow. That was where Karen hoped to be sent to open a clinic. The nearest hospital was over a hundred miles away and there was no doctor in the area. The Swedish Covenant had begun to raise money for the clinic. Jo had no doubt that Karen would get there and that life in Candle would be all at once bright and full of hope, and surely organized.

As yet Jo had not seen Karen so much as wash her hair. She shampooed it at home on Saturdays, and it stayed clean all week. Jo was always getting caught at lights-out with her hair in a sink, and later as she sat up in bed dripping in the dark, groping for bobby pins on the blanket, Karen's Pepsodent yawn reached her as a reprimand. Yet there was no real basis for Jo to feel that way, and she knew it.

Earlier in the month, when Karen came back from her first weekend in Oak Park, the whole family came with her. They filled the narrow spaces in the room, each holding a package of food—father, mother, grandmother, and a little sister named Anna with glasses and braces. Karen's mother had glasses too, and the same teeth. All of them had the look of good care, even the grandmother. She gazed up at Jo from bent shoulders, where four tiny red foxes circled the collar of her suit jacket.

Mr. Eckstrom, a tall, heavy man, grunted disapproval at their network of extension cords, then crouched to fiddle with the broken turn-off on the radiator. He had brought a box of tools. Anna plopped down on Jo's unmade bed.

"Sit down, Mormor," said Karen to her grandmother, "and stop staring at Jo."

"Svenska flicka?"

"Nope," answered Karen. "I already told you."

"No?" asked Mormor. She was plainly disappointed.

"It's all right, Mormor," said Mrs. Eckstrom. "She's a good girl anyway." She smiled at Jo apologetically.

"What does she want?" asked Jo.

"She wants to know if you're Swedish," Karen explained. "She thinks I should have a Swedish roommate. Don't let it bother you. She's nuts." Did she say that fondly?

"This is not a Swedish school, Mormor!" boomed Karen's father, on his knees by the radiator.

Mormor's hand shot up to her hearing aid. She fingered it painfully. "Heela teeden," she muttered. Then she studied Jo again. "Vy don't you eat? You got to get fatter."

"Oh, I eat a lot," Jo protested, smiling at her. When Mormor looked doubtful, she added, much too loudly, "I do! I do eat!"

"Jo, we hope you can come home with Karen some weekend soon," said Mrs. Eckstrom. She was sitting in Jo's desk chair, on the edge of it, since the back was covered with Jo's clothing—skirts and things that had been tossed there during the week. Jo explained about her weekend duties, noticing out of the corner of her eye that an old slip with a safety pin in the strap hung in plain sight.

"Well, Thanksgiving then, for sure," said Mrs. Eckstrom. "Will you come for Thanksgiving?"

"Of course. I'd love to."

When they left, the radiator had been turned off, the broken drawer glued and clamped, and Mormor had made Jo's bed. She had even plumped up the pillow and turned back the top sheet, ready for the night.

"Thank you," Jo said. She really didn't know what to say.

They left behind some of the most delicious cookies she had ever eaten—S-curves called spritz and ginger cookies called pepperkakka (said Karen, spelling it) and thick slices of dark sweet bread spread with butter.

Karen had offered several times to take some of Jo's laundry home to Oak Park with her own and do it there, but Jo said no. She could see Mormor muttering in Swedish over a tubful of grayed undies. In the basement of the dormitory there were set-tubs and wringer washers and lines strung up for drying, but Jo had not yet found time to get down there and do a whole load at once, so her laundry bag hung bulging and a little smelly in the closet. She soaked a few things each day in one of the kitchen sinks and draped them over the radiators at night. It was not the best arrangement. Her blouses picked up rust, and her sweaters dried with ridges in them.

Taking a bath was a problem too. The tub was occupied whenever she had a moment to use it. One tub was not enough for eight girls, and they were not allowed to use it during study hours. Jo was used to getting along without a tub. There was none at home in Garfield. She had learned to take stand-up sponge baths in a basin, with water heated in a kettle on the stove, and she had never felt unclean. But that Chicago dirt had to be soaked off. It glued itself to your skin and buried itself in your pores before you realized it was a force to be reckoned with every day. They all faced this. The city settled into them, into the fibers of their clothing, under their fingernails, and up their noses. Even when their windows were not open, it sneaked under the sashes. "Heela teeden," Karen would mutter, as she blew the dirt off her books. It meant "All the time!" she said. The big white blotters they had bought to cover the surfaces of their desks were smudged already.

Karen was snapping on lights and adjusting the curtains now on her side of the room while Jo tried to dispose of her notes. "What have you been doing over there in the dark?" Karen asked.

"Nothing important." It was not, Jo decided. That was the effect Karen's presence had on lots of matters.

The two of them still had not held a serious conversation about anything. They had such a lot in common, yet it was as if they had come to this ground by opposite roads and had not managed to meet.

At times Karen's road looked very desirable—compact, Christian, Swedish. No loose ends or wrenching decisions. Once Jo had asked her when it was she had given up the movies, and Karen said she had never been to one in her life. This was unbelievable.

"None?" asked Jo. "Not ever?"

"Only things in school—like Niagara Falls and how cotton is made, that sort of thing."

"Didn't you want to?"

"Oh, sure, sometimes. I could have. My parents never said I couldn't. But none of my friends in church went either. It didn't matter much. We were busy with other things and having fun."

Karen was saying this? She could find her way around Chicago as if it were somebody's back yard. If she were a farm girl, or a Mennonite, like several pink-cheeked girls at school with little caps over their chignons, such a protected life would make some sense.

By comparison Jo felt old with experience, certainly not because of all the movies she had seen, but because she stopped seeing them on her own. Her reasons had been mixed and maybe not totally clear, but it was her decision, made apart from her family. She had heard kids she mingled with at Youth for Christ rallies in Boston talk about consecrating their lives to Christ and throwing out the old idols. They quoted from Romans 12:2 a lot: "And be not conformed to this world: but be ye transformed by the renewing of your mind."

She had wanted to take that step. She had never been one to do things halfway. Even in kindergarten she had been the first to lift her knees high to the music when they marched around the room. When they learned to knit in 4-H, she wanted to start with a sweater, not a straight scarf. She hated to dust a room. She would rather spend a whole exhausting day cleaning the house, changing things around (to her mother's dismay), starching the curtains and picking flowers for vases, or not do anything at all. She hoped she was not proud of this quality. It seemed beyond pride entirely.

Now Karen was sharpening a handful of pencils, turning them in a yellow shaver she held in her fingers over the wastebasket. Jo felt special, chosen for hardness, going it alone. Karen had never had to fight. Her family and church were solidly behind her.

The sharpened pencils clinked into the jar one by one. It's up to me to bridge the gap, thought Jo, suddenly ashamed of her reticence. Karen had shared her possessions and brought her family. Jo pictured her own family in the room, come for a visit, Mother, Daddy, Loring, Yooney. They looked strange and out of place. What would they bring? Not fancy cookies—a box of prunes and water from the well.

"What are you smiling about?" asked Karen.

"Nothing," said Jo. But she knew exactly what to do. It was a wonder she hadn't thought of it before.

After dinner that day Jo located some pictures among her things, and when Karen was out of the room she pinned up one of them on the bulletin board, an 8 x 10 glossy of Loring's crew, posed informally in front of their plane. It had been taken at Casper Field in Wyoming. The crewmen sat on the ground with their knees up, ankles crossed, and the four officers stood behind, Loring among them. They were all hatless. Loring's hair, grown out at last after the first crewcut, blew in the Wyoming wind.

Karen noticed the picture right away, of course. She knew Loring was in the Air Corps and that he was overseas. Jo had told her that much. "Which one is your brother?" she asked.

"Navigator," said Jo. "Second from the left."

"Oh yes. . . . What kind of a plane is that?"

"B-24. Liberator. They've been bombing in Europe."

Karen examined the picture a minute more, said they were sure a handsome bunch, and then was gone, over to her desk. Jo was not certain what she had expected her to say or ask, but she was disappointed, and more than that, she was cross with herself. Bringing out the picture was a mistake after all. She had meant only to introduce Loring. Instead, it was as if she were making a big announcement, her "news." Now, with the picture up and the news not told, its significance grew even bigger. It hung in the room overpoweringly, this huge silent fact in her life. The crew smiled, their hair blew in the wind, the shiny plane behind them so new, so intact, every seam and rivet showing. In the first week after the telegram, she had tried a hundred times to take the plane apart, to see it falling, disintegrating, men tumbling out, unseamed, unriveted. Always they sprang back together, everything in place. They grinned now from the bulletin board. She wanted to put the picture away, but that would be an even more obvious gesture.

Later that evening Soup came in. "Oh, beautiful!" she cried. "Maleness! How I love it! Who are they?" When Jo explained and pointed out Loring, Soup insisted he and Jo looked just alike.

"No, we don't," said Jo, put off by Soup's excessiveness. "Loring has red hair."

"Are you Irish?"

"My mother is. But that's not where the red comes from."

Soup groaned. "Irish, Swedish, Italian. Everybody's something, and I'm nothing. Zero."

"You have to be something," Karen said.

"No, sir," mourned Soup. "I have no ancestors. Not one. No grandparents even. My mother and father weren't even born. You know that? They materialized at puberty."

"Hush!" said Karen, pointing at the door. Someone was moving around in the kitchen. "Jewel," whispered Soup, and quickly opened a large chart for Adolescent Psychology across Jo's bed. They were not supposed to visit each other's rooms in the evening unless they studied together, and Soup seldom studied. What she came for usually was to retrieve and convey information.

"Karen, Jo! Mr. and Mrs. America and all the ships at sea!" she would cry as she lurched through the door. She had a way of throwing her body forward as she walked. "Let's have three cheers for Buddy Shaw and God! . . . Ah, God I know, you say, but who be Shaw? A shy lad who keeps to himself, is he. A boy so tender he cries if the potatoes have been mashed. But today, my dears, he has lost all inhibitions. He's shouting for joy over there on the campus. You see, he earned five hundred dollars for school this summer, only to spend it all on—guess what? New teeth. Yes, yes, a plate. No laughter. Poor boy, he came to school empty-handed— though full-mouthed, you might say. Not a cent for his bill. Board bill, that is. But he came, trusting his Heavenly Father, and this morning the whole thing was paid by an anonymous donor."

If she had no news, Soup would tiptoe into the room. She would come up behind you and cover your eyes with her hands. Or she might give you a hard sudden back-rub between the shoulder blades. At least she did it to Jo; she hadn't tried it yet with Karen.

This night of the picture she would not settle down. She whistled under her breath and sang in a whisper on the bed. "He lives! He lives! Christ Jesus lives today!" She cracked her knuckles until Jo turned around. Soup waved at her happily.

"Got any more snapshots of your family, Shrimp?"

"You just don't want to study, Soup."

"That's true, but I would really like to see your pictures. You do have some, don't you? Everybody does."

"We're bothering Karen."

"Don't worry about me," said Karen.

Jo, reluctant, pulled her wallet out of a drawer and handed it to Soup.

"Furlough pictures," said Soup, spreading the snapshots on the bed. "They always make me cry."

It was a roll of film that had been taken in April on Loring's last furlough. They had each posed with him in front of the cedars by the porch. Jo wore his uniform and was lost inside it. They had been horsing around all week, the alternative to a strained courtesy. Now they were making wry faces at Daddy, who always took forever to focus a camera and prodded people into smiles with baby talk. "Ha-*ha!* Oos better smile, cause she's a-goin' of it! . . . Bootiful!" It irked Jo to hear him do that, but she tried not to show it, feeling his love behind the black box.

"Oh, just hurry up!" Mother complained, with Loring's cap pulled down over her face. She thought she took a terrible picture and always tried to hide. Her face was too thin. She had been pretty once, in a precarious way that had come loose several years back.

"He's a doll," said Soup. She was holding the one of Loring alone, back in his own uniform. All that week he had worn his old green plaid shirt with the holes in the elbows, though it didn't seem to fit him any more. It had hung by the back door when he was gone. At the end of the furlough he packed it away with his other things, shoving them under his bed in cartons, neatly labeled, as if he knew the same person would not be coming home under any circumstances and might not recognize the stuff.

Jo reached for the pictures to put them away.

"Wait, I'm not done," said Soup. She lingered. "How come your father looks so young? Even with white hair. What color did it used to be?"

"Reddish." The color of an old penny. He had freckles and blushed a lot. People thought he was a college student. "What? You look too young to be a father," Jo used to hear women say when she went selling with him. She had gone along whenever she could, to protect him from the customers he complained about, young wives of doctors and lawyers in Wellesley and Newton whose "minds were shut before they opened the door." She would demonstrate the Busy Kiddy, hanging by her knees and skinning-the-cat, never giggling or acting silly, even if she felt like it. Selling was hard for him. It was more like him to give everything away. "That man will pick up a hitchhiker and offer him the car," Mother would murmur, watching out the windows for his headlights on the quarry road.

They were all glad whenever he was sick and had to stay home. He kept getting things wrong with him that were funny and dreadful. Boils on his feet once. Then he had pyorrhea and paced the living room floor, rubbing teething lotion on his gums. They had to borrow money from Grampa for food and bills.

It was during this period that Mrs. Cannon persuaded him to drop selling and try his hand at writing. "Just the story of your own mental bootstraps, that alone would be valuable reading," she said. She got him to do a personal memoir and send it to *Reader's Digest*, because they paid the best.

"Wait," said Soup again, brushing Jo away with her shoulder. She was stringing things out as long as she could. "What a cute house. It looks like a summer cottage."

"It used to be a quarrymen's camp."

"What quarry?"

"A traprock quarry, in the woods nearby. My parents found the house when they were picking blueberries. Before I was born."

"Do you own it?"

"Oh, no. It belongs to some neighbors. The Cannons."

"Do you like it in the woods?" Soup wanted to know.

"In ways. My mother likes it. . . . I think they only meant to stay there for a summer, at first. There's no electricity or running water."

She should have known better than to say that. Soup was intrigued. Just like the mission field. How did they keep warm? Who lit the lamps? No bathroom? Wasn't there a telephone even? No. No radio? Yes, batteries charged by a little windmill on the roof, hitched also to an auto horn that would blow for emergencies. "Did you ever have to blow it?" asked Soup. No. No emergencies they couldn't handle themselves.

Then Karen came over. She sat down beside Soup and examined the pictures. "You look like everybody else," she commented.

"I know," said Jo. She glanced at the person who was herself in the snapshots. She had inherited too much. Too much was going on in a small space—wide mouth, faint horizontal lines already in her forehead, tiny dark freckles even on her eyelids, and dark eyebrows that got mussed at night when she slept. When she was twelve, she had practiced for weeks looking poised and peaceful in the kitchen mirror, and when she finally thought she could do it without looking, someone at school said, "You know what? You look like a leprechaun."

"People used to tell Loring he'd be a pretty girl," Jo said, going back to the desk with her wallet.

It had plagued the daylights out of him, the way people stared. She stared at him sometimes too, when they did their homework together under the lamp in the living room. It was a pressure lamp, and they both hated to stop to pump it. Loring would duck down to catch the fading light, and his eyebrows and lashes would turn amber. If he caught her looking, he bared his teeth and snarled, "Pump the lamp, Picklepuss."

"Pump it yourself, wise guy," she answered, and he grabbed her wrist and squeezed until she gave in and reached for the brass pump. She used to be afraid of his hard, sudden fists, but she never gave him the satisfaction of showing it. She often vowed she was going to give him one truly good wallop he would never forget, but then she would have to forgive him before she got the chance, because he would do something kind, like letting her get into bed with him if she was afraid at night (turning his back and making sure no part of them touched). Or he might bound in out of the cold air like a big dog, yell, "Where's the brat?" and whirl her around the room.

No, she meant more than looks. She was stronger than he was. Right up into junior high he came as quickly to tears as he did to fists. "Police those tears!" Daddy would say. It annoyed him to see Loring cry. He would tell him to learn to bark his shins on the raw realities of life and take it like a man. "Look at your little sister. She doesn't cry." She didn't, except now and then listening to *Death Valley Days*.

"You must be proud of him," said Soup. "It takes brains to be a navigator."

"I know," said Jo. "He's always been good at math and stuff. He was a pre-med at Tufts on a scholarship when he enlisted."

"When did he join up?"

"Year before last."

"Does he love the Lord?"

Jo turned to look at Soup to be sure she meant it. Of course she did, but the question seemed totally foreign in relation to Loring. Soup asked it again. "Is he a Christian?"

"Not to my knowledge," Jo said uncomfortably.

"No? Has he heard the Gospel?"

"Probably not. In the right way, I mean."

"Didn't you have a chance to tell him?"

"Not really. He didn't want to talk about it." She had always thought there would be a right time, the right mood, a time to explain it well, when his disdain had cooled.

"He refused, you mean," Soup said.

"Not exactly. . . . Maybe I didn't try hard enough."

Or too hard. Once at a youth rally in Boston she had heard a soldier talk about kneeling by his bunk in the barracks to pray in front of all his buddies. It had taken him a long time to find the courage to do it. He had been ashamed of Christ, he said. Jo saw immediately that she'd been avoiding a confrontation with Loring. For those two, three months since her decision, she'd been praying on her back in bed, looking as if she were asleep.

So that night she blew the lamp out, her bravado not taking her quite far enough for light, and Loring stumbled over her in the dark.

"Jeeezus Christ!" he swore. "What are you doing down there?" She answered, "It's only me," not meaning to be funny, and neither of them laughed. If they had, things might have been different. Loring stuck his head back over his side of the partition and said, "Don't flaunt it, that's all! Don't flaunt your holy-moly at me!" She felt the old sparks that flew so often between them and wanted to hit him, really land him one on the nose. She shot back, "It's none of your business anyway! Can I help it if you have to track through my side of the room?"

"He thought I'd gone off the deep end," she said to the girls. That was all she said.

"Does he still think that?" asked Soup.

"Oh . . . I suppose so. I meant while he lived at home. He hated anything fanatical." She was going to tell them what had happened to him. She would in a second, when she could do it casually, with her face and voice right.

"Do you hear from him?" Soup and Karen were still on Jo's bed. They were both looking at her, Soup's eyes inquisitive and Karen's simply blue, waiting for an answer. Karen was wearing a white turtleneck sweater, and Soup was wearing a green rayon blouse—was it size 46?— the shoulder pads dropping down off her arms.

"Oh sure, but not just lately," Jo said. "Mail doesn't always come through sometimes, you know. It's unpredictable from overseas. We've always gotten it in clumps."

She had really meant to tell. She was startled by her own reluctance and astonished that she had as much as told a lie. There was a clumsy pause while they looked at her. Correct it, she thought. Now. Soup said, "The Lord is taking care of him, Shrimp. We'll pray for him." Then there was another pause, and Soup whispered, "Oh no. She's found me again." A crooked step was crossing the kitchen floor. "Are you in there, Soup?" called Jewel softly.

"Okay! Okay! We're coming out!" Soup answered. Leaping from the bed, she grabbed Jo around the neck and pushed her toward the door. "Hold your fire!" she called. "I've got a hostage!"

That night Jo had trouble getting to sleep again. Each time she started to drop off, sudden images, provoked by the snapshots, roused her and her eyes flew open.

Loring charged down the quarry road in a cloud of dust, his knickers ballooning around his legs and his socks falling. "Stop!" he yelled, churning his arms at the disappearing Plymouth. "Come back with that car!" Daddy ran after him and led him home, talking, talking to him, Loring with his face hot and wet, crying into his bent arm. "But it's ours," he insisted, totally frustrated.

He had not seen Daddy drive home with the man in the car and hand him the keys. It was an hour before Loring understood (and years before Jo did) how the car could really belong to the other man, who was taking it back because Daddy had failed in his payments.

"Don't blame the poor man," Daddy kept saying. "He has his rights."

It seemed to Jo that Daddy was much easier on the man than he was on Loring. He shook him quite hard to make him stop crying and suggested a bucket of cold water might bring him out of it. " 'Oh, give me a place in the world's great fight!' " he recited in a deep voice. " 'A soldier's work to do!' " He was always reciting that.

Later Loring whispered in the bedroom, "Someday I'm going to be a doctor and give him all my money." She had forgotten that part. It fluttered into her memory now like an injured bird. She was being foolish. Loring himself would not feel sorry for that ten-year-old boy. It was wrong to let her thoughts get so morbid. She reached for something bright and calm. Tomorrow was choir, one of the best hours of the week.

Letter to Yooney: I am learning how to breathe. Yes, at last. Next time you stand to sing in church, watch the backs of the people in front of you. If they catch their breath up around the shoulders, that is wrong. Their ribs should expand, down low around the waist. Then you train your muscles to push the air up, up—not to the throat but to the eyes. The throat is just a passageway. The sound must float out of your eyes. My brain tells me to work at it too hard. I haven't found the right combination of control and relaxation. At our last rehearsal I was reprimanded for chin wobbles— that's a sign of tightness. I laughed, and the director said, "There. Now you've got it!" If I could sing and laugh at the same time, I'd be famous.

On the day after Clyde's "watch your eyes" note Jo found a letter from him in her post office box. It was posted and in an airmail envelope.

Dear Sister Jo. It must seem to you that I have been acting strangely. I am ready to explain. Maybe you have noticed that I am not a run-of-the-mill C.B.I. student. God seems to have set me apart for some reason of His own. You see, I know what it means to bear about in the body the dying of the Lord Jesus. I do not say this with pride. Perhaps He is preparing me for a ministry in which I shall face death regularly. Time is precious. I am appaled at the way students waste time around here, guys playing ball in the dormitory halls and horseing around. Never mind that now. The point is, I am trying to use every minute for His glory. Thus I rise at 5 A.M. to break open the Word. "No Bible No Breakfast" is my motto. There is no time for anything that does not further His cause. I long to be every minute on fire for Him. For the above reasons I am a celebate. Normally I do not even look at a girl. Colossians 3:3. The Holy Spirit controls my eyes. In view of this, you have been a great burden to me. Thus I have needed to find out what kind of girl you are, how closely you walk with the Lord etc. before I take any step. I find you puzzling. For instance, you attend a prayer band each day, but I have yet to hear you pray. What's more, there is something in your manner that bespeaks the old nature. I wonder if you are fully surrendered—even willing to die for the Lord. Nevertheless, I feel it is His leading for us to have fellowship in Christ. I do not have romance in mind at all, but a spiritual freindship, mindful of His presence. As to God's purpose in this, I know not. Let us begin by sitting together in the mess hall at some free-time meal. Soon? Pray and advise.

> Yours in His Conguering Name,
> C.
> P.S. Burn this.

At her first chance that afternoon, Jo hurried back to Harold Hall, determined to show this letter to Karen, regardless of anything. She was in the room. "Oh, there you are," she said, with an expression on her face Jo had never seen before, an anxious smile. On Jo's bed was a compact bundle, wrapped in a towel and sitting on another towel.

"I hope you don't mind," Karen said. "Someone wanted to use the sink they were in."

Jo opened the bundle and looked at the three tight rolls of white cotton and a shiny pink one, her own blouses and slips she had left soaking that morning.

"But . . . did you . . . you *scrubbed* them?" The clothes were very clean.

"I just swished them around a little and rinsed them out," said Karen. She was actually blushing. "Is it okay?"

"Of course. . . . Thank you. When did you do it?"

"I had a free period this morning. The blouses are starched, by the way. In fact, they should be just about ready for ironing."

They were perfect, the right dampness. Jo saw herself down in the basement laundry, ironing, the blouses glistening and smooth and smelling warm.

"I'll get to them quickly," she said, tucking the towel tight around the rolls again.

Karen turned back to her desk. In Jo's hand was Clyde's letter. That was the instant to give it to her, but the instant passed as she pondered whether or not she would be able to attend to the blouses before dinner, and the impulse to give Karen the letter was gone. The blouses were important; the letter was not.

"I'll do them after I practice," she said.

As it turned out, it was more than three days before she got to the ironing, and by then the slips had dried out and the blouses had mildewed.

In that time she never did give Karen Clyde's note and she never answered or acknowledged it. Instead, she fell in love, suddenly and overwhelmingly, with—of all people—Roger Honey.

It was as if a wind rushed through her life and blew open the doors, and there he was, before she could back off, pray, call for help, whatever could have prevented it.

It began with a curious experience in Beverly's room. It turned out that Beverly was the person Jo finally talked to about Clyde. Jewel was the proper one to go to with problems, of course. That was what a floor captain was for. But while she wore an air of wisdom, it seemed unlikely she would know anything about men. Soup was out of the question too, as were Ruth and Ruby.

Actually, Ruth was supposed to be in love with an ex-Calvary student named Barry. Last August, as Soup reported it, when the Lord put a burden on Ruth's heart to go to India, she broke up with Barry, because he was called to be a pastor in the States. Barry was in seminary now, in Dallas, and every week (said Soup) there was another letter begging Ruth to come back to him. *He* was sure the Lord meant them to be together.

It was hard to imagine Ruth in love at all, or Ruby either, as if they were above all that. Jo still mixed them up sometimes. Their lives seemed made of interchangeable parts. They both typed in offices in the Loop afternoons, they were both going to India to work with the Untouchables. They both used the word "precious" a lot when they talked, "precious Lord" or "precious Word."

It boiled down to Louise or Beverly. Louise was everybody's friend. Neighborhood children actually followed her down the street. She and Soup sneaked them into the dormitory and fed them snacks. Louise was openly fond of Charlie Higgins, the boy who stood on his thumbs. He lifted weights at the Lawson Y and chewed his milk. Jo could not imagine what Louise saw in him, and he seldom acknowledged her existence. Half the student body knew about her unrequited love and she didn't seem to mind.

Beverly too was an utterly sociable person. She bounced around school in crepe-soled oxfords, thick white socks pulled up over her stockings to her solid calf muscles, calling out her greetings in a strong contralto. She was a musician, engaged to a Marine overseas, and an

M.K.—a missionary kid. These combined to make her trustworthy and popular.

Jo went down to Beverly's room often to study music theory, and this is where they were, that day, sitting on the bed Indian style with their work in their laps, when Beverly said, "Is it true what I've been hearing about you and Clyde? That you're sweet on each other?"

"Oh my goodness!" Jo gasped. "You mean, people are *saying* that?"

"Oh, it's nothing," Beverly said. "It's just that Clyde is so super-spiritual. He won't cross a room without checking to see if it's God's perfect will, and he does all that talking about sanctification and celibacy. Everybody's waiting for him to fall madly in love." She was laughing as she talked, the way she always did, oiling her words with pleasant throaty chuckles.

"Well, he hasn't fallen," Jo said. "He says he wants a spiritual friendship."

"Ho!" crowed Beverly. "So that's it. Exactly what does *that* entail?"

"I don't know. He wants to sit with me some Sunday dinner."

"Oh, really, he's a sly one. Are you going to do it?"

"I hope not."

Beverly gave a delighted jounce on the pink bedspread. Her room was a pink photo gallery. Bob was everywhere, a strong presence, not only by way of photographs, but in the diamond on her left hand, his high school ring wound with adhesive tape on her right, his wristwatch on one arm, identification bracelet on the other. She wore a locket around her neck that opened to pictures of the two of them and shut to enclose them in a snug embrace. In the high school picture on the bureau hair rose off his forehead in a rippling cliff, and under a square of glass on the desk, against a pink blotter, were a dozen snapshots of him in his Marine dress uniform, his curls mowed down to a stubble. A print of Sallman's Head of Christ hung over the bed, looking rather pallid and yellow in all that pinkness.

Clyde was a sorry person, Beverly was saying. "He has no friends. I wonder if he's ever had. You must have heard what happened to him last year in his dorm."

Jo shook her head. Beverly was chuckling again. "One day when he was out the guys on his floor filled his room with trash from floor to ceiling. Right to the door."

"What a terrific idea!"

"Sure, and he deserved it. But if they'd treat him better, he'd be different."

"He scares me," said Jo. The admission startled her, and Beverly, too.

"Oh no, Jo, he's just odd. There always seems to be an oddball at Calvary. When my folks were here, it was a guy they called Little Marvin. He'd dress in a Boy Scout uniform and blow a bugle and say the Lord was calling him to Dearborn Street or whatever as he skipped across the courtyard."

"At least he was cheery."

"My father used to say God chooses the lowly to keep us all humble."

Show me a true believer and I'll show you a misfit, *my* father says, thought Jo. She was glad her father would never meet Clyde. But she could see the awful snobbery there, wanting only certain kinds of people to be Christians, to make your own allegiance look good to the world—to make *Christ* look good, of all things.

"Do you know about his family?" Beverly asked.

"No. Nothing." It hadn't occurred to Jo that Clyde even had a family.

"Our parents were students here at the same time," Beverly said. "Married students. Clyde and I were both little kids then, though I don't remember, of course. Jim and Carol Ross were here, too, the ones who were beheaded in Africa. My folks went to Kenya, and Clyde's went to Formosa. I forget which board they went under. But they only stayed six months. They were *sent* home by the board—dismissed, you understand? They tried to go back and were always turned down. . . . At least that's what my folks heard."

"What on earth happened?"

"I'm sure we'll never know. Maybe it wasn't anything spectacular, just being people who were difficult to get along with, like insisting their way was right, that they had more light and all. Missionaries usually try awfully hard to get along with each other, so they must have caused real trouble. Anyway, they've lived all this time at Clyde's mother's home, in Iowa, with the grandparents, and his father hasn't done anything except work on the farm there."

Jo stared down at her empty shoes, planted on the fluffy bath mat by the bed. "I have to tell him no," she said, "but I hate to hurt his feelings." He needed a friend. It explained all his queer behavior, the lack of grace, the odd combination of assertiveness and stealth. He had no idea how to make friends.

Beverly said, "He seems like such a bad testimony. But he does have a passion for souls. He's always out on the streets witnessing."

Said of anyone else, that might have been heartwarming. It made Clyde sound like a vampire.

"The Lord knows all about it, Jo. He'll show you what to do. He has a purpose in this."

"I'm not worried."

"Can you define an augmented chord?"

"Augmented?"

"You'll get that on the quiz."

Jo made an effort to gather her thoughts in the pink of Beverly's room. Someone from Africa ought not to like pink, though Beverly had not been in Africa for a long time now. She had gone to a girls' academy in Montrose, New Jersey. Bob was from Montrose.

"Augmented as opposed to diminished," Beverly hinted.

To Jo theory seemed much more like math than music, with its triads and dominant sevenths. The simplest things fled her mind, like how to change a chord from major to minor. Augmented? Bob, smiling at her from the frame, waited for an answer.

"I'm getting it," she groped.

Beverly scattered flag notes on the music paper. "Bob had to ask me out seven times before I went with him."

An augmented chord was a triad composed of two major thirds. Jo wanted to tell Beverly before she forgot, but Beverly was chattering,

66

blurring her words together. Bob had not a single musical bone in his body, she said.

"I thought I should marry a musician. We would be a Gospel team, you know. Sing and play instruments together. In other words, I was dictating to the Lord. When I stopped fighting, I had total peace about Bob."

"I see," said Jo. She was writing on the music paper, C-E-G#.

"Have you ever been in love, Jo?"

"Hundreds of times," Jo answered.

That tickled Beverly. She seemed to have forgotten about the augmented chord. She went to the bureau now and bent over from the waist, brushing her hair down from the neck. She was wearing a long flowered housecoat. Her oxfords and socks showed below it. "Which time was best?" she asked.

"A boy named Gary Ryan." It seemed entirely out of place to mention Gary now. Jo was surprised to have even remembered him in those terms. Beverly asked her something, behind the wall of hair. Jo didn't hear her. She had just caught a whiff, a gulp of summer night. Down by the frog pond they were slapping at mosquitoes and skipping stones, Loring and Gary good at it and laughing at her plunks. It came and went, as real as this pink room. A vague pain lingered, fading slowly.

"What made him different?" asked Beverly's muffled voice.

"Oh . . . he kept coming back, I guess you could say."

She had no intention of explaining that. There was a game she had played over and over—long ago, it seemed now. She had found it best to have an infatuation going whenever possible, not only because it kept a fresh supply of pleasant thought material on hand, but because the void was too quickly filled with fear, some member of the dark family that dozed along the corridors of her brain, waiting for a chance to rouse up and take over. If she was in love with somebody, her fears lost their power. So she chose boys she didn't know very well—always older, Loring's age—and made them into anything she wanted them to be, even changing their names to suit her taste.

In each case the game focused in on the moment when they, she and the boy, finally "knew." She had given herself to constructing these occasions while walking home from school alone. A favorite was getting knocked over by his bicycle, though it wouldn't be his fault, or hers either. He would help her limp to the doctor's office, secretly admiring the way she controlled her tears. She could make a boy so much a part of her thinking that in his actual presence she had to act as if she despised him to keep herself from blushing.

It always ended in disappointment. In time each boy would do something that revealed his true inadequacy and the whole thing would fall apart, leaving her empty and depressed. It took very little. He might spit on the sidewalk, or wear cotton in his ear for an earache, or get a haircut. A haircut, cruel and denuding, could strip a boy of prestige in an instant.

But Gary was never part of this. With all those fragile imaginary loves over the years, her affection for him had revived in reality every summer when he came to stay with "Aunt and Uncle Cannon, the Big Guns." It was never a question.

"Jo?" said Beverly.

"Yes."

"I said, where is he now?"

"Oh. In the Navy somewhere. Virginia, I think. I haven't heard from him in three years. He was never any good at writing. I'm not sure he can."

It was a joke, Mrs. Cannon's frustrated efforts to improve his mind. That was one of the reasons he spent summers with them. "What does she want? I read a book once," Gary would say.

"Did he love you, too?" asked Beverly.

It happened again, a sudden wind. Croquet at dusk, the three of them, at the level space below the house where the gold light held on a little longer. Moments before, with the sun going down, their shadows had stretched out rubbery before them. Smack! Mallet and ball, almost invisible. Then Mrs. Cannon's police whistle, faint and emphatic, beyond the pasture and orchard. Gary answers, "Coming!" plays for five more minutes and when Mrs. Cannon calls again, he plunges away through the juniper and sweet fern. He would be back in the morning, they always knew. Every day until September, when he went home to Pittsburgh.

"I was too young for him," Jo said, answering Beverly. "He was my brother's age. I used to chase them through the woods and the quarry. They'd hide on me." But she always found them—up a tree or in clumps of cedars, Coke bottles full of Kool-Aid tied to their belts. She would want to hug them both for joy, but she never did.

"He liked me," she told Beverly. "It was okay for him to think I was cute, I guess, because I wasn't his sister. He had no sisters or brothers."

Gary's face hung in her mind, joining the gallery in the room. His comical nose was too big, almost a man's nose even when he was nine and first came to Garfield. Now he and Loring lay very still on two cots on the screened porch, baseball on the radio between them. They were bare-chested, and their sweat smelled of juniper. The juniper that grew in the rocks around the house seemed to be melting.

She tried to stop it. It was unnerving for memories to be so real.

Beverly straightened up, brushing her hair back from her flushed face. "Jo, I meant grown-up love. Have you ever been *in* love?"

"I knew what you meant."

Several times a week they went swimming, on the other side of town, the three of them on Loring's bike, one boy on the back and Jo on the handlebars, facing the world. It was a mad, bumpy ride, careening between the cow flops in the pasture, then down the asphalt hills. At the lake they curved their bodies in surface dives, and raced for the float. Out there high school boys pushed each other off into the water all afternoon, glancing back at the rocks where girls combed their sopping hair, one knee up for leg profile. Jo swam back and forth, not one of the boys, and not one of those girls, either.

One night they went to the lake for moonlight swimming. She was fourteen then. It was like going to a place they had never been to before. Every tree and rock was transformed. No one was there, only laughter from a rowboat across the lake. The light was so clear it almost hurt, yet it was incomplete. You longed for sunlight and hoped it would never come.

They swam close to shore, breaking the surface with splashes that crackled. Afterwards, Jo and Gary sat on a bench. Loring stood at the edge of the water, skipping stones. The air was very warm.

Something special was about to happen. Importance—lovely, dangerous—lay heavy between them in the night air. Jo thought, she *knew*, that Gary was going to put his arm around her and draw her over against him. She wanted him to—and she didn't. The gesture would be too unnatural. She wished she were someone else, lithe and tanned. She sat there in the night, being that girl, and then his arm accidentally touched hers and that patch of her skin burned with the warmth of his and lightning flashed in her whole insides, so bright she thought it could be seen, like a firefly. He turned and looked at her, the tall, tan girl, and for a moment they tried to penetrate the moon shadows around each other's eyes. Then they laughed and it was over.

Who was the girl she had been? It made no sense for her to wish she were someone else with Gary, because she would be giving up too much. She knew him in a way no other girl ever would. She knew him almost as well as she knew Loring, and she saw them both through each other—Gary had given her more of Loring than she could have had by herself.

When he left for Pittsburgh on Labor Day, she found an old sneaker he had forgotten hanging on the clothes line and took it into the woods and kissed it. That was the last summer he spent in Garfield. So much had changed and he was part of the past now, that was all.

Beverly was dipping a comb into a glass of water to dampen her hair. "You know about Clyde, I take it," she said.

The transition seemed to reach back to weeks instead of seconds. "Know about him?"

"Yes, he's a medical discharge. Sugar. You know, diabetes. He was in the Army eight months before they recognized it."

"So that's it," murmured Jo. She had not known why he was discharged or actually cared enough to be curious.

"He's very sensitive about it," Beverly said. "It's very personal with him, the war and all. I heard he tried to give blood last week at the donor center and they turned him down."

So, even his blood was no good.

Beverly began to sing into the mirror as she combed her hair. She was singing low like a cello, ta-ta-da-tee-tum. Mozart? Jo watched her, glad to have her filling the air. She felt suddenly unsafe, target for anything. A hundred feelings . . . Clyde, Gary, Loring. It would go away in a minute.

Beverly spoke. "Clyde told me he would do anything to change places with Bob." She pulled her hair back tight with big clips, to straighten it during the night. "Just think, where Bob is now, it's tomorrow morning."

A basket on Beverly's desk was full of air mail letters from somewhere in the Pacific, Bob's location a secret. Jo slipped her shoes on. It was important to get out of this rosy room. "Thanks for the help," she said.

"That's okay. Goombye. Say good night to Bobski," said Beverly, cheerfully. She held out his school picture with the rippling hair. Jo hesitated, feeling foolish. She said, "What's the point? It's tomorrow where he is." The remark sounded oddly cruel. Beverly made a face and said to the picture, "Don't you mind that naughty dirl."

"I'm sorry," said Jo, and grabbed the picture and kissed it, startled to find only the cool flat pane of glass under her lips. She wiggled her fingers in a funny wave and shut the door on Beverly's laughter, and there she was, eye to eye with a sobbing African bush child tacked on the outside of the door, a cutout from a missionary pamphlet. For an instant sight and sound mixed, Beverly's chortle on the inside and the misery-stricken child on the outside. "Hopeless without Christ," said the caption.

That's silly, thought Jo. He's afraid of the camera.

The floor was quiet. Across the hall Louise's door was shut and there was no light under it. She had fastened up a poster with the letters J O Y on it. "Jesus first, Other next, Yourself last," it said. Ten feet down the hall Soup's door was opened into the room, but Jo knew what was on it. "Wildlife Refuge" at the top, postcards, magazine clippings, cartoons, church bulletins, and tracts. In the middle was a poem.

Only one life,
'Twill soon be past.
Only what's done for Christ
Will last.

The desk light was on, revealing a rumpled bed. Soup had been wrestling on it that afternoon with two neighborhood children, one white and one coffee-skinned with a forest of kinky orange hair.

"Holy Bejesus!" one of them had yelled.

"Oops!" reprimanded Soup. "Never swear in this building. Understand? Bejesus is *here!*"

It was against the rules to let children in from the street, but Jewel never said anything. The mother of these particular children locked them out of the home while she entertained her men. Soup taught them Bible verses. " 'Believe on the Lord Jesus Christ and thou shalt be saved.' You recite that to your mother," she told them. " 'Though your sins be as scarlet, they shall be white as snow.' " She was gone from the room now. There were potato chips on the floor.

Across the hall Ruth and Ruby had tacked maps of various parts of the world on the backs of the bureaus that divided their room from the passageway. "Go ye into all the world," they had printed on the maps, and "Here am I, Lord. Send me."

Now Jo was in the kitchen. Jewel's room was on the right, shut. Jo could hear her moving around in there. On her door there was nothing but a card that said: "Jewel Thorpe: Learning His Ways." Jo's own door was on the left, hers and Karen's. She was reluctant to go in. Karen was in there. She would be just through studying and putting her pencils back in the jar and shutting her books with a plump, neat sound like a librarian.

Jo felt petty and cross. She saw herself walking back the length of the quiet hall and yanking down off the doors and walls all the things people had put up.

On her own door in front of her Karen had taped a picture of Mt. McKinley, snow-covered. "How excellent is Thy Name in all the earth," she had printed under it. Jo herself had put up an elaborate drawing of a suit of armor, each section labeled from Ephesians 6:14-17, the "breastplate of righteousness," the "shield of faith," the "helmet of salvation." How could she have done anything so pretentious? Soup had drawn Kilroy on it, peeking over the shoulder. Jo ripped it off the door, thumb tacks flying into the kitchen, then tore it in half and walked into the room with the pieces in her hand.

Karen looked up over the carrot sticks with a quizzical expression.

"I don't like it any more," Jo said. "I hate it." She dropped it into the wastebasket. "My art," she explained to Karen, "not Ephesians." Then she was crankier than ever, for trying to explain, and because she really didn't know what it was she did hate or if she really did at all. She undressed, singing to herself, lest she direct her feelings at Karen.

Two hours later Jo crept down the silent hall to the bathroom, a place to put the light on and get herself back to Calvary. She had tried, in bed, to compose another letter to Yooney about tomorrow. It hadn't worked this time. Tomorrow's schedule eluded her. The cross mood was gone, and she felt vulnerable again, as she had in Beverly's room, an easy mark, rushed at by memories and feelings, the sky of her mind filling up as tiny dark clouds raced for the center. She had never felt so awful in her life, except for the day of the telegram. Trust, trust, she repeated. Let not your heart be troubled.

She liked the old bathroom. The sink was marble and the faucets, coated with green that never stayed scrubbed off (she ought to know—cleaning in here was her job), stood up high and slender. Jo fastened her eyes on those faucets, then on the tiny white tiles of the floor, then on a picture over the bathtub of Christ being baptized in the River Jordan. She tried to conjure some of her earlier anger, this time against the white robe and the rolled-up eyes and the artists who had planted these notions in everybody's mind, making Him less real.

She talked to herself busily about this, walking in a triangle between the sink, tub, and toilet. The mind wanted concreteness—"the visible expression of the invisible God." Immanuel. It meant God *with* us. He had to be a real human.

Then did He go to the bathroom?

Strike that. A worthless thought.

But did He? In the desert? In the *Jordan*?

"Stop this nonsense," she said out loud. What did it matter whether He did or He didn't? It mattered. Because if He did—which of course He did—it put a whole new light on things. But what light? If God Incarnate went to the bathroom, then . . . She must be crazy to pursue this. She reached for an abstract to balance her thoughts. Logos, Word. But the Word *made flesh*. Back again. Poetry rescues theology. (Who had said that?) Lamb of God. Lion of Judah. Lion/Lamb. Hunter/Victim. Sometimes you could only juggle from hand to hand the things the Bible threw at you. Two-sided truths. The Holy Spirit was like a breath, a wind. And yet Satan was prince of the power of the *air*.

Prince was too nice a word for him, *that* person. Actually, she questioned the existence of Satan at all. Yet she believed in evil. She had believed in evil long before she believed in God. Hovering trouble. A face at the window watching for the right chance. She knew about that. She explained this to the white trio, tub, sink, and toilet, who listened uncritically.

A bath might help, the shock of cold water, to lie back until your head is covered, then up, gasping and streaming. She had never been baptized. This fat tub was almost as big as a baptismal tank. She knew that because when the Baptist Church back home blew down in the hurricane, there was the tank, the Baptist mystery, where everybody could see it, full of rain water, a painted mural of a river standing behind it. Corey Byrne, the son of the Baptist pastor, had insisted she was not obeying "our Lord's example" unless she was immersed. He had offered his father's services, but she could not see herself going down into that galvanized tank, which had now (since the hurricane) been salvaged and built into the heart of the new little church. She said she would rather wait and do it in a river sometime.

Her mind was like a machine again, with no button to turn it off. She sat on the edge of the tub and tried to think only of how hard and cold the porcelain felt. Someone had left a can of April Showers talc in the corner. Jo drifted some onto the floor and pushed it with her toes. She hummed softly, to make a present sound. "Drop Thy still dews of quietness, till all our strivings cease."

It had been a luxury to go once in a while to the Framingham house for their baths, until Grampa began to keep the tub full of yellow drippings from the broken tap. Rather than waste that water or call a plumber, he caught it and dipped it out into the sink for washing and shaving.

In that house, such a thing was not surprising. Grammy and Grampa sat in darkness in the evening to save on the light bill, the eye of the radio shining dimly in the corner. The gas jets in the kitchen were used only in summer; during the winter they burned coal in the kitchen range to heat the house, and hot water came from a kettle. It was a depressing thing to get cold water from a faucet that said "Hot" right on it. Food sat around the kitchen, butter soft on the table, and several bowls of leftovers on *top* of the ice box (no ice), always seeming to be cabbage or turnip, covered with waxed paper held in place by rubber bands.

She had found it exasperating that her grandparents would live that old-fashioned way. Theirs was no house in the woods, like her own. It was in Framingham, where Garfield people went for permanent waves and to the movies. But for all the vague shame she felt, she had liked to visit. Grammy fed her molasses cookies as soft as cake, and Yooney was always there, glad for company. Grampa was a patient audience when you were learning some new skill, such as yodeling or raising one eyebrow.

Framingham had been Loring's home until he was three, and while he always said he didn't remember anything before Jo was born, when they approached the house in the car, he grew silent. She had never asked him about it, because you didn't ask questions like that, and because she knew. It was not the arguing, which must have been endless, trapped together there. Sometimes she wondered if Loring had seen a real tirade, though of course he hadn't, because Grampa hadn't had one since he lived in Maine.

Daddy had taken them one summer to see the old farm near Lewiston, and the one-room schoolhouse where Grampa had been the master for ten years and the three little Free Baptist churches where he had preached, dashing to them in a horse and buggy Sunday after Sunday. Those stark white churches with the weeds growing around them, so still and unspeaking—against those you could not imagine Grampa's fits of anger. But the first one had happened there, in the cemetery atop the hill, where he had suddenly "broken." "Dust to dust!" he had cried, and splattered the coffin of a friend with fistfuls of mud, one after another. When they tried to stop him, he fought them off, then bolted and ran from the scene.

That was the end of everything he was doing—the ministry and the school and the dairy farm. Daddy had made it a point to tell Jo and Loring about this, because he wanted them to understand that the trouble had been caused by "fanatical religious fervor." He wanted them to see where he had come from, he and Mother, who had been a foster child in the Fuller household.

After Grampa's breakdown, Daddy had had to quit school at age fourteen and tend the farm and the milk route, finally canceling his plans to study medicine. He did nothing but farm work, easing himself around his unpredictable father. "No one could cross him," he said. "If you did, he would fly into a rage, shouting for hours, then go away for days into the woods."

Jo was remembering some of those words from Daddy's memoir, which she had heard him read aloud to people, asking for comments. It had come back from *Reader's Digest*. Too honest for them, Mrs. Cannon said. It went out to *Atlantic Monthly* next, and then to others. It was called "A New England Tragedy." It always came back.

The Maine farm was sold in 1918, and the family moved to Framingham where Grandma got a job in the Dennison factory. Daddy enlisted and went off to France. "I had waked up," he wrote. "When I got it through my farmboy skull that this God for whom my father had burned out his life and for whom I had sacrificed my youth did not exist at all, going to war seemed sane by comparison."

Grammy died before Daddy wrote any of this, and Grampa did not really know what was going on any more. Yooney did her best to cope with him. "He's up attic," she'd whisper to them in the kitchen when they went to visit. "Locked in. Won't take anything but baking soda and water." And Daddy would go up and try to talk reason through the attic door, but Grampa never answered. In a year he was dead himself.

A resounding gong filled the bathroom. Jo jumped to her feet. Her elbow had knocked the talcum powder can into the tub, where it rang like the clapper of a bell. She stood shivering for a minute on the cold tiles, then put out the light and groped her way back down the hall.

Her bed was warm, as it used to be at home when she came back from the frosty privy at the end of the shed. Mother had made a sweater for the hole. She had covered a cardboard cutout with soft flannel. It hung over the stove in the kitchen, and you took it out there with you to sit on so you wouldn't freeze your bum.

Jo drifted off to sleep in a rowboat, her bare feet on the slimy wood in a little warm puddle of lake water. Not far away a noisy crowd of high school boys jostled each other on the float. They fell into the water with great shouts and scrambled back onto the float again. Loring and Gary were there, and Beverly's Bob, and several C.B.I. boys, among them Clyde and Roger Honey. All of them were sunburned and self-conscious about the water that streamed from their bathing trunks, and they all meshed together, not understanding that they were strangers and did not belong in the same world, in a dream or anywhere.

By morning she felt much better. The sense of impending danger was gone. When she saw Roger across the courtyard he seemed like an old friend she ought to shout to, a result of the dream, of course. Oddly, that afternoon she had her first direct contact with him. If direct is the right word; he was on the sidewalk, and she was five floors up.

Now it was Louise's room, which was not pink, nor any predominant color at all. Jo went in there late in the day to prepare a Flannelgraph story. It was Louise's Flannelgraph, for her outdoor class. Jo was going to borrow it later for her course in Child Evangelism, so she had offered to work on it, though it was a little too much like paper dolls to be called work.

The story was of Abraham and Isaac. First they colored the cloth-backed figures, the old man, the boy, then the crude altar, the bundle of sticks for the fire that Isaac carried on his back, the lamb, the thicket he would be caught in, and the knife Abraham would lift to kill his own son. Louise had already covered the flannel board with brown and purple felt mountains. The figures would stick to that as the story unfolded.

She was practicing, half playfully, making Jo the audience. "Abraham, behold me!" she cried (God's words), pressing Abraham against the board. He stuck there, his head raised attentively.

"Yes, Lord. I'm listening."

Then she was God again. "Take now thy son, thine only son whom thou lovest, and offer him as a burnt offering upon one of the mountains that I will tell thee of."

Louise's voice was nasal and sweet, almost childlike. She thrust out her little bosom as she played the roles. This delayed Jo's reaction. She laughed, and the next moment the horror of it struck her. She held up the little knife she had just colored and cut out. With that instrument a father, a loving, adoring father, was going to cut the throat of his only son and promised heir—a prince, whose name, Isaac, meant Laughter. They had studied this story in Bible Survey. They had been over it quite thoroughly, but until this moment she had not sensed what it meant. *Slit the throat of your cherished child and burn him to a crisp on an altar.* That was what God was saying. All the thousands of years that had passed since could not erase it.

Over on the flannel board the caravan prepared for the journey across the desert. The servants were lining up, the wood tied on Isaac's

---

back. What did the boy think this trip was for? A hike? Camping out with his dad?

"Louise, we can't tell this story to little children," Jo said suddenly.

Louise looked up in surprise. Her right eyelid shut and opened just a hair slower than the other. Jo had thought this was a wink on the first day. It threw you off, that eye. If Louise were to scold the daylights out of someone (which was unimaginable), her lazy eye with its lovely long lashes would be winking at you all through, saying she didn't really mean it.

"Why not?" she asked.

"It's too frightening," Jo said.

"Oh, but children love it. It's one of the most exciting moments in the whole Bible."

"But this is a *father* who is going to kill his son."

"Yes. It's a symbol of God giving *His* only Son. It helps children understand that."

"But does it? Don't they just see how dreadful it is?"

"Oh, no," said Louise. "First you make them see that this is not a mean father." Her own children especially, she said—slum children in her street class, most of whom had fathers who beat them, if they had fathers at all—first they must see that *this* was a father who cherished his son and would never wish him any harm. "They have to understand that Abraham believed all along that God would intervene. He just didn't know *how* He would do it."

"Do you believe that's what Abraham thought?"

"Of course." (Winking.)

"But then why do it at all?"

"On the contrary," said Louise. "He *acted* on faith. I've found something out about children—they can understand faith. You watch, they'll believe *with* Isaac that his father will not hurt him."

Prince Laughter was wearing a dark purple tunic. Jo had chosen the color herself. He was strong-looking, a young man more than a boy. When had he caught on to what was happening? Surely he'd been taught that his life was precious. Destined to father a nation. Isaac, get your sleep, drink your milk, wear a hat, come home early. And now to die like an animal?

"But would God ask for murder?" Jo mused. She was cutting out around the lamb now, his legs askew, ready to be caught in the thicket by the altar. She knew what Louise would say.

"He didn't. He provided the lamb as a substitute."

"He asked for the intent of murder."

"But He couldn't contradict himself. He had promised that Isaac would be the heir. Abraham knew that."

All right, Jo thought, she could see the adventure there. This was where the truth came out—to obey Him when it was the most puzzling and dangerous. She could see it clearly. It was like good singing, strong and abandoned at the same time. Then the idea was gone and what she saw was insanity.

"How do you *know*?" she asked, addressing the lamb. She was getting much too worked up about it. They were only cutting out a Flannelgraph, and it had become the most important thing in the world to get this straight.

"Oh, Jo, you funny person!" laughed Louise. "The lamb was there. Isaac was not killed. This was not a pagan nature god asking for human blood. That's the whole point."

"But it was so close," Jo persisted. "He raised the knife. Think what was going on there! Why did God have to ask for a blood sacrifice of any kind?" She sounded like her father. Back at home she'd hated it when he had confronted her with a question like that, pressing it on her, making her answer. Now she was asking it herself.

She was actually close to tears, and irritated with Louise, of all people. Louise stood by the Flannelgraph board, glancing quizzically from Abraham to Jo and back to Abraham again. Then she smiled. "Maybe because He knew the heart of man. It's like asking why there's blood in our veins. Oh, it's okay, Jo. The answer is in the library, I'm sure. We can look it up."

"I think I'm tired," said Jo. "I get looney when I'm tired." She crossed her eyes and made a face.

"Maybe you're getting your period," said Louise.

Then, in a matter of seconds, the mood in the room changed. Louise went to her desk for something, glanced out the window and exclaimed, "Oh, there's just the person I want to see!" Jo set down her scissors and went over to look. Roger Honey stood down below on the corner. Louise explained that Roger lived on the same floor as Charlie Higgins (the boy who could stand on his thumbs), and she had a little gift she wanted delivered to Charlie.

Though it seemed shameless and contrived (Charlie was still ignoring Louise's frank ardor), Jo entered wholeheartedly into the scheme. First, they got Roger's attention by tossing a big soft eraser at him. It was against the rules to yell out the windows, or throw anything for that matter, especially from the fifth floor. Then they held up a sign with WAIT on it, wrote a note, wrapped several pieces of fudge in it, found a silk kerchief, found string, made a parachute and dropped the fudge almost at Roger's feet.

They watched as he read the message and pretended to devour the fudge. Then he reached up with his hands as if to catch the next missile.

"Jump into his arms, Jo," said Louise. "Go ahead."

Seeing him down there, wearing his nice smile and a green sweater, Jo thought she wouldn't mind at all. He'd catch her too, if anyone could. You had that feeling about him. Was that trust? No, it was insanity.

When Roger had walked away with the candy, the kerchief, and the eraser, Jo and Louise stayed at the open window, leaning over the desk, while Abraham and Isaac and all their sacrificial paraphernalia lay limp and lifeless on the bed. The sun had been working hard all day to burn off a haze across the irregular line of the rooftops, and now, going down, it had given up. The city looked soft and brown.

They talked quietly at the window, wasting time in the fading light. They talked about boys, that subject again. Louise did a rundown on the "good eligible men" at school. There were only about a dozen as far as she was concerned. Charlie Higgins was one, and Roger Honey was another. "They say Roger's never been able to find a girl at Cal to take the place of the one he broke up with back home," she said.

"Why did he break up with her?" Jo asked, trying to sound casual.

"She wasn't interested in full-time service. That's what I heard. I guess she was pretty worldly."

"I see," said Jo. She could feel herself yielding to this, the idleness and chatter, the hazy brown city out there. They could hear the faint roar of a squadron of planes somewhere behind the blanket of mist and smoke, out of sight. It was "white sound," Loring had written. Inside a plane, feeling the vibration too, it could put you to sleep.

"What do you want in a guy, Jo?" asked Louise.

Jo pondered. Lately there had been a lot of talk at school about the ideal Christian mate—a person who would put Christ first and expect you to do the same. You were, in a sense, stewards of each other. It was a nice idea to think about, but Louise didn't mean that just now, Jo knew. She was referring to personal traits. It was almost like high school, talking with Gloria about boys, as they did endlessly. They had made a long list of requirements: smart but not egotistical, neat but not self-conscious. . . .

Now what did she want? Nothing she could list. He presented himself, the "right one," as six feet or so of warmth and color. Jo could feel him but not define him, except that he stood alone, free and uncluttered, part of the living present. She stared at him over the rooftops, this vague person, and watched Roger Honey take shape before her eyes. Louise was waiting for an answer. Her right eye winked. Her friendliness was a lovely thing. Charlie Higgins was a jerk not to see that. Jo thought she would like to hug her, but she smiled instead.

"I think I'd like a guy who can stand on his thumbs," she said.

When she passed Roger in the corridor the next day, her heart bolted into action. Their eyes met and they spoke, the way Calvary students always spoke to each other. It happened again an hour later. He seemed so amiable and harmless, and perhaps that was why she allowed herself to watch for him around campus. It was remarkable how quickly you could learn someone's whereabouts and doings. He took Homiletics in Darby Chapel while she was in Doctrine on the third floor. He passed her at the foot of the stairs after class. He sat thirteen rows behind her in chapel. He went to the library right after Men's Evening Fellowship.

She picked up bits of information about him. He came from Michigan, from an independent church called Bethany Evangelical. He had turned down a full scholarship to Michigan State to come to Cal. He was a good student.

In a day or two she began to test the possible ways they could accidentally discover each other. First she would catch him looking at her (thinking, "That girl is different") as they stood bunched on the steps of the post office at mail rush. He would slide away his gaze, as if it meant nothing, but the second time it happened he would smile, artlessly, as if they were old friends whose eyes happened to meet. Finally, they would be thrown together in some situation not of their own planning, like entering the door of the Pastry Shop at exactly the right moment and finding only one empty booth.

On Saturday night she was dismayed to find that she had brought him with her to the rescue mission. She could imagine him sitting there on a yellow kitchen chair, as clearly as if he really were, looking so great in his green sweater among the sleepy bums. He never took his eyes off her as she sang in the trio, and when she walked back to her seat on the platform, she could feel him watching her yet.

By dinnertime on Sunday she knew she was in much too deep.

Sunday dinner was free-time. Only then, and on Monday evenings, were men and women allowed to sit together in the dining room. Actually, there was not that much mixing. Free-time meals were a time of diffidence. Too much had been made of them. If a boy sat with a girl it was like a public announcement. Established couples sat together and a few brave males hammed their way into the women's side. Mostly the tables were solid with girls. They flocked together, the best way to avoid the uncertainty.

As a precaution, remembering Clyde's letter, Jo had tipped a chair against the table to save for Jewel, who had to be late. Clyde simply walked up, put out his hand, grabbed hers in its feeble return gesture and stood there behind the chair while they sang and said grace.

"It's saved," Jo said.

"Praise the Lord. So am I." It was a tired dining-room joke.

Jo looked around desperately for Jewel. No, she was looking for Roger. She was almost sick with the thought that Roger might see her with Clyde and think it meant something it didn't.

"It's for Jewel," she said firmly, holding the chair, but there was Jewel with a seat at the next table, waving at her and nodding. Clyde insisted on pushing in Jo's chair for her. He was the only boy with eleven girls, acting as if he had a date with her, dressed in his Sunday suit with one black chest hair curling like an ivy tendril through a crack between his shirt and a white paper collar. He wore the brown tie, and as he sat down beside her, Jo looked smack into the tie-clip. "Sharper than a two-edged sword," said the letters across the little open Bible.

Where was Roger? Maybe not there at all, out on an assignment, unable to get back by dinner. Jo threw one glance over to the men's side into the tide of dark Sunday suits. Clyde was talking to her, and Louise on her left said, "Jo, the potatoes." He was only asking her if she wanted the potatoes. "All right," she said. She held her face firmly. He would not get a trace of a smile.

He was saying something else, on her right. Whatever it was, she answered him with the barest nod. Beverly, across the table, kept nudging her with her foot, and Louise pinched her elbow and grinned directly into her face as she passed the chicken platter. "Watch it. It's hot," she said.

To make matters worse, Ruby was there. She sat at the end of the table in the hostess seat. She was wearing her Sunday hat, a round slice of brown felt with a dip over her forehead. The veil, turned off her face while she ate, festooned around her head. The dining room was dotted with dark Sunday hats on girls who had just gotten back from church or Practical Work in time for the meal.

"Well, well, Clyde," said Ruby coyly, "to what do we owe the privilege of your company?" Fortunately, Clyde didn't hear her. He was full of news, which he directed into Jo's right ear. There was an enormous Youth for Christ rally last night in Madison Square Garden. Did she know? Very successful, he reported. Twenty thousand in attendance. Jo ate too fast and bit her tongue. Sudden intense pain filled her head, and her eyes watered. She bent over her plate.

A girl across the way was also talking about the rally. She was from Newark. Her brother, who was one of the ushers, had called her this morning. At least two thousand souls came to Christ, she said with enthusiasm, including scores of servicemen.

"Do you think all that stress on numbers is right?" someone else asked. "There's so much emotion at a meeting like that. The decisions don't last."

"The Seventh Army is in the Vosges Mountains," said Clyde to Jo, bending in close, still reporting. He had trouble with Vosges. A particle of food landed—somewhere. In her milk? She scanned the tablecloth for it. It had to be in her milk. Anyhow, she wouldn't drink it now, just in case.

"Have you been following the Seventh?" Clyde wanted to know.

"What?" asked Jo.

"The Seventh Army."

Jo shook her head no, moving her shoulders slightly to protect her food. The pain in her tongue was abating much too slowly. The chicken and potatoes and peas were all thrown together on her plate, and in her mouth she swallowed them with blood. For an instant she saw Loring's dinner plate at home, all the foods neatly separated and eaten one by one.

"We're nine miles from Belfort," Clyde said. "Captured St. Gorgon and we're in the mountain passes."

"Jack Wyrtzen was the speaker," the girl from Newark said, "and Carlton Booth led the singing."

The dining-room host asked for their attention over the P.A. system. He wanted all the servicemen who were guests at dinner to stand. A half-dozen uniforms popped up here and there to applause and cheers. Clyde raised his fingers high in a victory sign. He made even the war look ridiculous.

Jo's tongue felt big. She leaned toward Louise, who smelled gently of April Showers and smacked her lips a little as she ate.

"But we smashed them this week, you know," Clyde continued. "One of the biggest bombing efforts ever flown over Germany. Thousands of bombs, thousands of heavies. We lost fifty-one."

A heavy was a bomber, Jo knew that. Liberators and Flying Fortresses, they were heavies. And strangely enough, a heavy was what they called a serving dish in the Calvary dining hall. There sat the thick oval bowl, "parked," she thought, emptied of mashed potatoes, its belly deep like a bomber's.

"Praise the Lord and pass the ammunition," said Clyde, pointing to the chicken platter.

Now there were several conversations at the table, all going at once, and maybe hundreds across the big room. The air rang with voices and forks and dishes. The heavies went around the table again, those with food left in them, moving awkwardly from hand to hand. Clyde was talking. Had he stopped at all?

"Do you want your moo juice?"

"What?" asked Jo.

"I said, don't you want your milk?"

"Oh . . . no." (Take it. You've made it your own.)

He drank it down. "I hope to God we wipe them out," he said fervently, in the next breath.

"What, Clyde?" asked Beverly. "Wipe out what?"

"The Germans. Don't you girls ever read the paper? Haven't you heard there's a war on?" He said it to Jo, not to the others.

"Things are going better in the war," said Ruby.

"No," countered Clyde. "We are overextending ourselves. In a couple of weeks we could be in the German woods. Do you know what that means? The German *woods*?" he asked Jo.

"Russia has crossed the Danube," somebody inserted.

"We ought to pray more for the Germans," Ruby said.

"Pray for the *Germans*?" Clyde said it to Jo, into her ear, as if she were a telephone. "This whole war has been caused by the theological poison that destroyed the Protestant churches in Germany. That's what made Germany what it is today—modernism in the churches, higher criticism in the seminaries."

"We ought to pray for Adolf Hitler," Ruby continued insistently. "Think what would happen if Hitler found Christ. The war would be over." The idea spun around the table and landed with a clunk, beyond imagination.

A crescendo of laughter rose from Jewel's table. Something funny had happened over there. A girl had a red face. She was looking for something on the floor. Jo froze. Roger was at that table. When had he come? He sat directly opposite her, with a clear line of vision over the heads between them.

"I'd sure like to be with that Seventh Army now," said Clyde.

Jo increased the angle of her back to him.

"We're glad you're here, safe with us, Clyde," said Beverly.

"Who's going to take out the heavies?" Ruth asked.

"I will," said Jo. She jumped up and began to gather the serving dishes on a tray.

"Well, the gentleman at the table ought to help, don't you think?" suggested Ruby.

"No!" said Jo. "I'll be fine, thank you."

She whacked things together in her haste. She could hardly lift the tray. Clyde tried to take it from her, but she wouldn't let him. The line to the kitchen was long and slow, and she thought her arms would break before she got there. In the kitchen, trays of dessert waited to be brought back to the dining room. It was cottage pudding today, squares of cake under a shiny sauce. She brought a tray of them to the table, then without a word to anyone walked back to the kitchen and out through the tunnel that connected the parts of the central campus building, a long winding submarine with low-hanging pipes and vents.

They were singing happy birthday to somebody back in the dining room. Jo glanced behind her to see if Clyde had followed. He hadn't, the tunnel was clear, but she began to run anyway. The heels of her Sunday shoes clattered and her tongue throbbed. Posters on the wall on either side blurred into a stream of color. She knew what they were—the Social Club programs, sightseeing tours, swimming at the Y, "FOOD IS A WEAPON. DON'T WASTE IT," the school newspaper begging for staff members. Missionary Union was showing a new film this week from the Sudan Interior Mission: "Leprosy—Africa's Open Sore. Pray, give, go."

She was running away. Her pride and cowardice were very plain and ugly to her. Lord, please forgive me, she said, still running. What was she doing? She hated this person she had just become. At the stairs to the main lobby she turned and began to run back toward the dining room. Repentance meant to turn and go the other way. The words were meaningless without the action.

At the table Clyde stood and held out her chair for her, as C.B.I. boys were expected to do. She tried to breathe normally. Roger was looking directly at her from Jewel's table, and as if to put him in his place, Jo poured milk into the glass Clyde had borrowed, filling it to the brim, and drank it straight down.

Clyde walked her to the dorm, talking all the way about the Seventh Army.

There were no leaves to turn, but it was clearly autumn. The geometry of the city had changed. Angles slanted in deeper and drew a sharper line. Karen, who said she had learned not to trust October in Chicago, brought her winter coat from home. On Sunday nights as she entered their room out of the crisp air, her Bible and gloves smelled of leather and faint perfume.

She was right about the coat. The wind along Chicago Avenue, though it whipped down out of a deep blue sky, had a new edge. Girls hugged their coats together and used their books to shield their faces against the biting eddies of dirt.

They came back from walks by the lake with red cheeks. It was beautiful right now, they said. One Saturday the Social Club held relay games and a tug-of-war on the beach. Jo didn't go. She had not been to the lake—even for a walk.

In the middle of the month teachers began announcing the dates of mid-term exams. It came as a jolt to everyone. Jo was far from ready. Her notes were disorganized, and she had lost her Doctrine syllabus. She had been losing a number of things.

"You and the White Sox," Karen said, as they searched the room in vain for Jo's wallet.

The wallet was returned the next day, found in the women's lavatory of Van Housen Hall. The syllabus was still missing, as were her best gloves, her Army Air Corps kerchief, a fountain pen, and two combs.

"Everybody's tired," Karen said. "We need a day off."

"I'll get over it," said Jo, and proceeded to walk in her sleep two nights in a row, which was a bit ominous, but mostly funny. Karen found her on the john at 4:00 in the morning. All Jo remembered later was the sudden blaze of light in the white bathroom and Karen standing there in her blue-checked pajamas with the retainer on her teeth and without her glasses.

"Do you know how long you've been in here?" she whispered.

That tied in somehow with Jo's dream, and she gave a crazy answer that registered with neither of them. There was a small wooden rack in the tub hung with somebody's stockings, and that was what brought her back to reality.

It happened the second time exactly the same way, except that this time Jo kept saying, "Where are all my ems? Where are all my ems?" She was half conscious and knew she was saying it.

"Lost your ems? Now you've done it," said Karen.

By the time they got back to the room, they were both wide awake. They tiptoed about making tea with tap water, which they sipped in their beds while the sky grew gray.

"Dayspring is at hand," murmured Jo with a yawn.

Karen shook her head. "Roommate, you're tetched," she said. It was one of their nicer moments yet. The next morning Jo left Karen a note: "This is good-bye. Don't come for me. I have gone to find my ems."

The sleepwalking stopped, and instead she began to sit up in the middle of the night and pull out all her pin curls. In the morning there were the bobby pins in a neat pile under the pillow and her hair was a mess. She had no recollection of doing it, only that she had dreamed unpleasantly of running. It was an obvious mirror of her daytime turmoil.

For she was "Clyde's girl." The label was on. Everybody knew it. Rules or not, he managed to be at her side. He waited for her, caught up, crossed her path, merged with her schedule, always with an urgency, a need to tell her something—a quote from a teacher, or news he had heard on the radio (Did she know Wendell Willkie had died?), what he got in his devotions that morning, written out. "See Romans 6:12. We are saved not only from the penalty of sin but from its very power. He has conquered sin! Praise God and live in victory!"

He gave her books to read, Thomas á Kempis, *Borden of Yale*, Jim Ross's diary—the last entry on the very day he and his wife were beheaded in the Sudan—and bits of research, on eschatology, Clyde said, stretching his mouth around the word.

She never knew how to behave. It was her Christian responsibility to be nice to him. She had decided that—not to yield to her pride and embarrassment. Yet to encourage him was misleading, and his very assumption that she would be nice, that he had a right to her attention, increased her disgust for him. There were times when even his Bible, a huge Scofield Reference Edition, hugged high on his chest, filled her with repulsion. When she saw him coming across the campus, the need to escape was overpowering.

He made her angry. He sat in judgment over other students. He was exercised about the spiritual climate of the school. There were not many "deep students" around anymore, not like when his parents were here. "There's not a Jim Ross in the bunch," he said, not one who would kneel before the sword. The standards of the world predominated. Guys talked of nothing but girls. He was making a list of girls who dressed carelessly. He meant to turn it over to the Superintendent of Women. Several times Jo saw his eyes stray to a girl's bust and lock there. Then he blinked rapidly and looked away.

More than anything he talked about the war. He clipped headlines from the Chicago *Sun* and folded them inside his notes. Verbs leaped out at Jo as she read them. Squeeze, strike, slash, grind, break, batter, hammer, crush! He sent her a map of Europe cut from the paper, adding his own code to the crisscross of roads and rivers and railway tracks and arrows that shot out of Nazi and Allied flags.

"The fighting is furious in Arcan," he said, thrusting the paper under her nose as they crossed the courtyard. Whatever was Arcan? "Arcan is the test. If she surrenders, we know the Germans are psychologically worn down."

There it was in the headlines. He meant Aachen. Aachen was being destroyed, house by house, street by street. Strong German counter-attack, "a savage and crucial battle." Shadowy pictures of German soldiers in long coats, captured, white hands in the air.

"Do you have anyone in the war?" Clyde asked, and Jo, knowing she could never mention Loring in his presence, muttered that she had a friend in the Navy. "In the Navy? Where?" asked Clyde.

"I don't know," said Jo.

His presence at free-time meals was the hardest to take. Jo had refused to have devotions with him ("fellowship" he called it) or go out on a date to distribute tracts, but dining-room privileges were hard to deny.

Even when she flanked herself with girls, someone would change places with him so he could be next to her. Even Louise and Beverly would do that.

But the whole idea was *not* to avoid him. She had only to see Roger to remember this. If *he* was anywhere nearby she turned to mush. Her heart raced, and she forgot what she was doing or saying, her hands would not button her coat, her feet landed wrong. Once she even sat down between two chairs, her skirt up, her books flying. In all her crazy history of crushes she had never been so self-conscious. There were times when she was sure he was staring straight at her, and always that was when something was wrong—her stockings were baggy, or it was too early in the morning and her eyes looked funny, one smaller than the other.

Even the letter *R* caused an inward stirring. His hands gripping a magazine in the library caused a dull ache in her chest. She knew what the back of his neck looked like. She'd need no other clue to identify him. His hair, dark brown, became soft and blond at the nape.

She often sat in the library or lounge in the hope that Roger would appear. She moved about like a displaced person, filled with remorse because she was not where she ought to be, not studying, not practicing. He was an idol of the worst sort. Every day she determined again not to submit to it. She searched for answers, thumbing through the New Testament, reading her favorite passages over and over. There was an edge of hostility to the usually friendly voices—Matthew, John, Paul. "Casting down imaginations, and every high thing that exalteth itself against the knowledge of God, and bringing into captivity every thought to the obedience of Christ."

She prayed constantly. "Forgive me," repeated her brain, "straighten me out, show me the way." Her prayers turned to wool-gathering: Was Roger at that very moment also praying, secretly in love with her, puzzled by the depths of his feelings? ("Oh, God, take this girl from me. She's filling my mind. I can't think!")

So she blew about the campus, in pursuit and pursued, looking for Roger, invariably overtaken by Clyde.

One morning she saw Roger's sweater coming her way in the courtyard sunshine. He was moving directly toward her, as if to speak.

She shaded her eyes in the bright October light. Was she seeing things? There beside him was Clyde's necktie and overcoat. They were coming over to her together. She could not even look. She shut her eyes. It was like being trapped in a sandwich, between the layers of her feelings and rationalities.

When she looked up, Roger was gone and Clyde was holding a map of Chicago in front of her.

"I want you to be the first to see this," he said. He had done some shading with a pencil down below the 49th Street Beach. It was the profile of a skull-like face, with the various inlets of the shore for nose and mouth, the Museum of Science and Industry the eye and in the center of the head like a small, rectangular brain, the University of Chicago.

"The antichrist," he said.

"That's crazy!" exclaimed Jo.

"Maybe," Clyde admitted, "but I'm convinced the antichrist is in the seat of learning, all over the world. Spiritual wickedness in high places. And I'll tell you something else. There's a group of our own students who go down there to the library at the divinity school. To me, that's courting Satan's attention."

He had lowered his voice and moved in closer to her. There were students all around them in the sunshine, and here she was on this alien island of Clyde's dark secret, where the air was bad. She thought she would suffocate.

She was an island of her own, a skirmish on a placid hillside. As she struggled in her room the songs of the whistler traveled up the radiator pipes. Often her roommate sang along, her voice rising smoothly from below. "O, could I speak His matchless worth . . ." That seemed to be a favorite. "I'd sing the characters He bears, and all the forms of love He wears." Listening, Jo saw her problems as petty and self-absorbed, not worth a thought—until they stopped singing.

"Expect a new impossibility every day," someone said in Morning Devotions. "Give it to Him and watch Him work." God would lead her out of this mess—*if* she wanted Him to. She wasn't kidding herself. What she really wanted was Roger.

No one knew about her struggle, she was pretty sure, and she had no desire to reveal it, though sharing burdens was encouraged at school. Sometimes in Women's Fellowship after dinner girls stood and asked for prayer for an "unspoken request," which meant it was confidential. She could not even do that. It was natural for people to try to guess what was wrong. Soup was curious enough. "How's Kewpie MacQuade?" she asked frequently. Once Ruth said, "I know you must be a real blessing to Clyde, Jo. The Lord is using you in his life." And Beverly, who was standing behind her, jiggled her curls at Jo with a knowing smile. Jo smiled back, thinking how little they knew and how at peace they both looked. Their hearts were in order.

That was the measuring stick that counted—peace. Absence of peace was a bad sign, and troubled waters were hard to hide. A spiritual person was at rest, and it showed in one's face and bearing. It went beyond being a soul winner or having a zeal for missions. To *trust* was the important thing. Not to trust was shameful, in the light of His love and faithfulness, or to doubt or be discouraged or downcast. You seldom saw such defeat expressed.

Troubles at school tended to be classified in two large categories: trials and temptations. It did seem to make things manageable to be able to say, "This is just a temptation," or "This is just a trial of my faith." Temptations came from Satan; trials came from God. They both came from His hand though, in the sense that nothing could touch your life that was not part of His plan for you.

Clyde was a test; Roger a temptation. But in either case, Jo thought she would far rather have it be a matter of her own weakness than something to toss off onto God or the devil. If she managed to get control, she wanted to feel she had done it herself, whereas she ought to give God the glory, since it would be only through His grace. She worked this over, sorting it out and covering the ground again and again, when she ought to be studying.

She was badly behind in her work. In her reading for Survey, she was stuck in Leviticus. She had read the sixteenth chapter a dozen times, her eyes reading, her mind elsewhere, and she was determined not to go on with it until she had managed to concentrate. She fell asleep trying. Her lecture notes were a shambles. She missed classes. It was hard to get up in the morning.

"Bell rang, Jo," Karen would say politely. "Did you hear it?"

"Yes."

"Are you awake?"

"Yes."

"Your eyes are still shut."

"I know."

Back in September she had gotten up gladly, though she had never been an early riser at home. Loring had been the first one awake in the morning. He would read in bed by flashlight, and when the sun rose he ate an apple, contemplating the drawings that filled his walls, dozens of tight sketches of early aircraft, every line done with a compass and ruler. Vickers Gunbus, Sopwith Strutter, Fairy Flycatcher. Jo woke to the crack of his apple. Sometimes in her sleep she forgot she was at Cal. She was home in her own room, and Loring was there. It annoyed her to be awakened from this.

"Jo, you're going to be late."

She and Karen often stood together in front of the mirror, dressing in the lamplight. Karen's hair came out exactly the same each morning. Jo's would snarl in her haste, or a garter would pop off her panty girdle at the last minute. While Karen read her Bible, Jo would be sewing on a button or racing down to the basement to press out a skirt. She was still dressing in the elevator. "Snowing down south, Jo," said Karen, and Jo yanked at her slip straps. Back on the dresser the cover lay off the deodorant jar and her hair was caught in a comb. If Karen returned to the room before she did, she would clean it up.

"I didn't want your deodorant to dry out," she'd say.

In Floor Fellowship Jewel had read snatches to them from the diary of David Brainerd, an eighteenth-century missionary to the American Indians. He was very young, only twenty-four, when he headed alone into the wilderness. Jo felt herself drawn to him, perhaps because he was from New England. She liked his honesty and quaint, austere language. He rebuked himself for an "unsettled, wandering frame of mind," as he tried to pray. His soul was "filled with surprise and anxiety to find it thus." He called it "barrenness." Sometimes he prayed for hours, whole days or nights, until he had "prevailed."

One night, when the luminous hands of Karen's clock said 2:00 A.M., Jo put her pillow on the floor and knelt on it, a blanket around her shoulders, determined to stay there until Roger was gone for good—all night if necessary. In less than five minutes she was asleep and slept soundly until the bell woke her in the morning.

"My goodness, you're up early," said Karen.

Jo hurried down to the bathroom to wash her face. Instead she began to clean the sink, and then the tub. She scrubbed furiously, using lots of Babo, rubbing and rinsing and doing it all again. Six-thirty in the morning. Here I am, back in the bathroom, she thought, determined not to cry. She would do the floor and the walls too.

"Hey, Jo!" called Louise through the door. "Save some hot water for the rest of us."

That very afternoon, as if to honor her chagrin, Jo completely wasted her practice time. Roger was often in the Music Building, playing his trumpet with different pianists who went out with him on assignments. He was there that day, on the same floor. She stopped to listen awhile. He was good on the trumpet, better than he was as an artist. He made lively arrangements out of old hymns. "When I survey the wondrous cross on which the Prince of glory died," he played, the clean brass mounting all other sounds around them. He always chose familiar songs, she had heard him say once, so people could think of the words. "My richest gain I count but loss, and pour contempt on all my pride." He played the second verse in minor, then moved into a higher, brighter key for the conclusion.

Jo considered the possibility of playing for him herself. In her mind, she put the two of them on the El, headed for a suburban church, loaded down with his trumpet and artist's materials, talking and talking as they clung to the straps. She could see them perfectly, Roger tall and leaning toward her. They would shout questions and answers over the noise of the train, gobbling up information. He had grown up on a farm, he told her.

He was the youngest of five brothers. They were always in trouble. (She was making this up.) His parents were strict Christians, and he'd been brought to church twice on Sunday besides Sunday school, and midweek prayer meeting, too. Once he set off a firecracker in the back pew. He'd hated church as a child.

Oh, she could sympathize with that, Jo told him, though her own situation had been quite different. She'd gone nowhere to church until she was eight. Her father had always said they would never go, until a new minister came to the Federated Church in town. "A fearless young modernist," her father called him. The first sermon she ever heard was about Immanuel Kant. She remembered because she thought it was spelled C-a-n apostrophe t, and was going to be like "The Little Engine That Could."

She might not tell him that. Maybe it sounded too cute.

Roger said church was apt to be an hour in which you grabbed at what second-rate excitement there was to get you through. Yes, said Jo, like saying "trespasses" instead of "debts" during the Lord's Prayer. Or her brother sometimes made her laugh by whispering, "Down the hatch!" during communion. The kitchen was the only room in the church she had liked. The other rooms had names that sounded vaguely obscene—vestibule, narthex, nave. But in the kitchen the faucets dripped sociably, and there were glass-doored cabinets where stacks and stacks of white plates were kept.

Sometimes before church started, she told Roger, she would wander into the kitchen and stare at those plates and pretend this was the home of a family with a hundred children. Their beds were the pews and their mother played the organ to put them to sleep. One day she found two ladies in the kitchen. They were cutting up bread in little squares and arranging it on the silver communion plates. It was the same kind of bread Jo had buttered for breakfast, from Cushman's Bakery. She could see the wrappers. One of the ladies was eating the crusts she had just cut off. She stopped chewing when she saw Jo. "Run along now and find your mother," she said, as if what they were doing was secret or illicit. After that she didn't like the kitchen either.

But how was she finally saved then? Roger wanted to know. So Jo explained about Yooney, her aunt who could do anything with her left hand alone—tie shoes and open cans and beat you in a tickling fight. After her grandfather died, Jo said, she had gone to Framingham on weekends to help Yooney, only they never did any work.

"Let's not be serious today," Yooney would say, and they would take a bus to Boston to Filene's basement or the Public Gardens. Back home in the evening they made those thick daring onion sandwiches for supper.

Once in a while they went to church, a different one each time, which was bearable, and when Yooney said she wanted to hear a Sheldon somebody speak at a youth meeting, Jo agreed to go. She had no interest, but she was glad to please Yooney.

"We'll make a day of it, maybe go to Bailey's for ice cream," Yooney said, looking so innocent with her right arm, thin as a bone, resting in her lap. Then she said, "You ought to ask your folks, you know." Why should she? Jo wanted to know. "The man's an evangelist," Yooney said.

"So?" said Jo. It didn't matter. She didn't intend to listen. "I thought I was impervious," she told Roger (in her mind that is), and he nodded, bent down to hear her over the noise of the El. She had never seen him this close. She had to work on that a little, how he would look inches away from her. She was not sure how much she would tell him, or if he could understand what her decision meant to her family. "If we had been Catholic, and I had turned Protestant. Or if we had been Jewish and I had turned Catholic—it was that kind of a blow."

She wasn't afraid. She had thought she might tell Daddy right away, when he came to take her home, but she didn't. Maybe she had wanted it to seep down first and be sure it was real. All day Monday the high plane held, but she told no one, not even Gloria. Her family was to be the first to hear. That evening at dinner she made the announcement.

"I've accepted Christ as my Saviour."

The steaming bowl in Mother's hand hung over the table. Daddy looked as if he had heard a noise outside and was waiting to hear it again. Then the bowl alighted, Mother retreated to the stove, and Daddy's fork went back into motion, too fast, as it was apt to do. Having gotten out the crucial statement in a normal voice, Jo began to tremble. She glanced at Loring's plate. A pat of butter was melting in the exact center of the potatoes he had just finished mashing with his fork. He was not eating. Maybe he was only waiting for the butter to melt. She blew on her own food, her hands clamped between her knees.

"I should have known," Daddy said. Meat loaf spilled from his fork. He tried to catch it, but it was gone, down to the floor. "I should have known Yooney would try something like that. Was it some revivalist? All the old tricks, I suppose?"

Jo didn't know what he meant. Sheldon was just a tired-looking young man in a brown business suit, rubbing his jaw as he sat waiting to speak, as if he had a toothache.

"Tell us about it," Daddy said. "Did he say you were going to hell?"

Jo nodded, avoiding speech.

"A hellfire sermon, no less," Daddy said.

It was, she supposed, though he had made them laugh through most of it. Should she tell Daddy that, or would he think it was a trick?

"What kind of meeting was it?" asked Mother, from the stove.

Jo shook her head. She didn't even know. An area-wide Christian Endeavor meeting, or something like that. She had seen that the others had come in groups, though there were not many more than fifty or sixty people there, a sprinkling of bored high-school students in that huge cold sanctuary. Their singing barely made a ripple, but their laughter echoed, surprised.

His jokes were not that funny. It was him. It was the *absence* of tricks. No one had taught this man how to act in church. He sprang to the pulpit and shifted impatiently from foot to foot. He hitched his pants and pulled his jacket up by the lapels and yanked it down on his shoulders. He cut off his own sentences and broke into his own words in a headlong rush to get it out.

You listened, that was the thing. There were no pauses, no notes, no piety. His voice was twangy and loud, but it was his own voice and not one he put on for the pulpit. Who would put on a voice like that? So they laughed in relief and listened.

Daddy was saying things. "Got your mind, did he? Got your tender young mind? Filled you with guilt. Called you a sinner."

Jo nodded again. He had told them they were "*dead* in sin."

"A religious experience is common when one enters the teens, you know," Daddy said. His plate was almost empty, and Mother hadn't even begun yet. What did Mother think? And Loring—it wasn't natural for him not to at least make a crack.

"Did he treat you to a tear-inducing description of Jesus hanging on the cross?" asked Daddy.

"No." The word emerged safely, without a squeak or a tremor.

"Well, then, share with us. What *did* he do?"

Jo shrugged. "He read a lot from the Bible."

He had *pounced* on it, really, page after page. She had never seen anyone handle a Bible with such recklessness and familiarity. Or heard anyone read it as if it were a real book with words that were meant to be read and understood. He kept it open. It rode in his hand like a big bird as he moved from behind the pulpit and down the carpeted steps to the pews, talking all the while. Why are you here? Tell the truth. Because you want to be? No? What's church all about, anyway? He was in the aisle, making them answer. God? Jesus? Who's He? Great teacher? Anything else? Good man. Died. *Why?* he asked it repeatedly. Why did He die? Do *you* know? Hasn't your pastor told you? Then what has he been doing in the pulpit? Hush, you say, he's right over there. Good. Ask him. Who is Jesus? Great teacher! (Snort.) The world is full of great teachers. Ask your pastor if *he* would die for Jesus Christ. Would he die for the namby-pamby lily-livered Jesus he preaches to you week after week? Of course he wouldn't. Why should he? Is his Jesus the same one who changed the course of history? Do you think this watered-down business you see in adults around you is being a Christian? My friends, whatever you do, don't let anyone fool you about Jesus Christ.

"So, you've gotten yourself saved," said Daddy. "How do you feel? . . . Forgiven?"

". . . Yes."

"Forgiven for what, for gosh sake? For being young and human?"

Maybe precisely.

"Did you feel so guilty?" asked Daddy. "What was your need? There has to be a reason for this. You should examine it. What did you want? Ask yourself. Clean bill of health? Rich uncle in the sky? Life eternal? What *hunger*?" Daddy set down his fork. "Do you understand why I'm doing this, Jo? I want you to think."

"I know."

"I want you to hear yourself say this. Hear how it sounds. First, you are a sinner. Is that right? Say it. I am a sinner."

"I am a sinner," said Jo, softly.

She was sure Loring would laugh, but he didn't. He was eating now, potatoes first.

"Bound for an eternity of hell, because the wages of sin is death. Say that," said Daddy.

"The wages of sin is death."

"Unless God forgives me," said Daddy.

"Unless God forgives me," echoed Jo.

"And He can't, you see, unless somebody *pays* for all that sin. And the price—hear this—the price is blood!"

"Daddy," said Mother.

"It's all right," said Jo. She was calmer. "The price is blood," she said.

"A primitive human sacrifice."

Was she supposed to repeat that? "God met His own price," she blurted, echoing Sheldon, of course. He had raised his voice, but he needn't have. His news was astounding anyway. Or was she just ready for it, one string in there tuned and ready to be played?

"Ah, but why does there have to be a price at all? There's the question," Daddy said. "What kind of a tyrant demands a punishment for what nobody supposedly can help?"

She didn't know the answer, but she had to say something. She said, "But it's free. Isn't that good enough? You just receive it." She sounded more defensive than she meant to. The words did indeed sound foolish in this house. The familiarity of the furniture, the stove, the pattern in the linoleum which two days ago she had walked on without knowledge of sin or salvation, made the words foolish. Meat loaf made them foolish. Then that disturbing moment was over, and she felt full assurance.

"If folks of a lower order can find comfort in immortality, then we must be tolerant," Daddy went on. "But you! You're young and free! Not you! Yooney can't help it. She needs it. Do you know what her favorite hymn is? 'Jesus, lover of my soul, let me to Thy *bosom* fly!' "

Loring's knife squeaked on his plate. Mother jumped.

"Grampa believed all this," continued Daddy's voice. "I suppose you know that."

She hadn't, not really. Things were falling into place.

"He was a Fundamentalist. That's what I was at your age—a Fundamentalist."

Bits and pieces were flying together.

"So that's what you are now, if you stick this out. A Fun-da-men-ta-list. Clumsy word, isn't it?"

Sheldon had not used that word. He had not given it a name at all. He was talking about a Person, not a category, and it was the Person she gave herself to, more than the idea, though she saw Him only faintly and maybe was mixing Him up with Sheldon. If she was, it didn't seem to be wrong.

"Let's start the hard way," Sheldon had said at the end. "Do you want Him as your Saviour? If so, I want you to slip out of your seat and walk down front. Right here. Think about it a moment. No bravado. This is not a show. It is taking the step from death to life. Will you come out clean and clear for the Son of God? There is no room in the cause of Christ for halfhearted believers."

She hadn't hesitated. It was only a matter of getting herself across Yooney's feet. Without looking to see if anyone else was coming, she went out into the aisle and found it full. Kids were coming from everywhere to the front, some of them crying, as if they'd been waiting for this moment all their lives. She knew *she* had. She thought, "True, true, true," all the way down front.

Daddy was still speaking. "All right. Here's what we'll do. Take a few weeks, a month. Go on back to Boston with Yooney. Go to revival meetings. Hear the preachers. Get a bellyful. If you last, we'll talk. But your intelligence will win out."

That's how he was going to deal with it. Not forbid her. He was going to appeal to her mind. All the endless argument she and Loring had heard over the years was to be directed at her now. Her new logic had given her the reason for all that talk, and now that she understood it, she was to receive its fire.

Jo glanced at Loring. He was still eating, his face expressionless. She had thrown a bomb into the house which might or might not go off. Anything could happen now. Did Loring know that? If only he would say something. He said, "I have things to do," and was gone, off on his own business. Usually he asked, "You want to come?"—down to the gas station to put air in his tires and see what was doing, or to the library to read *Popular Science*. She loved being in on the incidental parts of his life. Sometimes he let her hang around while he killed time in the Square with his friends, talking about baseball until the curfew blew. Now he never looked at her at all as he zipped up his jacket and went out.

Daddy pushed himself from the table, holding back a burp. " 'Scooz us," he said.

The trumpet had stopped. Roger had slipped out of her mind at some point in the telling, and Jo had not even noticed. He seemed quite distant, in fact, and she wondered if there had been a turning point in her feelings at last. But as she left the building there he was, standing in the open door of a practice room, his back to the hall. As she passed him, her throat full, she wanted more than ever to be rid of him, and more than ever to keep him at her side.

Shortly before exams began, Jo lost her keys. She discovered this after lunch one day and suspected Clyde immediately—not that he would take them, but that he might have knocked them out of her jacket pocket shoving in one of his notes. But there was no note.

She retraced her steps all over school, checked at the Lost and Found and finally reported to the Household Office. It would take two days to get replacements, they said.

It was a nuisance. To get into the dormitory she must either make sure she was with someone who had a key or else pound on the outside door until some poor girl on the first floor heard her and had the grace to open up. Sometimes girls unlocked doors for each other, slipped the latch for short periods of time, but this was discouraged.

"Last year someone from the street got into the foyer and did a grunty," said Soup, on the elevator.

"A what?" asked Jo.

"A grunty, a grunty. Eliminated a feces. What did you call it in your family?"

"Oh, we called it try-hard," Jo answered, before she could catch herself.

"Perfect!" boomed Soup. "Try-hard! Praise the Lord!" Leave it to Soup to make something of that.

It turned out to be a hectic afternoon with all that running and hunting, and as they stood in line at the top of the dining-room stairs that evening Jo felt suddenly faint.

Beverly suggested getting some air. "I'll go with you," she offered. "I don't like creamed chipped beef anyway."

Off they went up Clark Street, the two of them, past shadowy bars and palm-reading parlors. The night air was biting. Jo felt better immediately. It was good to leave Roger and Clyde and lost articles behind her for a while. Beverly was fun to walk with. She took your arm snugly and seemed to want to be in the exact spot where you were. Jo kept moving over. They began to weave back and forth on the sidewalk and got silly.

A group of foreign sailors with red pom-poms on their hats—Portuguese, maybe, Beverly said—walked from the opposite direction and whistled at them.

"Nize shape, bebby!" one of them muttered to Beverly.

She gave a funny snort and hugged Jo's arm tighter. The sailors laughed. They looked very young and unwarlike in their fancy uniforms.

"How can you fire a torpedo with a pom-pom on your hat?" Jo said, when they had gone by.

Then Dr. Peckham passed them in his old bakery truck and tooted.

"On his way home to dinner," said Beverly.

"Does he recognize us, do you think?"

"Sure. But he won't tell."

It was breaking the rules to be out on the street this way during dinner, especially since they had not signed out at the dormitory.

Pecky's truck was painted black, and you could see the letters on the panel beneath the paint: MURPHY'S BAKED GOODS. It had cost him fifteen dollars, he had told them in class. There were rumors about Pecky, that his children had either died in infancy or were not "right," that his wife was a terrible housekeeper, that he hadn't had a new suit in ten years, that once he brought a sandwich to school made of a pancake between two slices of bread, or Spanish rice between two pancakes. Jo had heard it both ways. He could eat what he wanted. She felt honored that he had waved at them. She said, "When that man prays, you suddenly remember God's got a brain." Beverly thought that was very funny.

At the Newberry Library ("Merry Berry from the Newberry Liberry," Soup was always saying) they cut over to State Street and continued north. They had heard about a restaurant with a trap door in the floor where young girls were captured for white slavery, and tried to guess which one it was. "No matter what they did to me, I would tell them about Christ," said Beverly. "Unless they cut out my tongue."

"The stones would cry out," said Jo.

They had been gone about half an hour and she was feeling a little weak again, so they started back.

"You ought to lie down awhile," said Beverly. "I'll stay with you."

"Nonsense," said Jo. "Go on to Fellowship. I'm okay."

So Beverly went as far as the dorm and unlocked the doors, then ran off to the auditorium. On the elevator Jo realized she had left her purse at Van Housen. She had to go after it, there was no choice, and since Harold Hall was empty (all the girls at Evening Fellowship), she pressed the button to leave the front doors unlocked.

When she got back, there was a man inside the foyer. For an instant she hoped it was Roger and feared it was Clyde, before she looked at him—that is, before her brain said more than "male presence." There was no way he resembled either. He was a stranger, quite young, dressed in black evening clothes and a camel's hair coat; she could see his black bow tie and stiff collar. He stood in the shadow against the dark wall and smiled and nodded politely at Jo, as if this were his home too and they met every day in the foyer going in and out. Jo's next crazy thought was that he had been blown there by a gust of wind from some lakeside night spot. He was rather a small person.

It was not until he began to move between her and the door to the sidewalk that the need for escape shot into her legs. Escape meant into the building, and that was where she leaped. He came too, but not as fast as she thought he would. He said something softly that she didn't quite hear. "My name is Peter." Was that it? She was able to slam the door and turn the lock before he reached it. They stood looking at each other on either side of the glass, he seeming not at all dangerous, but quizzical, as if she had shut him out of his own house.

"What do you want?" she asked through the glass. He didn't answer. He glanced around, perhaps to identify the building.

"You've got the wrong place!" Jo yelled.

He shook his head and smiled vaguely. Jo felt the whole empty building rise up behind her, narrow and silent.

"Go away!" she shouted. She waved her arms. "Get out of here!"

At that, he looked so startled and pathetic she was ashamed. Why hadn't she asked him what he wanted out in the foyer? Maybe he wanted a particular student and he thought this was the main building. She even thought he might be Ruth's Barry, come up from Texas to win her back to himself. But not in a tuxedo. All that went through her mind like a flick of light.

He had nice dark eyes. There was something sharp in them. Was it fear? Did he need help? She had heard of a man who had simply walked on campus and asked to talk to someone. It turned out he was on the verge of suicide.

She did not intend to open the door, but she could at least make some effort to show good will. She rummaged quickly in her purse for paper to write on and, finding none, pulled out a tract. It was not one she liked much, but it was concise and the headings were big.

1. YOU NEED TO BE SAVED.
2. YOU CANNOT SAVE YOURSELF.
3. JESUS DIED TO SAVE YOU.
4. TRUST HIM FOR SALVATION NOW.

In between there were paragraphs in smaller print, explaining, but he could see at a glance what it was and let her know if he wanted to consult someone.

She bent over and slipped the tract under the door, feeling now the pressure of his need, whatever it was. He picked up the tract and examined it. For a moment she thought he would toss it away in scorn. Instead he smiled at her. "Okay," she said, smiling back. And now she faced a new problem—how to get him over to the campus so that one of the men students could talk to him. She was figuring this out when he swung open his coat.

"Oh my goodness!" gasped Jo. "Don't do that!"

Just inches away from her he was holding himself against the glass, like a naughty child. Only what he held in his hands belonged to no child.

Huge and rigid. She thought surely it was going to break through the glass. "My gosh! My gosh!" she said and looked quickly away, up at his face. He was still smiling at her. She blushed intensely, her eyes watered, for him, for her. She felt as if he had unzipped his skin and shown her his heart, lungs, liver, his last vestige of privacy thrown at her feet. She turned her back on him and wobbled to the telephone on the wall by the radiator. It was too high up for her. She had to dial three times before she could get the 0 all the way around.

"Van Housen," said the switchboard.

"This is Harold!" Jo called into the phone. A buzz answered and the phone went dead. The man was still there. She could see him without really looking. Then he was gone. She heard the outside door. The foyer was empty, and the tract was on her side of the door, shoved through the crack.

She picked it up. He had written something in dark pencil all around the margin. "Fuck you holy virgin fuck you fuck you fuck you holy daughter of God. I'll be back."

She crumpled it in her hand and stared at the empty doorway, not sure what to do. She did nothing, except get into the elevator. It received her, a safe bronze cage. She was not a silly person, easily shocked. She had always taken some pride in that. There had been no undue modesty at home. Loring had thought nothing of taking out his pecker and shooting an arc into a juniper bush while she watched. They joked about his range. Gloria had never even seen a penis. She had no brothers. "Oh, it's nothing!" Jo used to say to her. No more than a thumb or a toe. But this! This she had never seen, this deformity, spectacle!

She rode to the fifth floor, then back down to the third, and slowly back and forth for several minutes, until she felt ridiculous hiding in an elevator. She went down to the first floor, got the night watchman on the phone and calmly told him there was an exhibitionist in the neighborhood wearing a camel's-hair coat.

"Any other details?" asked the watchman.

"Details?" asked Jo. "Oh . . . none in particular."

He said thank you for reporting. He'd watch out for him.

In the room she studied the penciled message again. It was a black scrawl. He had borne down very hard . . . "holy daughter of God." The coarseness and hate in the words were dumbfounding. She thought of his polite face. It made no sense.

The girls were back. The front doors vibrated, and voices scattered throughout the building.

"What's going on, Jo?" asked Karen, entering the room. "Beverly said you were sick."

"I'm fine now."

"How come you look so pale?"

"Do I? . . . I had a funny experience."

Soup appeared, drawn to the room by the scent of drama. "What happened?" She was delighted. "You saw what? A zip man? Here? You saw a zipper?"

"A zip man?" Jo had never heard the expression. It cast an entirely different light on things, as if he had performed some sleight of hand.

"Jack the zipper!" cried Soup.

"They don't usually attack, I've heard," Karen said. "You probably weren't in any danger."

"Start from the beginning," said Soup.

"He was waiting inside the front door," Jo began. "When I saw him he spoke to me. I think he introduced himself."

"What a nifty touch! What was his name?"

"I thought he said Peter."

"Unbelievable!" cried Soup, falling on the bed. She would not stop laughing.

Then Jewel was at the door, and Ruth and Ruby.

"You saw a sex fiend?" gasped Ruby. "In this building?" She wanted to hold a prayer meeting for him immediately, but Soup started to laugh again. "Put him on your prayer list," she said. "His name is Peter."

"Oh," said Jo as the light dawned. "Am I dumb!"

She never told anyone about the tract or the scribbled message.

He was on her mind for a long time. The threat of his return, looking for her, lingered. Several times she thought she saw him on the streets. Each time she entered the foyer her feet moved to the memory of fear. Whenever she tried to pray for him, she saw him again, standing exposed on the other side of the glass. The more she tried to erase that picture, the more clearly it appeared. It began to come to her at other times, distressing interruptions in a class or while she was in conversation. She would break off a sentence as she struggled to block it.

Then, perversely, her mind began to play tricks on her. The man became Roger. Then Clyde. They swaggered and posed, showing off, waiting behind pillars in her brain to jump out at her—look, look! It was the silliest thing that had ever happened to her, a tiresome bore. What did she care what their genitals looked like, or anybody's?

Once, fighting it, she said "No!" out loud in the Survey exam. Heads raised around her. She felt as if she'd broken wind. She tried to act as if nothing had happened, it was not she who had spoken. The whole thing was stupid. It was funny. She ought to laugh. Was she cracking up? Dr. Peckham had just prayed at the beginning of class, "Grant us the mind of Christ," and everyone was writing industriously about Moses and the fire on Sinai, and across the aisle Clyde MacQuade stood up, opened his Army coat and sported himself. Zip Man.

There was not a lot of discussion of sex around school, none that Jo heard. The subject was not ignored; she didn't think so. It simply did not surface a great deal, except remarks Soup made about the more amorous couples, and a lecture or two in Women's Fellowship on demeanor (boys are more easily aroused, quickly tempted, it's up to the girl to set the standard, how she sits, how she stands). Once titillating reports of the tensions in a similar meeting for men circulated among the girls. Evidently there had been confessions. Specific terminology was not used. Even

Soup avoided the word "masturbation." She called it "secret sin," rolling her eyes.

Now Jo began to notice how couples stood, the thrust of a pelvis, a thumb hooked affectionately in a girl's belt, fingers touching, finger games. She wondered, a cloudy idea, if sex was not an enrichment of all they did together at school. Or was it the other way around? Singing together, kneeling together, sharing their most serious thoughts, going off to the city to witness and work together, supporting and encouraging one another, brother, sister. It was a warm damp atmosphere for the birth and growth of intimate ideas. She was not sure that was wrong, and in spite of it sex was treated as secondary.

There had been a time when Jo and Gloria had talked of nothing else. For months they had hammered away at it, whacking out information. How does it start? What happens next? Until the nice little fires of guesswork were finally extinguished by the truth, as found in Gloria's mother's book, full of unmistakable diagrams, and they had taken turns, each discreetly alone in Gloria's bathroom, door shut and locked, examining their own private parts with a hand mirror, comparing them with the sketches and finding them complete but terribly unattractive and assigning the whole matter to the future when love would surely do its work.

That stage was long over with. It was all out of proportion to be harassed now in this disgraceful way, the biological facts flaunting themselves before her without desire or pleasure or even good sense.

Then, as if to make things as bad as they could be, it was not just Roger and Clyde involved in this perversion. The first time it happened, it was a what-if. What if she should sink so low, permit an image so unthinkable? But that was as good as thinking it. The picture was already there—Jesus on the cross, the loincloth slipping. She shut it out with a gasp. Yet it came back and began to repeat itself, especially during prayer, public or private, whenever she shut her eyes. It was a demonic distraction.

Soup had told stories once of nuns she had heard of who had imaginary erotic affairs with Christ. "That's what celibacy does for you," she said. It made Jo shudder to think of it. Certainly there was no connection between that distortion and this nonsense that plagued her. "I'm not like that!" she protested—to herself, who else? But her concept of Christ was stained. To feel close to Him, aware of His love, and to sing song with words in them like "He holds my hand" and "My Jesus, I love Thee, I know Thou art mine" seemed dangerous. Because being a Christian was *like* being in love, she had to admit that. But so much more. It was a matter of spirit. You couldn't love Him with your body. . . . Unless it was impossible to separate things that finely. It was too much to think about.

Jo was taking down her hair almost every night now. Karen said the bobby pins must be too uncomfortable. Jo knew the dream was causing her to do it. It was the same running dream; she was running at home, through the woods and the quarry and down to the lake. She knew she was looking for Loring, calling him home. Yet there was more to it than that. She was really running no place. There was a dreadful feeling of not going anywhere, or there being no place to go, or when you got there it would not be where it ought to be. Nothing was dependable. The ground slipped under her feet.

One night she was on Prospect Road, by the swamp. It was dark, and she was late for supper. She could barely see the lights in the Cannons' windows, and as she ran they receded, as if the house were a boat at sea and she a swimmer. She knew that if she ran forever she would not get there. She woke up gasping for breath, a clump of bobby pins held tightly in one fist.

She asked Jewel, offhandedly, as they were rinsing out stockings in the sinks, if she thought God still spoke to people in dreams as He did in the Bible. "I think He uses all parts of our minds," Jewel said. Then she added, "But it's tricky. The devil uses everything too, though I hate to give him credit." She went on a bit too long about it, as Jewel was apt to do. The safest way, as she saw it, was to know the Word and put your trust there. All else was dangerous. Satan was a wily deceiver. Jo wished she had not asked her.

That same week she escaped again to the Pastry Shop and sat alone in a booth at the rear. Several of the Pastor's Course students were in their usual booth, as she had hoped they would be. She had come here on purpose for this, to let their voices scrub like brooms through her brain. When she arrived the subject was pacifism and war ("Thou shalt not kill"), and in a few minutes moved on to the rest of the Commandments and laws of every kind, school rules, freedom and judgment. Their Bibles were spread open among the coffee cups, and they were thumping through them, back and forth, reading aloud and interrupting so often it was hard for Jo to keep the thread.

"Galatians. Look at Galatians!"

"I am not bound—"

"Jesus came not to destroy the law but to fulfill it. Not one *jot*—"

"Galatians. Listen. 'The law is our schoolmaster to bring us—' "

"Take the Sabbath, for instance."

"We are now *sons*, not children. Look at the first half of Romans."

"Could I please finish this verse in Galatians?"

"Take separation from the world. What if I were to go to a theater tonight? Am I really free to make that choice?"

" 'If meat offend my brother—' "

"But we cry 'Abba' *like* children. We are always children."

"We are under the law right now in this school. That's my point. We are not *trusted* to be under grace."

"Half the time I don't trust *myself*."

" 'Stand fast in the liberty wherein Christ has made us free.' "

"Could I—?"

Jo strained to hear them, relishing the argument, ideas colliding and multiplying. The bald one prevailed. Christian liberty had two foes—legalism and license. He was explaining legalism when she lost him. Clyde came in.

She could not believe it, that he would enter again just as before, and at a moment when his intrusion should cost her so much. Was she a magnet that drew him from any point on campus? Oh, go away, go away, she thought. He was at the counter. She ignored him. The bald one said something about Old Testament jurisprudence, and Clyde turned around. He saw Jo and came over and slid into the other side of the booth.

"You hear those guys?" he whispered. "They're the ones who read at the University library." His head was down as he spoke. His hair looked as if it might come out in tufts if you pulled even gently.

Something-something immanence, one of the boys was saying. Had they changed the subject? They were more subdued now.

"Playing with fire," said Clyde.

"But nothing means something," Baldy said. "Ex nihilo."

"Right. Logos. The power which creates the power by which—"

"Beware lest any man spoil you through philosophy and vain deceit," said Clyde softly, still looking at Jo.

The students at the table stopped and glanced over at him, then continued their talk. "Geological ages," she heard, and then Peckham's name.

"Darwinism. Peckham is a sellout." That was Clyde. The remark was obviously directed at the others, though he still looked at Jo and spoke softly. He tapped his fingers on the table. There were specks of foam at the corners of his mouth.

"Are you talking to us, MacQuade, or your girl?" asked Baldy.

"Anybody who's listening, including 4-D draft dodgers."

They laughed. Clyde's ears grew red, and he turned around to face them. "Afraid to die," he said, loudly. Then he seemed startled at his position, alone against four. His lips trembled. But he went on. "Half the

4-D's at this school belong in the war. You need more than big words over there."

"Wait," said Baldy. "Repeat what you said about Peckham."

"Never mind."

"Repeat it."

"He'd sell his soul to sound scholarly and up to date."

"You've got him all wrong. He's got nothing to hide."

"Oh yeah? Did you see him this morning?" Clyde's voice was beginning to shake, but he sputtered on. "This morning. He was up there on the platform during the prayer looking through his little appointment book. Yes, up there, looking through his little black book and saying, 'Yes Lord, yes Lord,' out loud. The big phony."

"Oh! Who cares? Why don't you just keep still!"

Jo had spoken. She was as surprised as Clyde's face. Before he could answer she was out the door. She could hear Baldy and the others laughing as she walked away.

Clyde avoided her the rest of the week. It seemed too easy. One clomp and he had retreated, injured. Several times she saw him staring at her with hurt dark eyes from across a room. In time he would come back, she supposed, and she would have to make a decision. For the present her anger cleared her mind. It hung on, a fine bright thing. She felt sharp and in charge of her judgments.

She gave herself to piano practice. Her first performance at a studio recital, before Mr. Cooch's other students, was due before the end of the month. He had given her a hard piece to get ready, a waltz by Chopin. Halfway through, the key changed to five sharps. She had been discouraged by it, but now she attacked it, getting control of the knots of notes one by one. She worked hard and felt good.

That Saturday Clyde was waiting for her as she came out of the Music Building and handed her, triumphantly but unsmiling, a whole cold newspaper, and walked away. Aachen had gone under the day before, surrendered, said the headline, outlined in Clyde's red ink. Between the print he had written, "Very important to talk. Mess hall. Tomorrow noon. Come in prayer."

On Sunday Jo bought a quart of milk on her way home from church and made that her dinner in her room. She stayed there the rest of the day, napping and writing a letter home. Louise brought word that Clyde was looking for her. "Let him look," Jo said. She was very tired. The edge had gone out of her anger. Writing the letter was labor, to find something to say that lifted only the top layer. Rereading her mother's last letter, she saw the same thing at work. How many chickadees were on the feeder, who was out sick at Dennison. Mother was a genius at two pages of cheerful nothing.

"The tea kettle boils," her letter went, "and there are deer tracks on the croquet court. One ought not to need anything more. I beat Dad at Chinese Checkers five times last night. His mind was elsewhere, per usual. Right now on the letter he is writing to you, want to bet? He is taking it through the seventh draft." She had fastened a tiny piece of green cedar sprigs to the paper with a straight pin. It was so much like her to do that.

Jo evaded Clyde until noon on Monday when he trapped her at last.

The woman's meal line gathered at the top of the stairs to the dining room, at the south side of Van Housen Hall. Before the last bell rang the staircase would always be full. This spot was out of bounds to men. They had their own line at the other end of the tunnel, where girls were not allowed. No one broke this rule, as the areas were carefully watched and the penalty was to be denied all social privileges for a month. So when Clyde appeared at the foot of the stairs just before lunch that day, an abrupt silence fell the length of the line. Heedless of that, he began to push his way up past the girls, his eyes on Jo, who stood above him in the hall.

There was no way to avoid any of it. "Watch out," someone said. Below Clyde by not five steps was a proctor. The girls around Jo fell back instinctively, and so did Jo. But Clyde had reached the top and was addressing her in a loud whisper. "Where have you been?" he demanded. "I've been looking everywhere."

Jo was watching the proctor. She was directly behind Clyde now, a tall woman who looked down on him. Her name was Miss Mackey, Grace Mackey. Students called her Amazing Grace. She was dressed as she often was, in a suit with gloves and a hat, as if she had just come from somewhere or was about to go. Her hair was in an updo, and her hat, a whole bluebird with wings spread, sat atop the curls on her forehead.

"What are you doing here, Mr. MacQuade?" she asked quietly. "Go to the gentleman's line, please. Someone will see you later."

Clyde hesitated, then left without another word, back down the path Miss Mackey had cleared on the stairs. Before Jo could feel relief or embarrassment, she found herself addressed.

"I think you'd best come to my office this afternoon," Miss Mackey said, still politely, taking a pencil and notebook from her purse. She looked directly into Jo's eyes. She had an unrelenting gaze that poured significance into her most casual greetings on campus. "How are you?" seemed like an inquiry after your soul's deepest needs. You wanted to look away and not involve yourself in that shameless give and take. But a swerving glance implied guilt.

"Let's see, your name is . . . ."

"Jo Fuller. But why . . . ?"

"Yes, of course. Jo." Did she look at you that way because she couldn't remember your name, a kind of signal of intense well-meaning anyhow? "Are you free at 1:00?" she asked.

Jo nodded, though she was not free, and Miss Mackey offered her a smile that precluded any further discussion. We will be firm but not unfair, you'll see, said the smile. The bell rang, and the line charged down to the dining room. Jo went in the opposite direction, to the girl's washroom in the tunnel, where she sat on a toilet in a stall, intending to pray. Instead, mortified and angry, she reviewed the incident over and over for a full half hour.

Out at a sink she washed her hands and rebuked herself for making so much of things. Her face returned to her askew from the warped mirror.

One cheek hung lower than the other, and part of one eye repeated. Gloria's aunt was a Rosicrucian. Once she had supposedly seen in a mirror the person she had been in an earlier life. She had smashed the mirror. Jo studied her divided eye, chilled. Oh, she could be so foolish. She wiped her hands and went to see Miss Mackey.

The door to the proctor's office was shut. Jo, about to knock, thought she heard someone crying inside and moved a respectable distance away. Moments passed before the door opened and the girl emerged, her cheeks wet and blotchy. The door closed again. In another several minutes, Miss Mackey appeared, her cheeks also flushed. "Come in, Jo," she said, smiling.

The room was surprisingly pretty, with flowered drapes at the windows. A plaque done in watercolors hung on the wall: "Yielding . . . yielding . . . until I am yielded." On her desk was another sign, visible from both directions. It said, "Keep Sweet." Miss Mackey offered Jo a chair in front of the desk, then seated herself nearby, companionably. "Let's have a short word of prayer, shall we, Josephine?" she said, and instantly shut her eyes. "Our Father, how grateful we are this day for Thy lovingkindness, for encircling us even this minute in Thine everlasting arms. Be present here, in the person of Thy Holy Spirit, as Josephine and I talk together for a little while. We remember that Christ said where two or three are gathered together in His Name, He would be there in the midst of them. We claim that promise now. In His Name and for His sake, we pray. Amen."

She raised her head and smiled, looking into Jo's eyes. "Well, Josephine."

"I'm sorry."

"What?"

"That isn't my name."

"I thought you said—"

"It's just Jo."

"Oh! Your mother wanted a boy!" Her voice was girlish, her vowels drawn in tight and her r's narrow. Jo measured her age across the space between them. Thirty-five? She was a good-looking woman. She had taken off the bird and looked better without it.

"Well, I thought we'd best have a talk. It's time, anyway. I've been watching you and Mr. MacQuade for quite a while. Let me ask you a question." She paused at length, so long it seemed she must have forgotten the question she had in mind and was making up another. "There is a good reason, don't you think, for compliance to rules we have agreed to obey before even entering a school?"

The question, finally articulated, lacked force. Jo hesitated, not sure she was supposed to respond. There was another silence, in which her answer, "Well . . . yes," sat like two small islands.

"Jo, Clyde is a young man who means well, as I'm sure you've found. We don't like to see him get careless about his decorum. He has a number of burdens to bear as it is. If the two of you are going to continue seeing each other, I must recommend some controls on when and where you meet."

"But we don't go together."

"You don't? . . . But you *are* interested in each other."

"Oh, not the way it seems."

"Who initiates your contacts?"

Contacts? "Oh . . . . He does."

"Do you want him to?"

"No, but I've let him."

"Then the interest is not mutual?"

"No."

"All right, I see. Does he bother you, Jo? We can talk to him, you know. We don't like students to rob each other of time and energy."

Jo looked up. Miss Mackey's eyes were intelligent. She knew Clyde. Of course she did. He had been here for a year. A proctor had to be careful. But surely she understood the dilemma. She was waiting for Jo to speak, and Jo felt drawn to her. The idea of talking, of telling someone everything, even about the Zipper images, however foolish that made her look, struck her as a most desirable and right thing to do. She thought, I am going to talk, I am going to spill it all, and she began.

"He does bother me, but it's my fault too, you see. He has no friends. It seemed right. Maybe it wasn't. Things have been a mess, to tell you the truth. I've never known exactly what to do. At least, I thought I did once, at first, I thought he needed . . . ." She stopped to adjust her perspective. Was this sounding self-righteous?

"Okay, kiddo, I see. This sort of thing is very delicate. You don't want to offend a fellow Christian, and sometimes fellowship with the opposite sex is very helpful to someone like Clyde, who . . . has probably not . . . perhaps has not had a chance to know many girls."

Jo didn't answer. The word "kiddo" was skipping around in her head and she had lost her train of thought.

"Jo, tell me if you care to . . . How do you *feel* about Clyde MacQuade? That is, do you feel, oh, ah . . . scorn or pity, say?"

"Both sometimes."

"Both? . . . Disgust?"

"Yes."

"Can we say there has been no love?"

"No love?"

"I mean, of course, Christian love."

"Oh. No. Not much love," said Jo. The desire to divulge everything was fading fast. She had to get back on the track before it was gone. "To tell you the truth, I wouldn't care if I never saw him again in my life."

Miss Mackey looked startled. Jo thought perhaps she was the first person to ever utter such words in this office. She had meant it as a kind of confession. It came out like a curse.

"That's a heavy burden," Miss Mackey said. She stood and walked to the window, looking down into the street. Her suit was plum colored, and her fingernails on the cord of the blind were well manicured with a clear polish. Jo glanced at her own nails. She had been biting the cuticles.

"Jo, what if you were to get to the mission field and find he is a fellow worker? Someone with whom you must work for years and years?"

"That would be very hard."

Miss Mackey turned. "How do you perceive your future with regard to Clyde, Jo?"

Future. Years stretched ahead with Clyde at her side, wet messages in her ear. "I don't know. . . . I want to do the right thing. . . . I mean now."

"What would Jesus do? Have you asked yourself that?"

"Jesus?" She said it as if she had never heard of Him before. "Oh. Jesus would—Isn't that different?"

"He would love Him, wouldn't He?" Miss Mackey came back and sat on the edge of the desk. She cocked her head. "Are you *willing* to love Clyde, Jo?"

"Love him?" The word snagged her again.

"With Christ's love."

"I'm not sure what that would mean. It's very complicated."

"Are you *willing* to love him romantically?"

"Oh no. Even Clyde himself hasn't—"

"I'm asking you about your own attitude, that's all. Are you willing to fall in love with him?"

"Oh, I couldn't."

"But God *could* make you love him. He could make Clyde attractive to you, if that was His plan. The question is, are you *willing* for that?"

"No. No, I don't think so. No, I'm not. No."

"I'm only pointing out the necessity of being sure your heart is right in all things. God knows what kind of a man you can love, or if you'll be happier and more useful to Him without a mate altogether. The whole thing, Jo, is to be open and surrendered."

"But what about Clyde? Is it wrong to—I wish I knew how to act with him." She was babbling, deflecting blindly.

"The Lord will take care of what goes on in Clyde's mind, Jo. You have one responsibility—to make sure things are right inside *you*. To be selfless, open to His leading. Do you see?" She paused. She wanted an answer.

"I thought I did."

"Are you happy in the Lord?" With her narrow vowels, the word was "Lerd." She wanted an answer again. "If you are not, then something is wrong. Are you fully yielded to Him, Jo? In every area of your life? Is He having His way? Don't answer me. Answer *Him*. Because it is not until we are emptied of our willfulness that the indwelling Christ can love out through us. There can be no barriers. We must die to ourselves daily."

What did that mean? What did it mean as it came from *her*? Jo saw a girl about her own size weeping over a coffin. It was warm in the room. Miss Mackey removed her jacket. A half-moon of sweat had darkened on her silk blouse under each arm. She draped the jacket over her chair.

"Love is the fulfilling of the law, the cross of Christ across the gap," she said. "Without His love we are nothing."

"I know," said Jo. "I know that." She meant it. She wanted to sound as though she did, but her stomach, with no lunch in it, growled in the next silence, going from high to low like a quickly emptied bottle. It was very loud. "Oh, excuse me," she said.

Miss Mackey seemed not to notice. "Okay, gal? . . . Then, let's go before the Lord with this, what do you say?" She bowed her head. "Why don't you begin, Jo?"

Jo wanted to cry. Oh, not again. She resisted. She thought of the girl who had been in here before her. Not again those waters. They rose powerfully, swelling in her head. Her nose burned. Her throat was going to burst. She knew suddenly that the crying in this office began during the prayer. If it were possible to separate Miss Mackey from her words, she might not mind crying. But she could not say "I see" to this plum-colored suit or give those tight vowels the yes of tears.

Miss Mackey was waiting. Jo said, "If you don't mind, I'd rather pray alone." It was bold. You never refused to pray when asked.

"Oh. Well, that's all right. . . . You'll take care of it then?"

"Yes."

"It's best to do it while things are fresh. Settle it with God. Never let a matter go unsettled between you and the Lord." Miss Mackey rose. "Here's a little secret, Jo. Pray *for* Clyde, not about him."

"All right. Thank you." The pressure of the tears had subsided. She wanted to say, "And I'm sorry, for a lot of things," but she wasn't sure what they were.

Another girl sat out there by the door, waiting for her turn. Jo thought of whispering as she went by, "Stiff upper lip, and whatever happens don't pray out loud."

Back at Harold, a pall hung over the fifth floor. Somebody had drawn the shades in the bathroom and kitchen. Soup was having a migraine.

"Light and noise bother her," whispered Louise. "She's trying to sleep now."

Karen was not in the room. Jo flopped on her bed to think, but in a few minutes she heard heavy running feet in the hall and then Soup gagging and hacking and flushing the toilet. She ought to try to do something for her, or at least express concern.

Soup's door was ajar. She was lying on her bed with a wet towel on her forehead. The room was dark and close.

"Can I get anything for you?" asked Jo.

"Hi, Shrimp," said Soup, without spirit. "No. Nobody can do anything. It just goes bang, bang on the back of my head." She was in her men's pajamas. The fabric was printed with hunting dogs and rifles. Jo recalled rubbing her mother's head when she had one of her sick headaches. They called it a "treatment" at home, a nice old-fashioned word.

Soup said, "Jewel claims it's the Lord laying me low where He can teach me something. She laughs, but she means it. Maybe she's right." She began to cry, and Jo, who had just backed off from the edge of that cliff, felt herself drawn toward it again. She concentrated hard on the tail of a hound who posed with a raised paw on Soup's chest.

Soup kept talking as she cried, and Jo couldn't hear all she said. Evidently Jewel had been trying to get her to lose weight. "Triumph over," Jo heard. "Control . . . greed . . . besetting." Finally Soup lifted the towel and said, "He must increase and I must decrease. John 3:30." Then she laughed and started to cry again. "If I trusted enough I wouldn't have headaches."

"Soup, would you like a back rub?" Jo asked.

"If you want to." Soup blew her nose on the wet towel. "It can't hurt anything."

She turned on her stomach. She had a very broad back. There was dirt in the creases of her neck, and her elbows were black. The loose pajamas caught under Jo's fingertips. She kept thinking, I can't touch her, I hate this. But it's Soup's body. She lives in it. . . . It was Clyde lying there, in those pajamas.

Soup was laughing into the pillow. "Think what it must have been like in the New Testament when they washed each other's feet!"

As soon as it seemed appropriate, Jo stopped and went to her room. She opened a window and took several long breaths, holding them inside her as long as she could. Then she went to the kitchen sinks and washed her hands, making mounds of suds with a new cake of Ivory, rinsing and doing it twice more.

After that she shut her door and sat at her desk. Loring's crew watched her, smiling bravely. The turbulence had to end. She said, "Lord, I'm willing for anything. I'm willing to love Clyde and be his girl and even to marry him someday, if that's Your plan. I'll spend the rest of my life with him—my entire life—if that's what You want me to do."

It was no help at all. She had thought such a surrender might bring peace. Instead she felt as if she had promised to commit suicide.

Instantly matters became worse. Clyde stopped all direct contact, advised perhaps to leave her alone. Instead he resumed the shadowing. He was back at the old bodyguard business of hovering nearby without speaking. For an hour on Tuesday afternoon he walked beneath her window on the other side of the street. He would slip out of sight, then back again. When she left the dorm to go about her business, he picked up her trail. She knew he would.

On Wednesday he followed her into the Music Building. She wasn't aware of it until she began to play and the light altered ever so faintly across the keyboard. When she glanced up to see what had caused it, there was the plane of his cheek just for a second, turning from the little window of the door.

It happened again five minutes later and then again. Each time as she stopped working and looked up, the window was empty. When she went back to the keys, the shadow fell. She thought he might try to come in, but he did not even knock.

She flew into Chopin. Mr. Cooch had whirled pencil marks around the spots where she was to concentrate her attention. *"Con anima!"* he cried out in lessons. "Oh! Oh! *Con anima!*" She must do better. He had to protect his reputation in Afghanistan, he said. The recital was three days away. She was nowhere near ready.

The shadow fell, lifted, fell. Jo scraped back her bench and ran to the door. The hall was empty. Music rang from the cubicles around her. "Let the peace of God rule in your hearts," sang the girl next door. She played the line through again and changed a chord, then fiddled with it some more. She was writing a song.

If Clyde was here, he was hiding in one of those rooms. Jo shut the door and went back to the piano. When the light changed again she tried hard to ignore it. But her concentration was gone.

What right did he have to haunt her and chill her this way? Why this cheek at her window? Of all the boys at school, why this one watching and waiting and clinging to her as if he owned her? Why not any other? Why not Roger? Really, why not?

She made it Roger, testing it out. Everything changed. The fear dissolved. He peered in at her, green-eyed, waiting for her to look up and give him a wave. Chopin saluted him. It was lovely.

Then the pretense struck her as ugly and warped. She was sick of fantasy. Oh, flesh and blood, she thought. Hair and teeth and eyelashes and breath of life. It was the real boy she wanted, here, inside the room, not at the window. Not a figment of her mind, not Roger the Zipper. The real boy, clothed and sane. She said it. Lord, I want him, up close, *here*. Is it so wrong? I want him, the real boy—here in this room. Or take him out of my life completely!

Her childishness was appalling. She snatched her music off the piano and whipped out the door and down to the next level, into the first empty room she found. In fifteen minutes the girl scheduled to use the room arrived, and Jo gathered up her things again and, checking the hallway for Clyde, searched out another room and set to work once more at another piano. The keys were cold. Her heart raced. She moved five times that afternoon. Here in this building full of music and safety she was like a groundhog scuttling in panic between the rooms of its tunnel. It was the exact opposite of Christian behavior. Her old fear seemed very close. It was only a memory. She knew that. But on Thursday she skipped practice entirely.

Her father's letter came on Friday. Jo held it lightly in her hand on the way to her last exam, Personal Evangelism. The envelope was fat and springy. Six or more sheets of onionskin inside. It smelled of Noxzema.

On the stairs she opened it and pulled out the crackling pages. Elite type, single spaced, with corrections and additions in his fine feminine handwriting. People charged past her, calling and waving their mail. The noise was deafening.

Dear John Anderson, my Jo:

There is no God. There is no Intelligence concerned with the affairs of men.

I have been writing this since September, when you left us for your greener pastures, and I cannot find a kinder way to begin.

An alarm sounded inside her, air raid alert. Doors and windows slammed shut, lights blew out. She assumed her old position, the one that had gotten her through a hundred grueling lectures, a solid unflinching front of wait-it-out. She was on the second page when she entered the classroom.

My greatest hope for my children has been that they would live for Truth, go after it ruthlessly, tooth and nail, with a consuming thirst that shoves aside dogma and superstition. Only then is the conquest of happiness possible. Each night I send a silent message west. "Science is the only basis for revelation!"

It is not only Loring's whereabouts that fills my mind at two o'clock in the morning, but my lovely daughter's mind there in Chi

Jo sat down in her chair and shoved the letter back into the envelope. Then she sighed and got it out again. All those lines of type, all that time. His voice continued, as if she had turned off a radio and turned it back on.

Concern about one's standing with an imagined God has crippled the lives of millions over the centuries . . .

Are you to ossify mentally at age 18?

She glanced ahead: the unreliability of the Gospel accounts (two pages to that), the escapism of a saviour, the scientific mind doubts everything. He had been through it all before. *Miracles*, Jo? Lot's wife turned to salt? Answer me. Yes, you say? Yes, and not lie? You believe the sun stood still for Joshua for a whole day? Do you know what would happen if the earth stopped turning for *one minute*? You believe Jesus raised Lazarus from the dead? Healed lepers with the snap of a finger? Think now . . . molecules, the skin changing before your eyes. Is there anything in your experience to warrant such a belief? Show me a miracle. Just one!

Mr. Baker was up front pulling the mimeographed exams from his briefcase. He looked like a young businessman, or a lawyer maybe. Students dived into notes for a last-minute review. "Shall we lift it up?" asked Mr. Baker. Pray and sing before the exam was what he meant. He began to sing, directing them with his hand.

> Are you to ossify mentally at age 18? Are you still my dear Jo, my beloved? I had thought you would be different from the general run of womankind . . . .
>
> Check your emotions coldly with your gray matter. Sorties of emotion can be excused as human weakness, but it is beyond me how you can rest your whole life on hysteria and still be true to whatever knowledge you have garnered along life's way.

Garnered! The word made her angry. She slapped the letter into the back of her notebook. Exams were being passed out. All notes and papers away, please, said Mr. Baker. No worry, no panic, he said, teasing them. Just a shotgun quiz. Bang, bang, I'm dead, said someone.

Question one: Quote, giving references, any Scripture you would show a person who thinks he must earn his salvation by being good.

Jo wrote, "Almost any section of Romans, chapters three through six, would apply. I would show this person chapter four, verses 4-5. 'Now to him that worketh is the reward not reckoned of grace, but of debt. But to him that worketh not, but believeth on him that justifieth the ungodly, his faith is counted for righteousness.' "

Once she had a thing all worked out to say to Daddy. It went: Just meet me. You be right, and I'll be wrong. But don't tell me that. Don't try to change me. Then we can talk. But to him that would be a game. He wanted her to face the evidence, he said, that's all, just look it in the eye. But she knew he wanted more than that.

"If the evidence shows your God does not exist, will you accept it?"

Yes meant more than yes. Yes was already a capitulation. She'd answered, boldly, "The evidence won't show it."

"Oh, is that so? Well, ain't we cawnfident?"

Sometimes she sat immobile for an hour, hardly answering him. He thought she was being smug. She was praying for calmness, holding on, careful not to show anger or frustration or emotion of any kind, because that was defeat in his eyes. That was what he wanted—to break her. It would prove something. Yet the agitation she felt seemed to come from *him* much more than from what he was saying. It leaped across the room and caught her whole.

"Are you afraid, is that it? Are you afraid *not* to believe? 'Square the shoulders!' Clarence Darrow said. Have you got the courage to face life without a myth to get you through? Or are you a fraidy cat after all?"

She knew what he meant by "after all." He'd always thought she was different. Even when she was little, she had not been silly, like most girls, afraid of things, squealing about cows and spiders and ghosts. Oh, she checked for spiders with a flashlight inside the toilet hole before she sat down, but that was not what really bothered her there inside the privy. It was not real animals, the unnamed creatures that snuffled about the shed or scratched under the house. If she kicked her heels on the wall, they scuttled off into the woods. Those were no problem.

"I don't think Jo is afraid of anything," Mother used to tell people. Even her friends thought she was brave because she dared to walk home alone after dark, or so they thought. She said good-bye to them as one by one they turned into their lighted houses. They were feeding their cats and setting their tables when she was just into the loneliest part of her journey.

If Daddy was home, he might come to get her in the car. There was a gate at the end of the quarry road, a great bedspring thing that sometimes was closed to keep the cows in. If she and Daddy were alone in the car, he waited behind the wheel (because if he didn't, the car would stall) while she lifted the gate off the hook and swung it open. It took every ounce of strength she had to do it.

"That's showing the world," Daddy would say as she climbed back on the seat, and she knew that she must never do anything to spoil his pride in her. Capable, sensible. Lots of gumption. That's what he thought. He had no idea what went on in her mind when she walked alone.

Sometimes Mother would meet her, and sometimes Loring, spelling SOS in Morse Code with the yellow circle of the flashlight. He never said anything about her fears, though he must have known. "They only want you if you're rich," he whispered in the dark bedroom, the first time she crawled into bed with him.

It had been in the newspapers. Jo had never heard before of children being stolen. She lay there, sharing the pocket of warmth Loring had created, passing his logic through her mind. It held until she went back to her own bed, where knowledge enclosed her like the cold sheets. If rich people's houses were not impenetrable, whose was? For a long time after that she forced herself to lie awake at night. Someone had to watch, for the whole family. So much could happen while you slept.

The second time she crawled in with Loring, he was cross. He had waked up, though she had tried not to disturb him. "What are you afraid of now?" he whispered into the dark.

"Nothing." Unnamed, she meant. No thing.

"You can't be afraid of nothing. It has to be something."

So she answered, "A face at the window," and it became that. It was as if having been born, her fear wanted an identity, and it was quite willing, she found, to change its name again and again, and its form. It had no shame. It didn't care what it was. It grew up alongside her, being what it could be, however ludicrous—an ape-man, a maniac escaped from Westboro State Prison, a stray Nazi hiding out in the woods. Once it was even an ear, coming from nowhere, nobody's, hanging from a tree in the swamp on Prospect Road, very high up. She never actually saw it again. It was only that she *might*. It could present itself in the front on your window, or you might kick it accidentally in the grass, fooled into thinking it was a toadstool. Once, in a moment of utter horror, she thought she had found it in the middle of a library book—*Anne of Green Gables*. It was a piece of dried baloney lying in a ring of oil. The strength of the ear faded finally, as she knew it had to, but not until it had taught her that one must not depend on things to be only what they seemed.

Getting bigger was not much help, for then she was expected to do more by herself, and the possibilities of danger increased. Home from school, she might find a chatty note on the table. "Hi, Dear! Dad and I at Framingham Laundry getting the sheets. Please put potatoes on at 5:00. Love a bundle, Mother."

Though the kitchen was full of signs of good human life, like a saucer of garbage in the sink, it meant nothing. Loring would be at Scouts or somewhere. Life outside—the chipmunks and the crows, utterly sociable, never without each other—was of no use to her. She was alone except for her fear, which stood in every corner of the house, worse now that she was old enough to deny it the silly forms it wanted to take, much worse as a possibility that patiently watched and waited for its chance.

When it was gone at last, it went without a struggle. Sometime after the Sheldon meeting she realized it had sneaked away, as if ordered out by a glance. She had wanted very much to tell her father. You asked for a miracle . . . ? But to tell him was admitting that the fear had been there in the first place, which would prove something too—that she was a certain kind of person to begin with, capable of all sorts of foolish notions. So she kept it to herself.

Question two: What would you say to a person who wondered why he should bother to be good at all if it didn't earn for him a place in heaven?

She wrote that she would show him all of Romans six, where Paul deals with the matter at length. She might get half credit for that. She was not thinking well. Her handwriting was cramped. There were extra mounds in her m's and n's. She erased. The eraser made a hole in the paper.

The recital was scheduled to start at eight o'clock on Saturday morning. At seven, skipping breakfast, Jo ran to the Music Building to get in one more practice session. She burst through the door to her room and almost fell on top of a boy and a girl huddled together on the bench, kissing. They broke apart, startled. The boy was Roger Honey, and the girl in his arms was a pianist who often played for him.

They stared at Jo for a moment, then the girl laughed. "Uh-oh," she said. "Is this your room?"

"Yes."

Roger made no move to unfold his arms or get up. There, not three feet from Jo (she had backed away), were all the details she had memorized, the jawline, the color high on his cheekbones. His eyes matched his sweater. In the light of this room they were startling eyes. The irises were rimmed in black. Jo had not noticed that before. The girl, pale and soft with a little double chin, snuggled against him. His cheek rested on her hair.

"I guess you want to practice," the girl said to Jo.

"I think I'd better," Jo answered. Her voice was mild and expressionless. There was a pause. Words flew up and fell down in her head like lost birds. She wished she could think of something witty to say, about the things people will do before breakfast, maybe. Her neck was hot. She said nothing.

"Okay. We'll go," said the girl. With a playful grunt she pushed Roger's arms away. They stood. Roger stretched and smiled. "All yours," he said, reaching out his arms.

Jo's heart leaped, until she saw he meant the room. The right thing to do at that second was to rush into that soft green sweater and burst into tears. She came so close to it the motion started in her muscles. She wanted to yell at him. You know more about me than any other person in this school! Don't you know that? What does this mean, this wretched charade?

"Do you practice at that piano every day?" asked the girl.

"Yes."

"You poor kid. It's the worst one in the school."

She hit B flat above high C. It gave a toneless yelp. Roger laughed, and they moved slowly toward the door, the girl leading, pulling Roger by the hand. He seemed moonstruck and helpless. He stopped and looked back at Jo, making a glum face at her, as if reflecting her own. "Are you going to tell on us?" he asked.

She thought of saying, "Not if you give me a nickel," but she just shook her head.

The girl pulled at him and he yielded, falling against her.

"Well, keep 'em flying," Roger said to Jo. "Won't you."

"Sure," said Jo.

And whoosh! All her love for him was gone.

They shut the door, and Jo dropped onto the piano bench, still warm from their bodies. She had met him in *this room*. She had gotten exactly what she prayed for. It was all over, whatever it was or might have been. She wasted five whole minutes trying not to cry. She was glad it was over, but it was sad to see him go, shot from her life so suddenly and completely.

The recital did not go well. Her foot shook on the pedal, and her hands were connected to nothing. A dozen students listened, all advanced. They were kind. Their faces registered only understanding as she stood and went back to her seat.

Afterwards Jo took a walk. She headed up Clark and turned West. Choir was meeting this morning. She ought to go back, but she kept walking. She still felt as she had at the piano, out of joint. Grit blew into her face, and she turned again, between buildings. It was a miserable-looking street, but the sun shone here. Children throwing a ball against some steps stopped to let her go by. "What are you doing here?" asked a little girl. Jo smiled at her and didn't answer.

She walked faster, knowing she should go back to school and wanting to, but not quite ready yet. A Negro soldier turned up some steps in front of her, avoiding trash and broken glass. He had a duffel bag over his shoulder. Sunlight caught on his buttons.

133

At the moment it seemed completely possible that Loring would suddenly appear, walking toward her in his uniform. A wonderful, freaky accident—to meet him on some Chicago street. It was the kind of thing that could happen in wars.

"Missing in action," she said, moving her lips. Separate those words from the war and they made no sense. Disappeared while doing something. "My dear Miss Fuller. I regret to inform you that your brother has disappeared. One minute he was right here doing something, and the next he was gone. Perhaps you will meet him on some Chicago street. Cordially yours, Adjutant Major Somebody."

Last winter she used to pick up the mail on the way home from school and carry it all the way without opening it. The house would be empty, Mother and Daddy both doing war jobs at Dennison by then. The breakfast dishes waited in the sink, along with a half-full pot of tea. She would pour herself a cup of cold tea, not bothering to make a fresh cup, add a great deal of sugar and evaporated milk, and sip it while she read the letters, first from Xavier University in Ohio, where he went for his initial training (Eager Beaver, they called it), then from Ellington Field in Texas, where they taught him to fly and shoot the stars, then Wyoming, Nebraska, Mississippi, and overseas.

"Up at 0200 every morning," he wrote from Texas. No heat in the glass dome—his position for contact flying. Four-to-six-hour flights, combat missions over western Texas, dry heaves for six hours at a time. He was airsick, of all things. No one knew what to do about it. He was going to wash out. His classwork was fine, but in the plane he went into a stupor of nausea. Would they care if he washed out? He apologized for failing. It was all a mistake. He'd be assigned to ground detail somewhere in the country.

Then the doctor gave him a pill that worked, and in no time, it seemed, he had his wings. He was almost as jubilant as he'd been when he made Eagle Scout at age fifteen.

What she missed now was the mail. She had gotten used to his bodily absence, but the letters had come and come. Over the distance they had insulted each other again. "Dear Fatso," he wrote, "Your letter was swell—well, fair—well, I read it anyway." She thought of writing to him now. She still knew his address by heart.

Lt. Loring P. Fuller
514 Sqdn. 376 Gr.
A.P.O. 681, c/o Postmaster
New York City

It made him accessible. She saw her letter getting all the way through to Italy, where the Fifteenth was still based and sending out its heavies. The letter would move around the base and at last be put with his things, his underwear and socks, neatly rolled and paired, his toothbrush and tube of paste, the leather portfolio she had given him when he went away, with its little window for stamps. All these waited for him over in Italy. Was it somebody's job to go into the barracks and pack those things in the footlockers of the missing men? Would he be careful, whoever he was? If there was dirty laundry, did he wash it? Or did it get packed away dirty?

The letter would not get there, of course. They would stop it somewhere and send it back with "Missing" written on it, in the handwriting of some very much alive unmissing soldier who had the safe dull job of returning undeliverable mail. Did he write "Killed" too when it was appropriate, or "Imprisoned"?

"It's not the worst," the man from the telegraph office had told them. He had driven his car over the quarry road and parked it beside Loring's own green V-8. Daddy was mowing the grass on the croquet court. Jo, standing on the porch above, smelling the cut grass, saw the yellow envelope held out and received. "Oh, Loring," she said, and his name slipped away into a hollow place in her mind, where she heard it call, her own voice echoing.

"Missing in action since July 8," the telegram said, "when his B-24 failed to return from a daylight bombing mission." You could have been fooled by that telegram. The plane had "not returned." It allowed for a hundred possibilities: the crew had taken off on a jaunt to Paris.

But there was nothing ambiguous about the letter from the ball turret gunner, whose wild scrawl reached them two weeks later from a hospital in England. "Mid-air collision, enroute to our target." He was contacting all the families of the crew, a prearranged plan for any one of them who might "survive," he explained. "We'd been giving them hell all week in Rumania." He had come down in his parachute. He had not seen any other chutes. "Over the Adriatic, west of Trieste," he said, as if giving directions to a search party.

In the atlas at Garfield Public Library the Adriatic was very blue. The Italian peninsula bristled with the names of coastal towns. Up there at the top of the Sea the water looked hardly bigger than a harbor. A string of tiny islands looped west and north of Trieste. One might even swim to shore, or be picked up by a fishing boat, out on a good July morning. So much was possible in a war.

She had come full circle and was standing in front of Harold Hall. Beverly swung out the door, sheet music in her hand. "Oh, Jo!" she said. "Hurry up! You'll be late for choir."

A Social Club Halloween party was scheduled for Monday evening free-time on the thirtieth. At dinner, sheeted figures walked from table to table and invited everyone to the ghost walk in the tunnel.

Karen said she was not going. She had too much to do. Jo was afraid Clyde would be at the party, and since she had a late paper to write for Ethics she decided to stay in the room with Karen.

By 7:30 everyone else on the floor had left. The two of them had worked silently at their desks for almost an hour before the buzzer rang at the end of the hall. Karen went to answer it. In a minute she called back. "For you, Jo. Prince Charming."

Jo met her in the kitchen. "Clyde," she said.

"Yes. He's at the outside door. Someone down there answered when he knocked."

"What did you tell them on the phone?"

"That I'd get you. There's more to the message. He's not going to leave until you go down."

Karen had never asked any questions about Clyde. Now she gazed at Jo directly. "Do you know what he wants?"

"He wants to talk," said Jo. "Something's on his mind."

It sounded mild enough, nothing to get upset about. She could understand that Karen would expect her to go down. They stood looking at each other for a moment, Jo not budging. Karen said, "You don't want to talk."

"No."

"Then why don't you just tell him so?"

"It's not that simple." Jo sighed, hoping her despair was not too obvious. "I suppose I should go."

"Do you want me to say you're not coming?"

"It won't work. He'll bother them on the first floor. It's my responsibility." Still, she stood there with no energy to move.

"Is there something we can tell him that will make him leave? I'll be glad to take the message."

"Would you?"

"Sure. What shall I say? No fibs. I'll tell him you're in general shock. How's that?"

"Wait. Let me think. . . . Tell him I'm in the bathroom. He's funny about bathrooms. Tell him I'm in the tub. Say I'm going to be in the tub all evening. Maybe he'll go."

". . . You're going to be in the tub?"

"I will. I promise, by the time you say that to him, I will be."

"Who am I to argue?" said Karen, and left. When she came back, Jo called to her from the bathroom. She was stretched out in the dry tub, fully clothed, a blanket underneath her and a pillow behind her head. She was reading. The light was excellent.

"Did he go?" she asked Karen. Down there in the big tub her own voice was rich and full. Karen didn't answer. "Any success?" Jo asked again.

Karen still didn't answer. She pointed at Jo mutely. Then she began to laugh, good solid ha-ha's against the tiled walls. She pointed to Jo's feet, still clad in brown oxfords, propped up on the old porcelain faucets, then she pointed to the pillow, then to the book, the bright cubes of sound coming and coming, resoundingly loud, a shouting contralto. Jo stared over the top of her book, entranced. She hadn't meant to be funny, and Karen's laughter seemed immensely generous. When Beverly laughed she charged her own batteries. Karen's ha-ha's were gifts from an unlimited resource, riding on a conveyor belt—"to be shipped to our boys overseas," Jo thought, letting out a queer machine-gun giggle. Now they both laughed. They roared. Karen leaned against the wall, then fell grandly onto the toilet, her head against the marble sink, her glasses in her hand. They stopped finally from exhaustion, gasping and wiping their faces.

"Do you intend to stay here all evening?" asked Karen, hoarsely.

"Yes, I said I would."

"Then why don't you take a bath?"

"Because I have my clothes on," said Jo.

Her voice squeaked uncontrollably, and they were at it again. They deafened themselves. The fat porcelain trio quivered and swayed and the shiny room was alive with dancing lights from their tears. The laugh-room, Jo thought. Excuse me while I go to the laugh-room. Then she knew she had gone over the edge and was going to cry. She struggled against it. What came out was a perfectly awful noise that had nothing to do with her feelings—just a noise issuing from her throat in short bursts. She knew that noise would go on making itself unless she found some way to stop it. She thought of turning on the cold water. Karen, her face serious, said, "Jo . . . ?" Then the buzzer rang again and startled them both. It rang several times while Jo got her breath and Karen watched her.

"That's Clyde," Jo said.

Karen put her glasses back on. "He wants to see you so badly. I never thought a guy could want to see a girl so much."

"It's all right. I'm going to see him." She knew she could. She climbed out of the tub and went for her coat.

Sudden cold air outside the dormitory. Sudden change in acoustics. Jo shivered. Clyde was leaning against the wall by the front door, the collar of his Army coat turned up and his Bible clamped under his arm.

"What do you want?" she asked.

"Not here. Let's find a spot on the campus."

They were silent along the sidewalk. Jo found herself two or three steps ahead of him, and when she slowed to match his pace (she was going to be nice) she could hear him rasping.

The corridor of Van Housen was full of couples and noisy groups. Students were dressed in quickly devised costumes, mostly hobos and witches. Paper-bag masks circulated around them. From below rose screams and intermittent music.

Clyde said, "Let's get out of here." He stopped to glance through the windowed doors into Darby Chapel, where couples were sprinkled throughout the pews. Then he continued on to the post office lobby. It was empty and lighted only at the exits. Still he seemed dissatisfied.

"What more do you want?" asked Jo.

"All right. Here, then." He lowered himself onto the stairs, and Jo sat down too, reluctantly, as far from him as she could get, against the concrete wall. If she needed to run, the hall was just around the corner.

Clyde huddled in his overcoat. "What I'm going to tell you is strictly private, is that agreed?"

"All right."

"I'm only telling you because God has shown me I should."

Jo didn't answer.

"Do you believe in divine healing?"

The skin on her arms stirred. She was surprised. It was a subject he had never mentioned before. "It depends. What do you mean?" she said.

"I mean, heal. Miracle. . . . Well, do you believe in it?"

"Jesus healed . . . and the Apostles. There are cases—"

"I detect an evasion. I am talking about now. This dispensation. Do you believe God heals in response to our faith?"

"Sometimes He does."

"Oh, the trumpet makes an uncertain sound! Is this the Word of God?"

"Yes."

"The whole book, or just the easy parts?"

"I don't know what you mean by the easy parts."

"The parts that require no great faith. Or are you one of those ordinary Christians who limit God's power? Jesus said, 'Him that believeth on me, the works that I do shall he do also.' Do you believe that?"

"I'm not sure I know what He meant."

Clyde snorted. Or perhaps it was just for practical purposes, because he stopped to blow his nose before he went on. "In case you don't remember exactly, it goes like this. John 14:12 and 13. 'And greater works than these shall he do; because I go unto my Father. And whatsoever ye shall ask in my name, that will I do, that the Father may be glorified in the Son.' Listen . . . I want that. Don't you? I want God's power in my life. He's offered His power and I want it, because we are disobeying Him if we don't have it. See?"

"Yes." She did see. As hard as it was to grant him an affirmative answer about anything, what he had just said appealed to her.

"Most of us go no more than halfway in our faith," he added. "You can count on one hand the Christians who have tested God's powers to the full."

She nodded. The statement itself raised questions, but the idea was right.

"Let me tell you something," he went on. "Sickness and ill health are of the devil. That's what the Lord has shown me, to put it succinctly."

A fine spray reached Jo's hand where it rested on her knee. She slid closer to the wall.

"If God does not heal in this day and age, it is because the church is weak and powerless," Clyde continued. "God cannot work in an atmosphere of faithlessness. This is no child's play. Satan is a prince of the power of the air, and the air is full of millions of microbes."

"I'm aware of that," murmured Jo.

"Those microbes," said Clyde, "are the principalities and powers spoken of in Ephesians six, verse twelve."

"Oh! . . . Nonsense!" He was taking it too far, down a side road of his own. She shook her head firmly, sorry for the ground she had given him.

He raised his voice in defense. "Martin Luther himself said it! Satan produces all the maladies that afflict mankind, for he is the prince of death. What's more, Satan rules the old nature—the mortal, dying nature in our bodies. And it's the old nature that harbors hereditary diseases, as in my case. I do not believe it is God's will for Christians to be sick, except as He uses sickness to teach us lessons."

He was holding his Bible against his chest and rocking as he went on. "Since I first fell ill two years ago, I've been asking God to show me why. Why did He order my discharge from the Army when manpower is so badly needed in this war? He's answered me. That's what I have to tell you."

"All right," said Jo guardedly. It was the microbes she was still thinking about, filling the air around them.

Clyde went on, rocking, almost reciting his story. "One day, just a while ago, I was praying for our forces in Germany, and my eye fell upon a verse in Jeremiah—'Order you the shield and buckler and draw near to battle.' But what battle? I asked myself, What did that mean? And then I remembered that in Ephesians we are told to take the shield of faith. Do you follow me? . . . I said, Do you follow me?"

"Yes."

"Do you know that place in Ephesians?—'Put on the whole armor of God'?"

"Of course I do."

"I knew exactly where my faith was weakest. I made a decision, a test. I put out a fleece. I would take myself off insulin for twenty-four hours, and if God wrought immediate victory in Europe, then I'd know *that's* what He wanted of me."

"Wanted of you?"

"The insulin. Giving up the insulin."

"Giving it up?"

"Yes."

"Stop using it?"

"Right."

"But don't you need it to—"

"To live? That's what they say. Sure, that's what they say."

"This doesn't sound right to me."

"No? Listen to what happened. I prayed all afternoon . . . all night. I was *over* there, in Germany, I know I was. I can't explain that experience. I was on the battlefield, fighting with my own company. Warfare through prayer. See? There's more than one way to fight a war! And the next day the news! Arcan had fallen. I gave you the newspaper that day. Remember? . . . Are you listening?"

"I remember."

He seemed to be finished, but Jo wasn't sure. She had not followed him completely and had no desire to ask him to repeat it. He was silent, hunched over his Bible. Noises of the party reached them faintly. Two ghosts poked their heads around the corner, waved, and disappeared.

Clyde took a ragged breath and went on. His voice was hoarse and weak. "And now I'm back where I was. The war is bogged down, and so am I. What God is asking me to do is very hard. It's very hard." He stopped again and put his head in his hands, muffling his words. "The next step—I mean, to ending the war."

Had she heard him right? "I'm sorry. I don't understand."

He shook his head. She could hardly hear him. "He's promised me strength, but it's a big thing. General MacArthur says only those are fit to live who do not fear to die." His voice gave out. He cleared his throat, then again, like a cold motor, while Jo began to comprehend.

He raised his head and looked at her. "I know He wants me to give it up altogether," he whispered.

"Oh . . . Oh, no. I don't think so," answered Jo, whispering back, hardly knowing what she said.

"Yes. That's what He's waiting to see—if I have the faith to trust Him to heal me."

"Are you sure that's—?"

"And if I do, you understand what it means, don't you?"

"I'm not sure. I . . . I can't hear you."

"The war hangs on it."

"The what?"

His voice broke through. "The war, the war! The outcome—of the whole war!"

"The *whole war*?" She was on her feet, almost shouting at him. "That can't be!"

He stood up and shouted back. "Of course it can! That's the *whole point*!"

"The whole war hangs on *you*?"

"Yes! If I—"

"The faith of *one person*?"

"That's the secret! It's the thing we're slow to get. That He works that way! He definitely does!"

Jo shook her head. She wanted to run.

"I suppose you think I've imagined all this," Clyde said. He sat down.

"I have a paper to do."

"A paper! Kindergarten stuff. Please sit down. I haven't come to your part yet."

"*My* part? Wait a minute!"

"Please sit." He changed his tone. "Please," he said hoarsely. "Won't you sit down? I wish you would."

Jo slid down onto the cold step again, shutting her eyes.

"God doesn't work through armies," Clyde said. "Not really. 'Not by might, but by my spirit, saith the Lord.' Through the faith of one small Christian—that's what moves mountains. I asked the Lord, why me? Why all alone? That was when He showed me how you fit into it all. He gave me another verse, almost a voice speaking, it was so plain. The verse was—"

He stopped and drew in his breath sharply. His hand flew up to his face. Oh, what now? Was he having an attack of some kind? Jo pulled back, her muscles tensed. And then he sneezed, two huge blasts in the echoey stairwell. She turned her head to the wall, but Clyde went right on talking as if nothing had happened.

"—in Matthew. 'If two shall agree on earth as *touching* anything that they shall ask, it shall be done for them.' I knew at last why He had brought you into my life. I want to tell you frankly, I didn't like it. I said, Why her, Lord? Is *her* heart right? Who is she to assume this responsibility? And He answered me again. 'Not many mighty, not many noble are called.' It's the weak of this world He chooses as His most effective workers. I'm no hotshot, and neither are you. Whether we like it or not, He has given us to each other for this purpose, to be partners in faith."

"Oh, no. No, I . . . no." She faltered. Though a hundred negatives cried out inside her, she could see a possible logic to what he was saying.

"Wait, before you answer. I have something to show you." He reached into his coat and pulled out a wrinkled paper bag. Out of that he took what appeared to be a wad of toilet paper. He was unwrapping something.

Jo said, "I don't want to—I don't like—."

"Syringe," he said. "Insulin. I'm going to throw this away, as a symbol, and I want you to do it with me. Agree as touching. Out in the street, down the storm sewer. Of course, I can buy others, but I won't. We'll act on His promise and *agree* it's accomplished."

"You should talk to someone. You shouldn't do this!"

"No one must know. Are you going to tell on me and spoil it? When I'm healed, then *I'll* tell." He gestured with the tissue full of glass things. "I want God's best! Don't you? I'm going to take Him at His word. He wants us to attempt the impossible. I don't want to be sick all my life!"

He raised his arms as if to grab her, and Jo, already flat against the wall, tensed to fight him off. But the move he had made was only a gesture of entreaty. She caught his misery then and absorbed it. Who was she, unsick, to hinder another's healing? In the dim light he was like a bad snapshot. She sharpened the lines and put a clear, composed light in his eyes. If healing would bring that, cut back through all the circumstances over the years and generations that had produced him as he was, she would like to be part of that. If that kind of healing was God's will, how could she stand in the way? How unthinkable to be the one who thwarted His purposes. It could be a noble, rich adventure, far-reaching, many lives touched. She wavered, yes on her lips. The wad of toilet paper was under her nose.

"This is a man-made device," Clyde said. "A compromise with the powers of evil. We cannot keep capitulating!"

The sharp new lines dissolved, and he was himself again. The vision had been hers, not his, *her* standards in operation. The idea that he might really change, or even *want* to, or *ought* to, was presumptuous and mad. They were both after the wrong thing.

"I can't do it," Jo answered.

She stood and started down the stairs and almost fell. For a second she thought he had done something to her. A thousand arrows shot into her right foot. Her leg had gone to sleep. The arrows became lead, and her foot was heavy and painful as she moved toward the hall.

"Wait a minute!" Clyde called after her.

"No."

"Is that your answer?"

"Yes."

"Pray about it, at least!"

"No."

"Ah! There! I was right about you all along."

Her sense of escape carried her through the night, overriding all other confusion. She slept exhaustedly, free of him at last. In the morning she saw her obligation clearly. Tell someone. Tell the Dean of Men or the head nurse. She planned to do it right after breakfast.

It wasn't necessary. As she left the dining room a boy handed her a square of paper. "From MacQuade," he said.

You don't have to worry. I am layed up in the infirmary with the grip. What's more, I took my shot this morning and expect I will continue. You should be glad to hear that I have joined the ranks of the Unfaithful, that great company of failures for Christ.

Kindly destroy this note.

She sent him a get-well card.

🙰 TWO

---

*A garden enclosed is my
sister, my spouse; a
spring shut up, a
fountain sealed.*

Song of Solomon 4:12

TWO

In November things changed for Jo, totally and all at once. It might be that her life, released from Roger and Clyde, went into another gear, as if to make up for lost time.

Here is what happened. Early in the month a hundred missionaries moved into the school for World Evangelization Week. Classes were cancelled. Days were packed with slides and films and world geography. Certain urgent phrases charged the air: unevangelized tribes, unreached millions, postwar challenge. It was an intense seven days, with morning lectures, private conferences all afternoon and special presentations in the evenings.

A number of students acknowledged calls to the foreign field. Soup committed her life to Mexico. She was ecstatic and talked of nothing else. She made plans to add missionary subjects to her schedule. "Listen to this," she said, deep in the school catalogue. "Linguistics, Tropical Diseases, Pagan Religions, Obstetrics—I'll never make it. And Minor Surgery? Please! Setting bones, removing bullets! Lord, my heart fainteth!"

Jo liked the missionaries. Their lives consisted of extremities which they accepted as a matter of course. They delivered babies, repaired trucks, shored up washed-out roads, navigated swollen rivers, learned unwritten languages, translated Scripture, rescued abandoned children, all in the process of presenting the Gospel. Some of them had been very ill with malaria and dysentery. They came untanned from tropical countries and spoke of their trials offhandedly.

At the end of the week a particular woman spoke, a linguist who had been working under Wycliffe Translators in some part of Latin America. Afterwards, Jo could not remember the country or what the woman looked like or what she said. What impressed her was the abandoned love and enthusiasm the woman expressed for the Indians among whom she had lived and worked. Yet it was not her work she talked about, but those people, *her friends*. She could hardly wait to go back to them, she said.

As Jo listened to this animated woman, the mission field appeared to her in an entirely new light—not as a sacrifice but as an honor. At the end of that evening she stood with other students to repledge her willingness to go anywhere in the world, in any capacity. The text of the meeting was "Behold, I set before you an open door, and no man can shut it."

At last she had a "definite call," and it was apparently the answer to everything. Because what followed next was startling. An odd hunger woke her early each morning, and kept her awake for a long period of private devotions before breakfast. She thought if she could swallow the Bible whole it would not be enough. Standing in lines at meals and at other small breaks throughout the day, she began to memorize it, starting with the Gospel of John. She meant to memorize the entire New Testament, book by book, if it took all her life.

Her idea of prayer began to change as well. It was like breathing, she found, a running, unbroken contact with Christ. She felt very close to Him and was careful to let nothing cause a barrier. She read a pamphlet about Brother Lawrence and practicing the presence of Christ. "Jesus Only" she tacked on her door. "The living realization of Christ," she wrote in a new notebook. She had begun a spiritual journal, writing out her thoughts each day. Certain phrases intrigued her. She wrote them down and tried to unlock them—things like "Dwell deep in Christ," and "Filled with all the fulness of God."

She talked about God more freely now and said the words "the Lord" without effort. To her surprise, she found it was not hard at all to pray out loud in prayer bands and fellowships. She did it frequently, in fact, sometimes at length.

Her sensitivity changed. Social Club parties, chatter in the dorm, even studying for her courses began to seem like a waste of time. She had reading she wanted to do instead: *The Christian's Secret of a Happy Life* by Hannah Whitall Smith and *Born Crucified* by L.E. Maxwell. To be sure, she was still stuck in Leviticus, but she had discovered the Song of Solomon and read that over and over.

She did study. She worked hard. She practiced the piano, if not with more ease, with more diligence. Matters like laundry were still a nuisance, but it didn't matter. Clothes were not important. Even eating became just a necessary function. She hardly tasted her food. She was still tired a lot, but that was nothing she noticed much. Many things were of no consequence. The Zipper images disappeared. She slept better at night, and seemed to stop dreaming, or at least had no memory of dreams in the morning. She felt like a house swept clean. Roger was laughable. Clyde, when he emerged from the infirmary, hardly looked her way, and she said, "Oh, hi, Clyde," off-handedly, whenever he did.

People noticed the change in her. Ruth said, "Jo, you've grown so much spiritually. It's a blessing to see it." It bothered Jo a little to win Ruth's approval, but what people thought was not serious anyway. In fact, she had begun to detect in others the shallowness and self-concern that she had just left behind. The girls on the floor annoyed her often. Qualities she had noticed in them earlier now seemed to predominate: Beverly was silly, Karen aloof, Soup coarse. She felt advanced and special. Then that shocked her, that it could be so easy to become judgmental, and that pride could be the by-product of an experience so good. One had to be on guard all the time. She prayed for humility.

One thing she knew with certainty: She never, never wanted to come down off this mountaintop, back to the valley of her old defeated life. This plane of living, she was sure, was what God intended for His people, and she meant to stay there on it, at the top, whatever the cost.

❧ THREE

---

*Awake, O north wind; and
come, thou south; blow upon
my garden, that the spices
thereof may flow out.*

Song of Solomon 4:16

Early in the evening of the Saturday before Thanksgiving Jo stood with eleven other students at the school corner on Chicago Avenue. They were waiting for a streetcar west to Halsted, where they would change and go south to West Madison, then walk to Des Plaines Street and the Anchor of Hope Mission.

The car was late. "It's a sign of the end times," joked one of the boys. "In the last days there shall be lousy trolley service."

They were all in a good mood, in spite of the cold wind and the fine mist that penetrated their coats like rain. The long veils on the girls' hats fluttered to the westward, and they held their hands over their ears and shifted from foot to foot in their high heels. George Winthrop, their group leader, wore red ear muffs. Jo's throat was scratchy, and she wished she had put on a warm scarf. Yet it was funny the way the wind kept after them, like a mean tease. It mussed their hair and sneaked up under their coats.

"Oops!" the girls cried, holding down their skirts.

"Oopsadaisy!" cried a boy in falsetto. "Stop that, you wicked wind!"

He got a laugh, so the other boys had to try it. They struck girlish poses and held their knees together. In a minute they were singing:

Aroodle-de-toot! Aroodle-de-toot!
We are the girls from the Institute!
Oh, we don't smoke or drink or chew,
And we don't go with boys who do.

Then the trolley came, ta-clank, ta-clank, along the avenue. Its wires sang and sparked in the wet air. It looked wonderful with the warm lights in the windows.

There were no empty seats, as was usual on this trip, and Jo stood in the aisle. Smells and sounds slid around her, damp clothing, cigar smoke, voices that pressed hard over the scrape of the rails. Curses leaped from the jumbled conversation: Holy Jesus! Christ Almighty!

Jo didn't mind the cursing. Maybe it was better for His name to be used that way than not at all. But sometimes, closed in by people she would never see again in her life, she felt harassed by the idea of numbers, all the countless nobodies who to themselves were the focal point of the whole world, hugging their meager seventy years and going from one unlasting moment to the next. Who was going to tell them there was so much more? The urgency of this enveloped her. Once recently, when the aisle was less crowded, she had walked the length of it passing out tracts. But always she left the trolley wondering if she had missed an opportunity to witness.

A Calvary girl just ahead of her was talking to her seatmate, a young woman. An earnest exchange was going on over an open New Testament. Jo wondered how it had begun. That was the most difficult part. First, to be sure you were led to speak and not blundering along on your own, and second, to know how to start in a way that was not an abrupt intrusion into the innermost being of someone you had not so much as seen before. "Do you know Christ as your Savior?" seemed rude and shocking, even when asked with courtesy. Some kids did it successfully. They went to U.S.O.'s or the Illinois Central Station for just that purpose, and came back with reports about people they had been led to speak to. Jo had never approached a stranger herself, held back always by the harm it might do, offending someone.

If only the truth could be emanated, she thought. If it could simply drift from you whole, with all its meaning clear, and place itself in someone else's brain.

The car stopped, and several people got off. Jo turned to look for an empty seat, saw one right behind her, and dropped into it, in that second catching a glimpse of a Negro woman next to the window. The impression was overpowering, and Jo fought a desire to turn and look again. Full rolling breasts and expansive arms under a coat trimmed with white fur.

A tall hat of white rabbit bound in swirls of sparkling blue net. The rest was a confusion of parts, black satin somewhere, leather, gold, silver—purple lipstick, purple nails. Something dangled, looped, caught the light, and flashed. When the woman moved to make room for Jo on the seat, all sorts of things jingled and rang. She would burst into music maybe—spontaneous combustion. Even her gum seemed alive, snapping between her teeth and giving off a fruity smell.

Jo fastened her eyes on the back of the seat ahead of her, then she yielded and glanced sideways at the dark window. What she saw was her own reflection, looking like the ghost of a mouse. Their eyes met in the glass, hers and the woman's, and the woman smiled and spoke. "How come you got that Bible wi' you on a Sa'dy night?" she asked.

Jo turned to face her, forming an answer. The chewing gum was green. "Where's the meetin'?" the woman asked. Her consonants were so soft it was hard to understand her.

"At a rescue mission on Skid Row," Jo said. It was happening. She was going to witness to this woman. Careful, careful, she thought. Let the other person lead. No, let the *Holy Spirit* lead. She had learned that much in Personal Evangelism, but she was not sure she would recognize either leading.

"You the preacher?" asked the woman.

"Oh, not me. One of the boys. I'll sing in a trio and give my testimony."

"Sure. Testify."

"You know what that means?"

"Oh, Lord, I guess!" She laughed and leaned toward Jo confidentially. Her coat fell away, baring two mounds at the edge of her neckline. Without lowering her eyes, Jo could see a shiny pendant resting on one of the round surfaces.

"You mean . . . you've heard the Gospel?" Jo asked. She had started to say, "Are you a Christian?" but remembered it was a wasteful question. Unless people were Jewish, they were apt to say yes.

"Have I heard the Gospel!" the woman answered. She laughed again, as if they were old friends sharing a joke. Was it a joke? Was she sarcastic? "Sweet God, yes!"

"You mean, you know the Lord?" Jo asked, still uncertain.

"Know Him! Yes! Praise Jesus, I sure do know Him!" Her voice was quite loud and people were turning to look at them.

"You mean . . . Christ is your Savior?"

The woman grabbed Jo's hand and squeezed it. "Oh yes! Hallelujah, He's my Savior! He died for my sins, praise His name."

She knew the right things to say, all right. But something was amiss. Jo wondered what question she could ask without showing her doubt. Are you a new creature in Christ? Old things passed away? Then how come . . . ? She would never dream of asking it: How come you flaunt your body in this incredible manner? It sounded like something Clyde would say.

The car was stopping, and Jo could see it was the corner of Halsted. The other students were moving to the front. Yet surely she must not leave this conversation so unfinished. She turned to speak again. The woman looked as if she might embrace her. "What about you, girl? Are you born again?"

Jo said, "Of course," but in the surprise her answer sounded lame.

"*Are* you? Transformed by His grace? Flooded through and through with His love?" The woman's voice was louder than ever, a shout, and people all around were staring at them and listening.

"Yes . . . I am," said Jo, wishing she could be more convincing. Some of the students had already gotten off. She had to end this quickly and in the right way.

"Aren't you glad? Isn't He wonderful?" asked the woman.

"Yes, He is," Jo said. She had to hurry. She reached into her purse and handed the woman a Gospel of John, new and red. "I'd like to give you this if you don't mind," she said.

"Why, thank you, honey. Now you wait. Hold on." The enormous pocketbook unsnapped, and the woman's hand plunged all the way to the bottom. Her bracelets slid and clanked, and the sparkler fell off the mound. Things in her purse began to erupt at the surface, wallet, compact, mirror, hand lotion, cologne, hair brush, candy bar. Jo moved into the aisle, apologetically. Up came the hand, holding out a stick of green gum.

"Why, thank you," said Jo, and laughed. As she turned to go, she waved, and the woman grabbed her hand again.

"Listen, little girl. God loves you, no matter what. There is no bottom to His love, no top and no sides. Don't you ever forget that."

"I won't."

"Our Father is going to give you a blessing tonight. See if He don't."

The car started up again. Jo fell forward. "Off! Off, please!" she called, but the driver didn't hear. He kept on going, across Halsted and on along Chicago Avenue, with Jo nudging her way down the aisle. When she reached the front, and the car stopped at last, they were five blocks from Halsted. She climbed off and began to run.

In the middle of the very first crossing she stumbled and turned her left ankle in a streak of pain. She hobbled to the sidewalk and removed the shoe. The heel was half off. She stood there a minute, her stockinged toes on the cold pavement, trying to shove the heel back onto its nails. It wouldn't go. Her foot was hurting badly. She settled her toes carefully into the cockeyed shoe, but it no longer fit. Both the shoe and the foot had changed. The shoe turned in. The foot wanted to turn out. It was a foolish shoe to wear tonight anyway, a sling-heeled pump with a bow on the toe.

Now there was no hope of hurrying at all. She had no money for a taxi, and none was in sight anyway. She could catch a streetcar back to Halsted, but that meant crossing Chicago Avenue. There was a great deal of traffic, and she was afraid to try it at a cripple's pace. Nothing to do but keep going as well as she could. Surely the group would wait there at the transfer corner long enough for her to appear.

She ventured along slowly with a minimum of weight on the burning arch and ankle. No self-pity, she told herself. It was slow going. The wind came full against her in strong, resistant gusts, carving her face with cold—cheekbones, chin. After many minutes she could see the bridge at the corner of Halsted where steam from the trains in the railroad yard below split in half and rose in white puffs on either side. No one was there.

She crossed and stood wondering what to do next. She ought not to walk down West Madison with all those drunks. She ought to get a car east back to the school and phone the mission. Someone could take her place in the trio.

But there was no reason to give up so easily. What would she be proving about herself if she retreated in the face of a little wind and inconvenience? More than likely someone would be waiting for her at the West Madison stop. If this was a test of her fortitude, she meant to pass it.

So she waited and waited, moving stiffly back and forth through the puffs of useless steam. She reconsidered the decision and imagined herself alone on Madison Street, limping past the drunks and the rows of saloons and flophouses with the preposterous names—House of Rothschild, Workingmen's Palace, Starr Hotel. Calvary girls were never encouraged to be out by themselves in any part of the city. Folly could wear the mask of courage.

Yet here she was, a candidate for the mission field. If she questioned God's protection now, even this much, what about the future, when danger might be a daily threat? This was nothing compared to that. She would go to West Madison and do her job.

Then it came at last, as of course it had to, a trolley with "Halsted" on it. The door slipped open, and a pocket of warm air wafted from the interior. It sucked her in. She fell with relief onto an empty seat.

There was nothing to fear anyway. The men who stumbled along West Madison and Des Plaines were half blind, bent inward on their own insatiable needs. They would not even see her, helpless themselves, even the younger ones looking so old. There was a fragility about them, as if they were held together loosely by something other than muscle and skin—the grime in their clothes or the drink in their veins. Just possibly it was the safest section of the city. In a matter of minutes, however long it took to hobble those three or four blocks, she would appear undaunted at the mission door, and the bright good light would flood across her. They would have started the service, the students on the platform singing and one of them leading, waving his hands vigorously, urging the men to participate. "Jo! Thank goodness!" the girls would whisper, passing it on: "She's here. She made it!"

Jo slipped off her shoes and held first one foot and then the other between her hands. The swollen ankle throbbed and was tender to touch. She wondered if she could stand on it again. And where was she now, anyway? The area was unfamiliar. An old woman with a kerchief tied under her chin sat across from her. "Excuse me, have we come to Madison yet?" Jo asked.

"Madithon?" shouted the lady. Her upper teeth were gone. Her pink tongue shot in and out of the gap. "Oh, we patht Madithon way back there!"

On with the shoe, the foot howling resistance, her heart pounding in self-reproach. She stood by the driver, asking him to let her off at the next stop.

"Are you lotht?" called the old lady. Jo shook her head no, and climbed down the high steps into the cold air and over the tracks to wait for a trolley in the other direction. It was a slovenly neighborhood, surprisingly deserted. Traffic was much thinner here. Across the way several small stores were closed for the night. She took flimsy comfort in the sight of framed pictures in a photographer's window. The store next to it was unoccupied. A blue-starred servicemen's flag hung alone in the display window.

She wished it were not so dark. The streetlight nearest her was out. Some broken part of it rattled in the wind. Other than one dog, there was no sign of life. On a Saturday night in Chicago, where was everybody?

A car braked at the corner like a sharply drawn breath, then swerved down Halsted and slowed beside her. She stepped backward. For a second she thought the car was empty, driving itself, then as it pulled away dark shapes loomed against the windows. She moved from the edge of the sidewalk back under the overhang of the pharmacy behind her.

In the process she missed a taxi. Its yellow bottom had flipped around the corner before she realized she could have hailed it and asked the driver to wait outside the mission while she went in for the fare. She was not using her brain. There were alternatives to consider. One: Walk back to Madison. Keep moving. But it might be several blocks, and the pain in her foot was getting worse. Two: Find a telephone. She had enough money for that. There was a light in the back of the pharmacy. She tried the door and knocked, peering in. A life-sized girl on a Squibb's vitamin display smiled at her from the locked warmth. She returned to the sidewalk and leaned against the window again. ALL MOST EVERYTHING 1/3 OFF read a sign inside the glass. Under that the lower half of a manikin stood, wearing a truss. She could see crutches in there too, like a bad joke. The doorway was better. She went back and huddled under the overhang, her collar up and her hands in her sleeves like a Chinaman. Oh Lord, send humans, she prayed.

Instantly, voices and hard-heeled shoes approached from the side street. Two soldiers paused at the corner, laughing, their uniforms a beautiful sight. Jo opened her mouth to call them and saw, just in time, how very drunk they were, drinking yet, sharing a bottle. In a moment they crossed Halsted and disappeared around a building.

No more taxis. No trolley spitting arcs of light far down the street. Shouts echoed from a distance, blocks away, and then a siren, so far off it sounded like a mosquito. She studied the second-floor windows for slivers of light she might have missed around blackout shades. No living occupants.

The greatest joy in the world now would be to take off her feet and put them in her pockets. She was vaguely ashamed of being victimized by the cold, as if it were a weakness. She had read somewhere that hell would be isolation in misery. She was doing a paper on hell for Ethics class—hell as part of the problem of evil, that is. It was her own idea for a topic. In her mind now she wrote: It is the end of hope that is inconceivable. To spend eternity in a night that went on and on, streetcars never coming, with those terrible stores around her, the wind never abating . . . .

This frame of mind was not helping. She could do better if she tried. She turned her thoughts to warmth and comfort. They homed in on the kitchen stove, oven door open. When she was small enough she sometimes had a bath there in a galvanized tub set on newspapers, towel and pajamas hung over the door. Everybody helped, pouring in water, heating more. Even Loring, who was too big (or thought he was) for the tub, made suds, heaping them up around her. It was her job, her part in the family, to take this bath and be fussed over, with her hair in a peak of suds and Daddy holding the mirror so she could see. Then she would be wrapped tight in a towel until the buttons on her pajamas had cooled so they wouldn't burn her, while Daddy held her and sang old songs: "There's a long, long trail a-winding, into the land of my dreams."

Her purse and Bible were wet and slippery. The mist had changed to icy rain at some undetected point, and the sidewalk had darkened with it. She was shivering very hard. So all right, Jo, let's have another toasty memory, what do you say?

When Loring was eleven he fell through the ice on the frog pond. (This is toasty?) The water was shallow, so there was no danger of drowning, but he was wet through and ran home in his heavy, freezing clothes. He was not even able to cry, he was so cold. Even his eyelashes were coated with ice. Daddy was at work. Mother threw herself into a whirl of efficiency. She stripped him, sent Jo for blankets, ripped towels off the line over the stove, rubbed his hands, put his feet in a basin of cool water. You would think she was almost glad he had fallen in, to give her a chance to come to his rescue. That afternoon the three of them celebrated. They baked an Indian pudding and sat down to eat it hot from the oven.

All she ever wanted was to have her own family, Mother told them one night when Daddy was late. (He was often late, but still she worried.) She would do anything to keep them together, no matter what happened. Her own history would never be repeated. Maybe that was why she wrapped them so. When they got older they were always pushing away the scarves she wanted to wrap around them. At night she tucked them into bed so tight they felt like mummies. Was that to keep them from flying off into the night?

Maybe something like that haunted her, because when the wind blew around the house, sucking at the walls with strange whines, Mother couldn't sleep. She sat in the kitchen doing a crossword puzzle by a kerosene lamp. If you got up to go to the bathroom on a windy night, you could count on Mother's being awake. She hated the wind because on the night of her own father's death the wind had howled around the neighbor's house where she had been sent to stay. She was four years old, and it was her only memory of her early years, a wound sandwiched between years of emptiness.

"Wind is nothing but moving air," Loring said during the hurricane. His voice was very calm, though he had to raise it above the roar. "It's caused by an uneven heating of the atmosphere." Daddy was not at home again, but Loring was sixteen and a long way from cry-baby days. He showed them how the dish towels always moved a bit on the line over the kitchen stove. The fire had been turned off for safety, but you could still see it. "When the hot air rises, cooler air comes in to fill the vacuum." Wind speeds could be measured. A gale was ten or eleven on the Beaufort wind scale and this storm was probably a hard gale, not a hurricane. Hurricanes usually blew off to the east before they got this far north. Still, the wind was warm, which meant it had come from the tropics. He began talking about the equator and polar easterlies, and Jo couldn't understand him any more, but it was a comfort to hear him going on about it as the cedars outside bent almost parallel to the ground, and the damp warm air, full of the dangerous smell of splintering trees, filled the house.

When the Congoleum lifted three inches off the floor and billowed there, whistling and undulating, Loring said, "That's good. The wind is moving *through* the house, in and out the cracks. We won't blow over." The house sat on a rock ledge, and it did not budge an inch. She had not really been afraid it would. That was not the sort of thing she was afraid of. She'd always wondered if Loring understood that. "You can't be afraid of nothing," he'd told her. She was not afraid of drunks on West Madison. She was not afraid of wind, or of being here alone.

Then why did she feel so forsaken and unsafe? She ought not to. She ought to trust. It was her own fault. . . . But she was not *afraid*. She was only remembering. The old enemy could not come back, she was sure of it. If the wind would stop for just a minute, she could adjust her thoughts. If it would stop cutting through her this way. Her brain was not working right. She had heard of people going crazy with the cold.

Someone coughed, not far from her, a terrible sound, raising awful things. Car lights picked up a figure on her side of the street, shuffling slowly, bent over with the cough. He paused to spit, then moved on again, coming her way, barely mobile. Twice more he stopped to hack and spit, almost collapsing with the convulsion. Now he was beside her, not three feet away. He had something tied around his head. A woman's stocking, under his jaws and up around his ears, as if he had the mumps. He wore no coat. He held the lapels of a suit jacket closed with one hand. Shuffle, shuffle, almost a crawl. There were rubbers on his feet, tied on with a string. No shoes, no socks. Jo could not believe this. He walked as if his feet were stumps. And then he vomited. It gushed, bloody, projecting from him. It splashed on her legs. She almost cried out. He stared at what he had done, then wiped his mouth with the back of his hand and shuffled on. She watched him go, his despair like a ball of ice in her stomach.

It was not him she feared. Not anything she could see. It had no name. She refused to give it one, because that was what it wanted. It would take any identity you gave it—an ear, a face at the window. It rode like a smell on the wind and rattled in the dead streetlight. Keep your head, she whispered. Don't call it anything, because it is nothing. It has no power. Oh Lord, keep me sane. I reject it in Your name. She pushed fragments of Scripture to the surface, hunting for the right one. Who shall separate us from the love of Christ? Shall tribulation, or distress, or—what came next?—peril, or . . . Her brain was paralyzed. For I am persuaded that neither life nor death, or was it death nor life, nor angels nor—principalities was in there somewhere—nor nakedness nor sword?

It must not come back. . . . But it was on the way. It had only been biding its time, waiting for a moment when she was too cold to think straight, her faith sputtering. No, it was *nothing*. Why couldn't she get that into her head? It was only the wind. Prince of the air. Dark prince. He spoke in the trolley wires. Down the street his chariot sang, arcing blue lightning, flicker, flicker, as at the edges of a storm. She must not get on. But it was already here. She limped to the edge of the curbing. What choice did she have? It knew how to do this, how to trick her. She would get on his trolley. She had to. But she would resist him yet.

"Let me off at Madison," she said to the driver. She spoke to his back as she dropped into the seat behind him. He nodded. Or did he? "Let me off at Madison, please," she said again, louder. No nod. How could he be so rude? Who do you think you are? she wanted to demand. Who are you, making people wait and not even apologizing? Answer me! She wanted to pound him on the back with her Bible.

He did not let her off. He simply did not. Nor did she recognize the street as they went by. In an unaccountably short time they were at the corner of Chicago Avenue. The sight of the bridge over the railroad yard filled her with despair.

"I told you Madison! Madison!" she cried to the driver as the car stopped. "What do you think this is?"

"Girlie, I never heard you," he snarled. She limped off the car and it rode away, yellow-windowed, and there she was doing what she could not do, standing again in the relentless cold. She was not alone this time. A scattering of men and women were watching her cry, a girl with a Bible under her arm who had just lost her temper at a streetcar conductor. She strained against tears, needing to blow her nose and having only a wadded Kleenex, good for nothing but a wipe. Her hat was crooked. She could feel it slipping to the back of her head, her hair in a tangle.

At some time beyond her reckoning she was on another trolley going east toward Calvary, barely conscious of getting on, feeling like a ball caught up in a game that streetcars play, scooped up and dropped or kept waiting at their will.

"That was some night," said Karen. She was standing by the bed with a cup of coffee from the dining room. The saucer was on top, to keep the coffee warm.

"What night?" asked Jo.

"Seven times I put the light on because you were shouting."

"I don't remember a thing," said Jo. It was difficult to speak. Her mouth seemed to have changed shape.

"But your eyes were open. I said, 'How are you?' and you said, 'My throat is an open sepulchre, Romans 3:13.' "

"I did?" Jo laughed, and reached quickly for her throat. It hurt. Her head weighed a ton as she sat up to receive the coffee. Something was wrapped tight around her foot. Someone had put an Ace bandage on it—when? "What day is this?" she asked Karen.

"Monday."

"Have I been sleeping all this time?"

"Oh no. We talked when I came in last night. You told me about getting lost. Don't you remember?"

"No." What *did* she remember? Soup, the only one home, wide-eyed in her doorway as Jo dragged by, putting her to bed, getting her a hot water bottle, elevating her foot, calling the mission. After that, nothing.

Karen touched her forehead with an icy finger. "You're feverish," she said.

"I guess I am," Jo admitted. Something else was wrong too. She did not like at all the way she felt.

"You ought to see the doctor," said Karen. "He's here this morning. There's an outbreak of grippe. Lots of empty places at breakfast. Can you walk?"

"Of course."

Refusing Karen's assistance, Jo got herself to the campus. A dozen students sat in the waiting room of the infirmary with thermometers in their mouths. Jo's temperature was 102°. The doctor was gruff. Students were careless. They sat in drafts and got their feet wet. He swabbed her throat and sent her back to bed again, assuring her there was no real harm to the foot. The swelling had gone down. A nurse handed her a can of grapefruit juice and some aspirin. The infirmary beds were all full, she explained, but student nurses were working the dormitories. Someone would keep an eye on her, and her meals would be sent on a tray.

So back in her room, Jo slept again, in and out of consciousness. Lighted trolleys zigzagged in her mind. Dreams mixed with the sounds around her. She thought she heard the broken streetlight rattling on Halsted Street, then realized she was at the old quarry back home, running between the coils of rusty cable and abandoned machinery. Parapets stood against a darkening sky. The noise was the tin roofs of the deserted sheds whacking in the wind. "Go back, go back!" she called to herself, and turned and hurried the other way, down the road to Calvary, where someone was washing out a metal wastebasket at the sinks.

Voices drifted in from the kitchen. Louise said, "My mother saw Alice Faye on the street once. She's ugly." And Ruth said, "Honestly that was such a blessing. He opened up the whole book of Philippians." The warbler in the room below did a bobolink and a robin. "We're praying for you, Jo," said Ruby. "Don't drop it," said Daddy. "That's my big girl." Jo had the windmill on her head, charging the radio batteries. The room was unbearably hot. Karen opened the window, and a child's voice below yelled "Sold American!"

"Are you all right, Jo?"

"Oh, sure, fine." Had she ever felt so vile? Even her eyeballs ached. And that other awareness, the sense of distance, as if she'd lost contact with a friend. She had to explore that soon.

"Do you want something to eat?"

"No, I'll just snooze."

A paper bag rattled explosively. "Hi, there. My name is Florence Nightingale."

"Hi, Soup." Jo opened one eye and shut it again. Soup had a new pimple on her chin, coated with iodine. There were more bobby pins than usual in her hair. When her hair got dirty she sprayed it with Brilliantine and added more bobby pins.

"Oh dear, your eye has pierced my disguise. I should have known you'd be too clever for me." She laid a cold orange against Jo's cheek. She had brought a big bag of them.

"That's really nice of you," said Jo.

Soup bent closer. "I can't hear you, my dear, you mumble so."

"Thank you."

"Thangoo, she says. Gracias, señorita." Since her call to Mexico, Soup kept saying things like "uno momento" and "adios, amigo." She dropped to her knees by the bed. "Oh Lord," she quavered, "raise up this Thy humble servant or send someone else to take her place."

"Thangoo."

"Not at all. Good-bye. I must trip the light bombastic."

The nurse was a senior, a Mennonite named Gertraud Schoen-some-thing. Her nurse's cap replaced the little black one she usually wore on her hair. "You're the only one sick on this floor, Jo," she said. "How did you manage that?"

"Oh, it's nothing," said Jo. She smiled at Gertraud, who had a red nose and a space between her front teeth. Jo liked her big blurry face. "I'm getting up soon," she told her.

Karen peeled an orange with her fingernail while the radiator sang. "And all the forms of love He wears . . . ." It sang and sang. It had a fine voice.

Now three of them on a bike, Karen, Jo, and Jewel. They ride into the living room. Grampa is there, smelling righteously of Lifebuoy, and Ruby, with her skirt up shamelessly, mending a stocking on her leg, her hand spread inside it.

"What have you made of your life, after all?" Grampa asks. Daddy is borrowing money again. Oh, she wishes he wouldn't.

"My children will think for themselves, as free as the breeze," Daddy answers. "I've not given them a lot of mealymouthed dogma to deal with."

Grampa says it would be better for Daddy if a millstone were hung about his neck and he were cast into the sea, than that he should cause one of these little ones to stumble!

"Unless the Lord tarries," says Ruth-Ruby. "Maybe He'll return soon."

"I don't want Him to come back yet," Jo tells her. "I am much too young."

"Mere yarns," says Daddy. "It is monstrous to the human intellect to believe such nonsense."

"Unto the Gentiles it is foolishness!" cries Yooney, astride the bike, her thin right hand resting demurely in her lap. "But unto them that are called it is Christ, the power and wisdom of God!" She speaks right up to him.

"Christianity is a baby's religion," Daddy asserts, kneading his side and burping. He thinks he has appendicitis.

"You bet it is," says Yooney. "And I can quote Jesus on that."

It was really Jewel, in the kitchen. Mother was there with her, wearing red ankle socks. Everybody was talking at once, and Mother was at the sink peeling potatoes with the quick tiny motions she had learned at a foster home, where you were made to peel the peels if you got too much off. "You hear?" she whispered, her fists down on the iron sink, paring knife upward. "They are all like that, the whole Fuller bunch. Cram it down the other guy's neck, *prove* it, *prove* it! Now I ask you!"

On and on the voices go. Down on the croquet court Jo and Loring can still hear them, everybody polite, nobody cross, though surely they will burst or melt or fly apart. The smell of pot roast is heavy on the air. Daddy's voice prevails now, insistently, asking reason to triumph, and suddenly Loring smashes his mallet against a wooden ball, the "greenie," and sends it sailing far into the woods.

Wait! This is no dream! It's a memory, perfectly restored. Now Loring turns to Jo, and with Daddy's voice still floating on the pot roast, he raises the mallet again and chases her (how she runs, thinking, "He won't! I know he won't!") all the way to Cannon's pasture, where he splatters the center of a fresh cowflop.

"Jo . . . Jo! Wake Up!"

"What's wrong?"

"You're groaning something awful and grinding your teeth. Are you all right?"

Behind a filter of lamp light, Karen was almost invisible. "Don't, Jo! Don't rub your eyes like that. I can hear them squish!"

On Wednesday night her temperature was down. Gertraud, wearing witch hazel like cologne, dropped in about 10:00, after her stint at Cook County Hospital.

"Can she go home with me for Thanksgiving?" asked Karen.

"Tomorrow? That really wouldn't be wise," said Gertraud, shaking the thermometer.

Gertraud left, and Karen dressed silently. Her dress and slip crackled with electricity. Her dress was dark blue wool, and it wore a fuzzy aura. Jo's eyes were not right yet.

"I'm sorry about Thanksgiving," she said. "I don't think I could eat anyway."

"I'm sorry too," said Karen. She hung up her dress.

"What did you cover in Survey today?"

"We finished Numbers. Don't worry, I took good notes."

When Jo awoke in the morning Karen's coat and suitcase were on the bed. She was straightening the room.

Jo lay still, listening to herself. She was cool, her throat was not sore. Where had it all gone so suddenly?

"Don't do my side," she said to Karen. "I'll take care of it this weekend. Be sure to tell your folks I'm sorry."

"There'll be another time. Get well quick."

Karen left, and Jo pondered. She felt good, all but that other feeling. Bereft. That was the word. She had to get to the bottom of it. The praise service was at 10:00, and if she set her hair with cologne she could make it. That was what she needed to do more than anything. Then, after dinner, if she was not too tired, she would clean the room and start to catch up on her reading.

First a bath. The tub was in use at the moment. Beverly was in there, singing the alto part to Mozart's "Alleluia!" The choir was to sing it this morning. Without Jo. She sat up to test her voice and knew instantly where the cold had gone. Not far. It had slipped six inches down into her chest.

Let it sit. She was tired of being sick. If she breathed carefully she could hardly feel it at all. She got up suddenly and began on the room. The desk was littered and over the back of her chair was the heap of clothing she had been flopping there for days before she got sick—skirts and sweaters and slips. The wastebasket overflowed with Kleenex and orange peels.

Soot had gathered on her books. She blew it off and lined them up across the back of her desk, the big Bible atlas, *Cruden's Concordance*, dictionary, theory text. Her fingers were reluctant to grab. Now the notebooks, bulging, papers protruding, the edges of them soft and ragged.

Under one notebook lay a button off her coat and a spool of thread to sew it on with. There were many other things on the desk—the wrapper off a Devil Dog, a used Band-Aid, half a shoestring, a pile of missionary pamphlets, and dozens of reinforcements for the holes in her looseleaf notebook, little white doughnuts, spilled. She stared at it all for a minute, then jammed down the contents of the wastebasket with her foot and swept everything into it—the reinforcements, the literature, and the thread and button too.

She was finished. All her energy had been used. The grippe was still in charge, controlling, omnipotent. Back to bed, where the hollow in the mattress was still warm. She could not afford to give in this way.

Soup was in the doorway. "As the door turneth upon his hinges, so doth the slothful upon his bed," she read. She had looked up a bunch of verses with the word "bed" in them. "Let the saints sing aloud upon their beds . . . . Woe to them that work evil upon their bed . . . . If I make my bed in hell, behold thou art there."

"Don't worry, I'm getting right up," said Jo.

"You want me to stay with you this morning?"

"No. You go. Don't miss the music. I'm all right. Maybe I'll come later."

The building rang with holiday noise. Shrieks of laughter rose into the room. The warbler, or her roommate, did a vocal exercise, skipping up and down a small mountain, higher and higher. Then gradually the noise lessened. The front doors thundered as the dorm began to clear out.

Jewel came in. "I'm going to stay with you this morning, Jo."

"Oh no, thanks. I feel fine."

"Sure?"

"Yes, really. Don't worry."

Jo lay in bed and stared dully at the disorder in the room. November sunshine played with a rayon stocking that hung down off the pile on the chair like a forlorn leg. It was still attached to the garter, and the garter was sewn to the old girdle with green thread. The sight was depressing. She shut her eyes. She'd been evading the truth all week. Things were bad. She'd come down off her November mountain. The Lord seemed far, far away and unavailable. Halsted street had defeated her, and she was ashamed. All right, all right, it was more than that. *He* had abandoned her there, when she was helpless and needed Him most. How could He have done that? She was angry with Him—and like a sullen child she had not spoken to Him in five days.

Dear Lord, she said. In the quiet room her inner voice was sudden and loud. Dear Lord, she repeated more softly, let's get this straightened out.

There was no sense of contact. Dear Lord, she began again, forgive . . . .

Italy crawled along the water, its wrinkled stocking pulled up over the knobby calf. The sea was blue, Yugoslavia vaguely pink across the channel. The water sparkled in the morning sunlight where mists had begun to break and lift. A strip of yellow beach stretched for miles. She ran. Oh, hurry. Now the beach was rocky as she progressed straight up, which was north. Tiny islands showed green. Trieste was on the other side, a vertical cluster of buildings. She must go over there. But as she poised to take the leap, the sunlight disappeared, and she was running through the quarry. Wake up! Do not dream this dream! She forced her eyes open, back on the Italian shore. Only it was not shore at all. It was a line drawn on paper by a man, a mapmaker. Trieste was a circle with a dot in it. The sea was pale blue ink. Over the flat wilderness her own voice called. Crows answered.

The bell in the hall rang sharply. Jo was sweating, her pajama top wet. She raised her head and listened. Not a sound. No voices, no water running. Her nose breathed with a faint staccato whistle. She kicked off the blankets and stumbled into the kitchen across an elastic floor. "Is anyone here?" she called.

Someone else had to be here, someone else sick or a late sleeper on another floor. She grappled with the impulse to run, then without another thought limped to the elevator and pushed the button to go down. At every floor she stepped off and called hoarsely, amazed at how weak her voice was, shocked at its lonely sound in the building. On the first floor, still getting no answer, she ran from door to door, pounding, then aimed for the basement stairs. All she wanted was one girl in the laundry, one whole earthly girl in her pajamas, hair in pin curls, the iron all business as it clumped cheerfully on the board.

There was no one there. The basement was quiet and unlighted. She ran back up and was part way out the door into the foyer, headed for the street in her nightclothes, barefooted and Ace-bandaged, when she saw what she was doing and retreated into the hall. In the elevator she rose slowly to the fifth floor.

She was all right now. She had a firm grasp on herself. The impulse to cough gathered in her chest, but she would not let it happen. She rebuked herself all the way to the kitchen and into her bed. Glad you're back, said Loring and the crew from the bulletin board. That was a close one.

Karen's radio sat on the table between their beds. Jo turned it on, accepting the first sound that rode into the room, and got up to get a glass of water. It was time to take aspirin. The important thing was to keep fighting and not to allow herself to sleep or to be in a position or attitude where it could overcome her. She leaned on the sink as she drank. "Don't sit under the apple tree with anyone else but me," someone sang on the radio in the bedroom. Her class in Garfield had sung that at graduation, along with "My Buddy" and "I threw a kiss in the ocean," tears in their eyes. "A wartime class," the principal had called them. They would need courage. Jo washed the glass and let water run into it, hot then cold. Oh, keep talking, keep busy, don't stop. Now Helen Forrest was singing.

Here I go again
I hear those trumpets blow again . . . .

She used to try to sing like Helen Forrest. If she spread her arms she could almost do it. Loring had taught her a quick dance step to this tune, around and around the kitchen floor.

Cross—step step aslide,
I hear those step step pullaway,
Twirl and back again,
Dip and a chance on love.

"Relax your grip, Pinhead," he would insert in her ear. "You're dancing, not drowning."

It was almost like slapping him in the face when she stopped dancing, though he treated the matter with aloofness—except once. He was the boy she had enjoyed dancing with the most. He was different when he danced, not the person who separated his potatoes from his beets. He let things happen all mixed together, and they came out right. Other boys filled you with worry, especially the younger ones (her own age) who were just starting. They were trembly, and their hands made a hot place in the middle of your back. They were jailed inside their sweaty bodies where the music couldn't reach. But Loring always seemed surprised at what his feet were doing, and it gave him a loose, comical air. It was the same when he began to drive, and with girls. Girls and cars liked him. Cars hummed, girls laughed, and his constant state of pleased surprise kept his touch easy.

Here I slide again,
About to take that ride again,
Starry-eyed again,
Takin' a chance on love.

"Atta way!" Daddy would cheer. He and Mother loved to watch them dance. Sometimes Jo and Loring would grab them and try to get them to dance too. They couldn't; their feet turned to wood. "Our muscles never learned," said Daddy. They didn't play much. Croquet now and then, checkers. They never went to parties. Mother admitted to being too self-conscious. Daddy had often said she ought to get over it and learn to be outgoing.

The floor was wavy again. Jo went back to her bed, but not to lie down. Jewel had left a jar of Vicks and she began to rub that on her throat as she listened to the radio. She talked to herself, keeping busy. All the world's songs were about love. Above everything else in the world people were worried about being loved. Get it somehow, get loved! She could do a paper on this sometime. Love divine, all loves excelling. Helen was still singing. "Ridin' for a fall again. Gonna give my all again . . ." The smell of the Vicks mixed with the sound of the song. Jo thought she could smell the song and hear the Vicks. "I see a rainbow blending now . . . ." Bright burning song in a blue jar. "Takin' . . . a chance . . . on . . . love!"

Daddy overcame his own shyness, Jo had heard him tell Mrs. Cannon, "by sheer determination." But Jo knew he kept a little notebook in his breast pocket with jokes written in it and a list of things to talk about, as if he didn't trust himself completely. Once at a Grange supper he pulled out his notebook and read aloud to people at the table when the conversation lagged. Jo laughed hard, afraid no one else would. She saw how nervous he was. Loring did not laugh. He did his Mad Russian act—"Very fonnya, very fonnya!"—and blushed at his own freshness.

She was still rubbing in the Vicks when the news came on. It was raining everywhere in the world. There were torrential rains in the Philippines, and a direct report "with the Third Army" gargled through the phlegm-filled air waves. "Sloshing forward . . . wet to the skin, mud . . . ." The voice slipped away and came back. "Enemy large-scale withdrawals from . . . . Weather is costing us dearly." It faded completely.

How had she happened to be listening to the radio that Sunday night? It was February. Maybe the weather was bad, because she had not gone to Boston to church. She was at home. The four of them were around the lamp table, all busy, and she was playing with the radio dial, seeing what was on. Lively full music sprang into the room.

We have heard the joyful sound!
Jesus saves! Jesus saves!

Surprised, she instinctively flipped the volume down, though no one had objected. It was the *Old Fashioned Revival Hour* from Long Beach, California, said the announcer. She'd never heard it before. It was like having new friends drop in on you. The music was good. Even Daddy liked the male quartet. He said, "That's a good bass." He admired a deep voice. Loring, studying hard from a big biology text with Tufts stickers all over it, seemed oblivious to anything in the room.

Then the preaching began. Jo turned the dial lower, but not much. Maybe she should have turned it off. She was asking for trouble. She wanted it on. Not just for herself. She thought that quite surely her fingers had been directed to this place on the dial. God had planned this—the Gospel in this house. She could see Daddy shifting his position in his chair, having all he could do to put up with the fervor in the voice. She nudged the volume down more and put her ear closer. The name Jesus buzzed through . . . Jesus . . . Jesus. Then suddenly the man began to cry as he talked. "Come to Jesus, all ye that labor and are heavy laden, and He will give you rest! Oh come," he pleaded. "Lay your burden at the foot of the cross."

Loring leaped to his feet and hurled his book to the floor. It landed with a thunderous crack. For a second or two they stared up at him as he hung suspended over the lamp there in the middle of the room, his eyes wild.

"Garbage!" he yelled. "Shit! Turn it off!"

"She's only listening," protested Mother.

"Only listening! Look at her. Groveling! Don't you see? Why don't you stop her?" he demanded of Daddy.

"Calm down, Loring," Daddy said. "There's no need to yell."

"Yes, there is! Do you know what she does downtown? She passes out leaflets to people. She might as well join the Salvation Army. No dancing, no movies! It's abnormal. Do you know how much time she spent on her knees last night, like some half-witted grandmother? Holy Christ, my sister's a holy roller!"

"I know what she does," Daddy said. "But I see no good in this display of emotion."

"Get your own radio then!" Loring shouted at Jo. "Listen in the backhouse. Take your crap out there where it belongs."

"Turn the radio off, Jo."

She already had.

"Sit down, Loring." It was an empty order. It had been years since Daddy told Loring to do anything. He was an adult in the house. He earned his own money and paid board. He did not sit down. He shouted across the top of the lamp at Daddy. "I want to know what you're going to do about it! I want you to tell me."

Mother's crochet cotton spun out across the floor. She went after it, moving self-consciously, as if she were on stage. She rolled it up and stuck the crochet hook through it and set in on the table on top of the stitch directions, which was a tiny clipping cut from the newspaper with pinking shears. They were all silent. Daddy was putting a medication of some kind on his fingernails. He had picked up a fungus. The smell of the medicine, like rubber cement, rose in the lamplight. The room was crowded, jammed with furniture. There wasn't enough room to put everything, a pile of magazines on a chair, too many pictures on the walls, the surface of the sideboard covered with vases and candy dishes and a mail basket and a fruit bowl with two tennis balls in it. This had never bothered Jo before. Now it closed in on her. They were all squeezed together in the lamplight. Loring stood staring at Daddy, waiting for an answer. You could almost hear Daddy's mind forming words, though he seemed to be concentrating carefully on the ends of his fingers.

"Above all," he said, "we must be careful not to allow ourselves the indulgence of emotion. You surprise me, Loring, with such an outburst. I thought you'd gotten over that. What do you think I should do? Lock her in the house? Burn her Bible? You know as well as I that would only fan the fires of zeal. She'd thrive on the persecution. There is only one way to reach Jo, and that is through her intelligence. Let her listen to that high-grade moron on the radio there if she likes—and all the others. Let her have it, up to the ears."

"You're wrong!" cried Loring.

"You think so? You think I don't know whereof I speak? I know the lies Jo tells herself, the fear she has of renouncing them, lest it be true, lest there be a hell, a heaven. I was like that. Until I wrenched myself away from my father's God. Tyranny of mind, that was how your grandfather raised his family. He manipulated us all. You children have never known that. You've been free to think and to dare. Yet with all that freedom, Jo has chosen to imprison her mind. The shackles of emotion. She'll yield to sanity one day, surrender to reason—when she just once opens her mind."

The lid was on, but something leaked out. You could hear it in Daddy's distinct consonants and see it around the edges of his being, the rims of his eyes reddening, his foot twisting. It seemed to come from his fingers in the fumes of the medication. Daddy being eaten away at his extremities by this force. Anger. And something else. What was it? It reached for them, passed through them to the dark corners of the house, then out through the walls. It filled the woods around them, hid in the bushes, and snuffled around the shed. It scratched at the windows asking for a name. If they looked up, they might all see it.

Loring's voice beat against it. "You can't do it with talk! When will you see that? We're all sick of talk!"

"Please, Loring, we can't have this from *you*. If Jo is going to let her ideas be dictated by her feelings, regardless of reason or veracity, I must be able to count on you to respond with sanity and control."

"Sanity! *This* is insanity!" He flung his arms to encompass the lamplight. "Sitting on our asses letting it happen! That's crazy!"

"I insist you lower your voice," said Daddy. "It's a wonder the Cannons don't hear you."

"To hell with the Cannons!" He roared it down over the cedars and junipers. Something outside plunged into the underbrush.

Jo could stop this. She knew she could say right now, "Forget it. I give up. Don't hurt each other. It's not important." Yet at the same instant that she realized her power to settle things, she knew she could never do it. It was a lie and a betrayal. "If any man love father and mother more than me, he is not worthy of me." If it tore them apart, she would not give up. She felt torn herself. "Asunder," she thought. An ancient word, a Bible word, no doubt, though she couldn't remember ever reading it.

Daddy was still talking. "Why is it that I can't have a rational conversation with my own children about sensitive matters?" The sentence rode out on sibilance. "Perhaps it would be best if we dropped the subject now. We'll talk again when we can do it without emotion."

But he continued himself. Loring stood frozen in his position over the lamp while Daddy quoted Emerson and Ingersoll. Mother slipped out into the shed. Jo could glimpse her out there with a flashlight, poking through a pile of old newspapers for an empty crossword puzzle.

Loring stood motionless until Daddy was done, then shook his head, or Jo thought he did, one quick little movement, before he straightened and left the house. The car door slammed. They could hear him speed shifting all the way down the quarry road. Late into the night he came back, the motor gentle, easing the knob on the front door, and tiptoeing across the floor.

The radio beeped a time signal. It was noon. The news came on again, repeating the same headlines. Jo dressed hastily, removed the Ace bandage, and went to the dining room for Thanksgiving dinner, smelling of Vicks.

That night she awoke just in time. She had drooled into her pillow, that was what woke her. Disgusted, she flopped the pillow over, and the dream with which she had been wrestling was thrown off onto the floor. Up on one arm, uncovered, she dozed again, and in another dream struggled fiercely against the first, fighting its return. She awoke from that shivering with cold, her eyes glued shut, gasping for breath.

Realizations came slowly. She knew she had been frightened, but it was dream fright, and her present actual danger occurred to her in stages. First, the sense of space was all wrong. There was no ceiling, or the walls were gone. She rubbed her eyes without mercy, forcing them open. Two rectangles of light hung side by side not far away, her window and Karen's. The ceiling dropped into place. Now a car passed, five stories below, a sigh of sound. It was Thursday night, Thanksgiving. All right. Eyes and ears working together, identifying space and time. Part of her was awake and working well.

The smell in the room was smoky and ought to be explored, her awake self said. She would check it out when her legs agreed. Her legs were reluctant to swing themselves into the darkness. There was a good reason for that, because there was no floor. She had missed that fact until this second. The horror of it fueled her heart—kerchomp-hiss! Back and forth, up and down, a machine. She opened her mouth to call. Jewel! Anyone! Nothing came out. Her breath was entirely cut off.

Karen's window was open. A damp banner of wind swirled in and touched her, and with it came the smell again, powerful, burning flesh and hair. The danger was unquestionable. She expanded her chest as far as it would go against the bonds that tied it. The gag fell away. "Baked sneaker," she said out loud. That was what they called the smell. It came from the stockyards when the wind was right. That's all it was. It was nothing.

She felt foolish, but she was smarter. She would not be fully awake and safe until she had gotten out of bed and shut the window. To do that she must get to Karen's side of the room. It took a long time to gather the courage. It was dark and turbulent down there between the beds, and the space was getting wider. "Now or never," her calm self told her.

She flung herself over like a bridge, from her bed to Karen's, and hung suspended, unable to move. The dream was down there, waiting for her. It had slid under the bed from the other side. She knew it was the running dream, but just now she saw it only as a dark hulk of fear. She recognized it unmistakably. The familiarity of its bare face was almost a comfort. At least it was something she had fought before, hand to hand, hundreds of times. Then she saw that even that acceptance was a tactic it used to fool her. If she gave in, this time it would really win. It would have her forever.

She was dreaming yet.

Shut the window.

Very slowly, with extreme effort, she inched her useless legs over Karen's bed and swung them to the floor on the other side. They landed on something fluffy and benign. Karen's slippers. She put them on, and in them walked to Karen's desk, straight into the cold wind. She was awake at last, really now, for the first time. All the rest had been dreams within dreams.

Karen's luminous clock said 3:20. The carrot sticks and the jar of yellow pencils were to the right. Jo expected them to glow like the clock, but they showed no color at all in the darkness.

Down below, the street gleamed moistly in the headlights of a single car. Several blocks away a trolley clattered. A searchlight swung against the horizon, and across the city some sort of machinery made the noise she had heard inside herself—kerchomp-hiss. It faded in and out with the wet wind. Mostly there was a great sense of sleep. Only the smell was really awake, dispensing energy.

Karen kept a cardigan on the back of her chair. Jo pulled it around her and snapped on the desk lamp—just as she could have snapped on the lamp by the bed, if she had found her wits. What quality of sleep had she been in to fool her so completely?

And how did she know that even now she was awake? Was the light really on, or was she fooling herself? When does one state tip into the other? There was no way to be sure that the desk and the sweater were real, the street really down there, the kerchomp far away and not within her. She was sweating, and her breath was short again. It was coming back, the dream, swelling toward her from the floor. I can't stand this, Lord, she said. Don't let it come.

She pulled out Karen's concordance and opened it to F. It took forever. Her hands would not work, and F seemed to have disappeared from the alphabet. Now she found it. FAS FAT. So many verses with "fat." FATHER, FATHERS, FATHERLESS, FAULTS, FAVOR, FEAR. There were a thousand verses about fear. With FEAR, without FEAR, FEAR God, FEAR not, FEARED greatly, FEARFUL, FEARFULLY, FEAST. Back up, back up. Luke, Acts, Romans.

> render f. to whom f. is due
> I was with you in weakness and f.
> What f.! What vehement desire!
> God hath not given us the spirit of f.

That was the one she wanted. 2 Timothy 1:7. She swished her way through Karen's big study Bible to Second Timothy. "For God hath not given us the spirit of fear; but of power, and of love, and of a sound mind."

She opened Karen's drawer and found a 3 x 5 card (they were stacked neatly right in the front) and wrote the verse out many times, on each side of the card, until it was fixed in her memory. Then she shut the window, picked up the card, and slid under Karen's covers. In that safe place she fell into sleep, the light still on.

When she awoke in the morning, she found the card in her hand, covered with a scrawl of unreadable words. She had been dreaming all along. Either that, or she had lost her mind. And what about now, this moment? Staring at the card, appalled by the wild irrationality of her own handwriting, she could think of only one thing to do—put herself in the presence of the sanest person she knew. She dressed.

"Well! Are you through ailin'?" asked Jewel, as Jo walked through the kitchen in her coat.

"I don't know," said Jo.

She had heard that Dr. Peckham was holding special visiting hours today, on this holiday Friday. That was where she took herself, to the hall outside his office. A long line waited there, mostly men students wanting conferences on term papers. Her errand seemed inappropriate, but she stood there an hour, still in her coat, her sense of urgency prevailing.

When her turn came and he met her at the door, she knew it would be all right. She introduced herself.

"Oh, sure. Hello, Jo," he said. He was even shorter than she had thought. She got his coffee breath full blast. It didn't matter.

"Excuse the mess," he said, as they went in. "I think the girl who cleans is mad at me because I never pick up. Are you a tidy person, Jo?"

"Only in rare spurts."

He laughed, and so did she. She liked her answer.

The desk was piled layers thick with mail and student papers. He was very slow at correcting papers. Sometimes he lost them. He had that reputation. Several open books were scattered over the pile. Bookcases of varying sizes surrounded them in the room, anything that would hold books shoved in wherever it would fit. From one corner a stack of magazines had cascaded onto the floor. A paper cup of coffee steamed on his desk; there was another empty cup beside it and several in the wastebasket at Jo's feet.

"Tell me why you've come," he said, in his froggy voice.

For one precipitous second she almost said, "My brother is missing in action." But she caught herself in time and said exactly what she'd planned. She said, "My father is an agnostic."

"How interesting," Pecky replied. She was sure he meant it. He even sounded glad. She sped through a series of reactions. She felt special because her father was an agnostic. Not every student could say that. She suspected Pecky knew she felt special, but he was not critical of that. He knew she had mixed feelings about it. He knew that was natural. He liked her.

"Have you got a letter from him there?"

She was holding it in her hand. "Yes. He wants me to answer him. I never . . . . I never know how, really. Would you be willing to read it perhaps? It's a little long."

"I'd enjoy that. Would he mind?"

"Oh no. He says in there somewhere to show it to my teachers if I like. . . . He means that as a challenge."

Pecky's hand, when he took the letter, was small as a boy's, nails bitten. He seemed not at all dismayed by the letter's thickness.

"Will you excuse me while I look through it?"

"Sure."

He bent over the letter. He seemed to wrap himself around it. Jo got up and went to the bookcases and began to read titles, authors first, as she had recently learned to do. Von Harnack: *What Is Christianity?*, Orr: *The Christian View of God and the World*, Pfeiffer, James, Ritschl, Schleiermacher, three books on the letter to the Romans. On the shelf in front of her she saw another empty paper cup, stained brown, and then another, with a thick green island of mold in the bottom. The smell of the stale coffee and the old books together resembled tobacco.

Pierson: *Many Infallible Proofs*. She liked the sound of that. One whole bookcase, more organized than the others, held only history books. Another held two sets of encyclopedias, intermixed. There were books on archaeology, geology, astronomy, and rows of commentaries on the Bible. Her eyes moved slowly around the room. It made her feel relaxed and well to be here. She laid her hand on the wood of a shelf, thankful for its reality. A dozen little men with torches in their hands raced across the colored spines of a Modern Library set: Aristotle, Dickens, Shakespeare, John Donne.

Her eyes moved from the little men to a picture on the wall above of Peter and John running with the news of the resurrection. Their faces were frightened, and their clothes were wrinkled and messy, as if they had had a bad night.

Pecky was speaking. "Have you tried to answer this letter yet?"

She turned to the desk and shook her head.

"Have you been through it before with him?"

"Yes."

"And he always wins."

"Oh, always."

He nodded, smiling. "He's had more practice."

"If I could just give him one convincing answer."

"To put him in his place? Or to win him?"

". . . Both, I guess."

"But, you see, you wouldn't do either. Why not just thank him for the nice long letter, tell him you are studying hard and someday you may be able to answer."

Jo was disappointed.

"Is it really a case of answering?" asked Pecky.

"He insists on answers," she said. "I know I should answer this somehow."

"I'm not sure that's what he wants. There are any number of people who could counter him with statements fully as reasonable and factual as his own. But do you think that would change his mind?"

She didn't know what to say. She had never thought about it that way before.

"It wouldn't bring him any closer to the truth," said Pecky. "I mean, it's a mistake to let a discussion of God be reduced simply to a rational argument. Making faith intellectually respectable can be a trap. We must always come back to mystery. . . . I'm not sure your father wants that route."

Jo sat down in the one chair that had nothing on it, by his desk, perching on the end of it because she felt suddenly a little shy. He was really talking to her. He saw her as he talked. She was charmed by this. Maybe it had never happened before. She could take her clothes off and not be embarrassed, because he would not see any more of her than he was seeing now. She wanted to laugh, and dropped the impulse into the wastebasket at her feet before it became an interruption.

"We are all agnostics," Pecky said. "Some are able to believe, by the grace of God. Probably your dad is a humanist, if we can use a label safely."

"I don't know. He calls himself a freethinker."

"Oh yes. The term was popular a while back, in the twenties. The problem was in staying free to really think. Freethinkers were apt to set a premium on one kind of thinking and therefore were not free at all. In metaphysics especially we have to watch out for that."

Pecky's finger was conducting the rhythm of his speech: loop, stab, hold. He stopped, his finger in the air. "Is this what you really want to talk about?"

Jo nodded.

"This is what you came for?"

"I want to talk about the letter."

"The letter or your father? You see, I can't give you a blow-by-blow answer. I shouldn't. What we can try to understand is what he really wants." He stopped again and looked at her as if he expected her to speak.

She said finally, "I don't think I know what you mean."

"Well, possibly he wants two things. He wants to be sure you are not damaging your life by a Christian commitment—what he sees as closed thinking. And he wants *you* to approve of *him*. Of his ideas. . . . Does that surprise you? There isn't a father who doesn't want that of his child. For some it can become an obsession. When the stakes are high, as I think they are here."

She shook her head, puzzled.

"I'm not sure I'm helping you, Jo. Wouldn't you like to tell me more about yourself and your family? You *know*, but I can only guess."

"I just want you to talk," she said. Maybe she sounded a bit desperate, because he studied her, then grinned and said, "All right." She sat back in the chair, wondering if she ought to take notes.

"There's always a danger in arguing mostly for the sake of ego. Don't get drawn into that. You must not need to prove that you are right.

Perhaps he does. Or, to put it another way, perhaps it undermines his own security to find there are intelligent people who believe in God with some confidence. But if he were here he might object to that, so it's unfair of me to be saying it. You tell me. What would he say if he were here?"

"That we should believe nothing that can't be proved scientifically."

"So? If you can't prove something to him, admit it. You can't prove the miracles of Christ. All right, that's no shame. You began your relationship to Christ in faith, didn't you? Must it be different now? Yield your father a point when you can. That's not a loss of ground. He is right when he says that terrible and unexplainable things happen in the world. What kind of a God is this anyway? The problems are enormous. Yield the point gracefully. . . . That's dying to self, hey?"

Wait. Stop the train. Those words again. When Miss Mackey said them they died. Pecky said them, and they came to life. She wanted to talk about that. But he was back to the letter, scanning it intensely, looking cross, as he so often did. The letter was a mess already, crumpled and smudged. The onionskin rattled like static. "Insist on sharing the initiative. Why must *you* always be the one to answer *him*? Send *him* to the books."

"I wouldn't know how to do that."

"Choose an area where you have some agreement. How about the ethical teachings of Jesus? Does he accept those?"

"Oh yes. He says that's all we need."

"Fine. Hang the miracles for a while. The teachings alone are astounding. They've become commonplace to the world, but Christ's ideas were remarkably fresh when He spoke to them, and still are. He understood the heart of Old Testament law. Take alone His concept of the Messiah as liberator. Magnificent. His own sense of freedom. Only the truly free can serve. 'I have come to release the captive,' Jesus said. Who was the man who could say such a thing?"

He offered her some things to read. The name of a Russian theologian passed through her ears in a swish and was gone.

"Could you spell that, please?" she asked, feeling dumb.

He laughed. "Are you putting me on the spot? I can't spell."

"My father reads Hume and Huxley sometimes," Jo said, hoping it was relevant.

"Thomas Huxley perhaps? Or Julian?"

She hadn't known there were two.

"Well, they are formidable," Pecky said. "But they are men, struggling with ideas, as we all are. Don't forget that." He shook the letter. "God doesn't expect everything from you, Jo. You're not supposed to have it all—unbroken faith, wisdom, smart answers. We have this treasure in earthen vessels. Our reason is limited, so is feeling. So we have faith—suspension. We *believe* God revealed His love to us in Christ. There is no substitute for that."

Pecky set down the letter. Jo hoped he was not finished. Not yet. She wanted more. But . . . but. Oh, something to keep him talking. "But," she said, "why does God leave it to faith, something so important? Why not solid evidence?"

"Because of the nature of belief, that's all I can say. It's how we're made. The realm of the spirit is as much a part of our lives as the physical. Man wants the unknown, the peril of belief. Like love. Look around you and see the bridges of faith man has built. All kinds. Even fear is a kind of belief. Fear and faith come from the same place within us. It's the touch of grace that makes the difference."

Oh, but there. But, you see. Jo drew in her breath to start a question and coughed instead. Pecky waited for her. "Are you all right?" he asked. She nodded. He sat still. There were others in the hall, but she saw he was going to respect her decision to stay longer or go. It was up to her.

So she stood, and so did he, but not too quickly. What a civilized person he was.

"There's just one other thing."

"Shoot!"

There's this other thing . . . this terribly important thing.

He smiled at her, waiting.

"I'm stuck in Leviticus. Sixteenth chapter."

"Oh. Why don't you skip it? There'll be other days. Leviticus is behind us anyway. That's why we read it, to understand that."

She moved toward the door, and he extended his hand. "Come and see me again, Jo. Next time I won't talk so much."

"It's been just right. I . . . thank you."

"Oops. Your letter."

He fumbled putting it back in the envelope and got it part way. One page was torn. He gave up with a laugh and handed it to her. What a lovely man. Maybe I'm in love with him, she thought. It made her proud to think they were both Christians. She felt a compelling urge—to go to the center of Clark and shout "Good news, everybody!" She considered that seriously as she stepped into the courtyard. Did she dare? Yes, she did. It was a crucially important thing to do, ring bells, tell the world!

She would just be a crazy girl, for sure. And the compulsion to tell, to shout—how do you keep it? You can't live with that burden pressing so upon you, not letting it out. If you don't respond to it, it goes away, because it has to. But even so, even if she told everyone she met for the rest of her life, there would still be thousands and thousands who would never hear in time. It had always been like that. Great masses of people who lived and died without hope, and just a few who heard and were given the heart to believe. And people like Loring, for whom believing was an act of insanity, what about them?

She was at the Pastry Shop. Her exhilaration was fading fast. She ordered coffee, though it was almost lunchtime, and smoothed out the letter to give her hands something to do. The Pastor's Course men were in there, struggling with the Trinity and the nature of Christ. "Everything hangs on the resurrection," said Baldy.

She wished they would shut up. How windy they were. She fought the urge to cough. Pecky had said something about fear, and she had forgotten it already. She wanted to run back to his office. She hadn't told him what she really needed to at all. I'm in some kind of trouble. I think I am losing my mind. That's what she meant to say. Can a Christian go crazy? I have strange dreams that are not dreams. I'm terribly afraid. May

I stay here? she would ask him. She'd be his cleaning girl, do his typing, stuff letters back in envelopes, anything, dust his books—just to be there. Sleep on a pile of magazines! She would read there, all day, the rest of her life. She saw herself saying to him, "Please! Please! This is where I belong!" She was holding him by the lapels, sobbing and begging, making a spectacle of herself, please, please, please, let me stay!

Her father's letter lay in two-inch pieces on the Pastry Shop table, and her mother's handwriting was on it, fragmented. "ter. Ne" said one piece. She had written something on the back of the last page, and Jo had never seen it until now.

She put the jigsaw puzzle together. "Just heard from Mrs. Cannon that Gary Ryan has been stationed at Great Lakes Naval Center. Near Chicago. Maybe he will get in touch with you. Here is his address." Jo put that together too, and put the pieces in her pocket to save.

Perhaps it was now that Jo began to lose track of time, days and nights (since she could not allow herself to really sleep) blurring together. It must have been an evening shortly after Thanksgiving when Beverly was called down to the phone on the first floor. She came back bent over with sobs. "Man mine! Man mine!" Jo thought she said. She was blurring her words together in tears the way she did when she laughed.

It turned out to be "land mine." Bob had been killed. His folks had called from New Jersey.

Far into the night they could hear her crying in her room. Jewel and Louise were with her. The rest of them had gathered in Soup's room to pray before bed.

In the morning, as Jo was brushing her teeth at one of the sinks, Beverly appeared beside her. She looked the same as always in the flowered housecoat, with her towel over her arm. She smiled faintly at Jo and ran water in the sink.

"Are you all right, Beverly?" asked Jo, around her toothbrush. She thought she would be changed somehow.

Beverly's curls shook as she nodded. "I'll be okay," she said.

"I'm so sorry . . ." Jo began.

"He's with the Lord. I can't begrudge him that, can I? I just wish . . . I'd rather have him here dead before me than not to come back at all. You see? You wait and wait . . ."

"I understand," said Jo.

For a minute she was afraid Beverly was going to cry again, and then she was afraid she would laugh, but she didn't do either. She washed her face. Her thick-soled oxfords peeked out from under the flowered robe. Jo went on brushing her teeth.

On the following Sunday afternoon Ruth rushed up to tell them that Beverly was playing beautifully in the auditorium. Jo threw on her coat and went over. The interior of Moorehouse was dim, except for the light at the Hammond organ, where Beverly sat. It was a minute before Jo saw that other people were scattered about the room. Song after song soared from the organ, and now and then, when they knew the words, the students sang along as she played. "Someday I shall hear God's call of love . . . Calling to the land of endless day. Someday . . . Someday . . . When the shadows flee away . . . Someday when the shadows flee away."

In another few days Beverly seemed to have stripped herself of Bob. The ring, identification bracelet, and locket were gone. In the pink room every picture had been put away except the one with the rippling hair.

Louise said, "I hope it doesn't boomerang. She got over it so quickly."

But Jewel thought everything was all right. "She's settled it," she said. "It's in the Lord's hands."

Waiting outside the bathroom in the hall, Jo heard Ruth and Ruby talking in their room behind the bureaus. Ruby was saying it was clear that Beverly had loved Bob too much and the Lord had to take him. Ruth said, "Not too much, but maybe too preeminently. Bob had first place in her affections. I think she knows that now. She has victory over it."

The floor seemed quieter that week, partly because Beverly was subdued and Soup had a prolonged migraine, and partly because everyone was tired. The whole school seemed tired.

"It's the end of the term," sighed Louise in the kitchen. "Finals are coming. . . . And it's the war. We're all so sick of the war. It's so sad, and it's time for it to end, that's all." She was buttoning one of Charlie Higgins' shirts onto a hanger. She had just come up from ironing in the basement. "We're all so sick of the worry and boys dying and runny rayon stockings and pennies that aren't copper and brown-outs and black-outs."

"We can't talk that way," rebuked Jewel. "We can't let down. Things are easier here than anywhere in the world. They're having a terrible winter in Europe, freezing and no food. We can't imagine how awful."

"Oh, I'm just beefing a little," said Louise. "I don't mean it."

Then it snowed, and instantly the mood changed. A rich, thick fall mounted quickly on rooftops and windowsills. Boys scraped the side-walks and left three-foot heaps along the curbing. Caroling began on street corners and in a couple of days the Social Club had set up a tall tree in Van Housen lounge.

The choir scheduled extra rehearsals for their performance at the December graduation in three weeks. Jo had been forced to drop choir and trio both. Her singing voice was in bad shape from coughing. The cough was gone now, but the cold hung on. Her nose felt bulbous, and she had a red mustache from blowing. She dozed in almost every class and fell asleep during any prayer that was longer than a minute or two—and always during her own devotions. Some mechanism under her kneecaps triggered sleep.

She slept at night too, in spite of herself, but in her sleep she set up a waking guard against dreaming, like a watch on ship deck. She still dreamed. She dreamed about dreaming, about *not* dreaming that one dream. It was as if she had not slept at all.

For all her dreadful weariness, some parts of her life were in order. She was making hard decisions with dispatch. She would not go home for Christmas vacation. The tickets would take all her remaining money, and she needed it for a payment on next term's board bill. Going home was an extravagance. It was not an easy choice to make—she could hardly think about her parents' reaction.

Soup said, "Jo, the Lord has been speaking to me. I have extra money, you know. Let me pay for your trip east. Shekels are shackles. I want to use it."

Jo told her no thank you, she just didn't feel right about that. Then Daddy offered, on the end of one of Mother's letters, to send train fare "one way only." Jo wrote back a rather spiritual-sounding letter, though she knew Daddy wouldn't like it. She said it was the Lord's will for her to stay at school, and it was Him she must answer to. She explained that she had employment in the dining room over vacation and needed to be near the library. She had been given extensions on her unfinished papers. It all added up right. She did her Christmas shopping in the bookstore and mailed the package home.

Her second big decision was to drop piano. It happened at the senior recital of one of Mr. Cooch's other students. The pianist played Grieg's Concerto in A minor. Mr. Cooch was at the second piano. The girl's arms seemed very long. Jo thought, calmly, I must give up piano. She had missed hours of practice and lessons she could not make up. Cooch had already assigned her to a student teacher in January. There was no doubt. It was right to let it go. Yet she was full of regret. What had started out as a fine adventure for the Lord had come to a dead end. She had not measured up. Sitting there at the recital, she thought all music had gone out of her life.

Afterwards in a visit to the Pastry Shop, Louise scolded her for being a sourpuss lately. "I know," said Jo. "I'm sorry." It was like being whipped with a bunch of daisies to be scolded by Louise, worse than if someone had been mean about it.

"Is something wrong, Jo?" Louise asked, spooning up her ice cream soda. Her right eye winked.

"Not really," said Jo. "I'm just tired."

It was hardly the time to get a note from Clyde. The only notice she had taken of him in weeks was that they both blew their noses in class.

The note was a copy of a cablegram he had sent to Field Marshall Montgomery, "since he is known to be a Christian," his explanation said.

Sir: A warning from God. Do not underestimate the strategy of the Panzers. A trap is being set. We have advanced too fast.

Respectfully yours
in Christ,

Cpl. Clyde MacQuade
Honorable Discharge
United States Army

That same day, Jo overheard an entirely different kind of Pastry Shop discussion. The tone was sober and low-voiced.

"I think they wanted to be caught."

"Suspended?"

"What else? It's not a first offense."

"The draft will get them now."

She gathered finally that two Calvary boys had been drinking in a café on Clark Street.

"Nobody's surprised," the talk went on. "It's been evident from the start that those guys weren't serious about being here."

That week the school was alive with rumors—a girl had stayed out all night, a boy and girl were found together in the girl's room, boys were smoking in the boiler room. The trouble seemed remote. These were not students Jo knew. There was talk of a fist fight in the boys' dormitory—"A thing just of the *devil*!" Ruby exclaimed. She said she thought a lot of kids had lost sight of the Lord.

Suddenly it was very close, right under them. The warbler and her roommate were gone. They'd left together. It was a while before Jo was certain of what had happened. Louise said, "They were lovers. They went all the way." No one talked much about it. Even Soup skirted the subject.

"Is it a sure thing, do you think?" Jo asked Karen.

"They admitted it," Karen said, matter-of-factly. "It happens at every school. It's bound to."

"I guess so," Jo answered. Those girls had been sitting in classes, going to prayer bands, eating in the dining room, and all along they had this overpowering secret.

The word "revival" began to surface about the school. A guest speaker preached on it in chapel. "This people's heart has grown dull and their ears are heavy with hearing," he charged. Certain words and phrases began to poke up with increasing frequency out of prayers and devotional messages. You heard them stirring about in conversations: deeper life, higher ground, confession, outpouring, renewal, infilling.

Soup brought news of a prayer marathon or relay—she didn't know what to call it—a continual unbroken chain of prayer, day and night, by one or more students at a time. It had begun quietly in the men's dorm, and it was growing. About fifty kids were involved now, she said. Some of them had prayed all night.

"I think the Holy Spirit is moving among us," said Ruth in an awed voice at Floor Fellowship. But Jewel said, "Now is the time to be wary."

One day after lunch Jo studied a new sign on a student bulletin board.

> The world has yet to see what God can do *with* and *for* and *through* and *in* a man who is fully and wholly consecrated to him.

Under this someone had written, "Are *you* blocking the way to revival?"

She stared at this a long time, feeling the pull of both directions. Which of these persons was she? It was no contest at all. She was a long way from the person in the first quote, a long way from where she had been even a few weeks ago. So swiftly she had come to this, down off her mountain, scraping along on the bottom of her existence. It seemed not at all improbable that if someone were actually blocking the way to revival at this school, it was herself. The idea weighed a ton. She dragged it around with her the rest of the day, thinking of nothing else.

By morning of the next day Jo had all she could do to dress. The initiative involved in that process, toe into stocking, arm into sleeve, took almost more strength than she could produce. She knew she must go that day to see Pecky again while she could make the decision to do it.

At exactly quarter to 9:00 it was too late.

Chapel began at 8:15. To her surprise, to everyone's, Dr. Peckham was the speaker. A guest had cancelled. Pecky had agreed to fill in. Jo felt this was significant. She sat ready with her notebook and pencil, feeling hopeful.

It was the shortest chapel message they had yet heard. He began by saying he had been getting a lot of questions lately about something called the "victorious life" or "the life that wins." It went by many names and involved some special act of God which would bring power and blessing. He had been asked if he believed in such an experience, and his answer was yes, he did, but if he must name it he would rather call it "the life that loses."

"As I get the picture," he went on, his funny cross face just over the top of the pulpit, "the life that wins is a shining life in which we are endowed moment by moment with unquenchable joy and a new strength of character. We want to be like Christ, we say. We want to have His heart . . . to be courageous, serene in the face of adversity, powerful in soul-winning, steady and unmovable in faith, free from the tyranny of self, flesh crucified, all in our places, with sunshiny faces.

"But friends, it may not go that way. If you ask for the heart of Christ, yours may be broken. If you ask for the eyes of Christ, you may be horrified at what you see. If you try to embrace all mankind, as Christ did, you may be consumed by that love. Touching broken lives means to be touched back by the world's misery. The healer risks infection. The diseases are fear, loneliness, even insanity. If we fight injustice, we are identified with the condemned. We will bear about in our bodies the paradoxes of mankind, the yeas and the nays.

"To be a Christian in the truest sense may mean to live on the edge of a cliff, shocked and dismayed at our own weakness, failure, and evil. We go there as pilgrims and pioneers, and only God can keep us safe on that wild frontier.

"If we understand all that when we talk about the abundant life, then we are ready for business.

"But do I mean we should give ourselves to a life of sorrow and sackcloth, or sit looking for trouble, or that you should not be lighthearted and young? Of course not. Christ said, 'My joy I give unto you.' We mount up with wings as eagles. The fruits of the Spirit are joy and peace.

"What we have then is a flat contradiction. Dead in Him. Alive in Him. 'As dying and behold we live; as chastened and not killed; as sorrowful, yet always rejoicing; as poor, yet making many rich; as having nothing, yet possessing all things.' That's the life that wins.

"But how will I know? How can I tell when I've got it, when I'm filled with the Holy Spirit? . . . I don't think we will know. I don't think we'll even ask, or give it much thought. We won't say, 'I've got it!' or 'Ah, now I am like Christ,' or 'At last, I am godly.' That will never occur to us, because we will only seem to be more human."

He sat down, and one of the music teachers rose to lead the singing and close the service. Chapel was over. Or so they thought. Before the organ struck its first note, a student, a boy, stood up in the back and began to speak, his voice traveling faintly over the rustle of hymnals and people.

"I have a message for each and every one of you. I want you all to know that it is I standing in the way of revival at this school. The power of God has been blocked by unconfessed sin in my heart."

It was Clyde. He went on as students turned and strained to see him. "Satan has gotten ahold of me. I have become a platform for the work of the enemy. My thoughts have been vile and fleshly, and I have lost the power of prayer." He asked them all to forgive him for whatever damage he had done in their lives.

He left the auditorium, out the back way. In a second, two other boys got up and went out after him. The teacher at the microphone called for composure and led them in prayer. He committed "the heart of this troubled boy" to God's care and love. They sang.

Jo's insides turned to liquid. She was awash with revulsion at Clyde's words, and mortified that she had entertained similar thoughts. She stood with her head down during the hymn.

As the last syllables hung in the air and they turned to reach for their coats, someone else in the back of the room began to speak, another boy. Jo couldn't hear at all, but she caught the tone. It was another confession. Gradually, students sat down as he went on. ". . . without compassion," Jo heard. The boy's voice broke, and he stopped.

The room was completely still, one sharp hyphen of silence. Then with a stir, almost a rumble, dozens of students stood up everywhere and began to talk at once. They stopped, raggedly, then some started again, stopped, then one at the front and one at the back were both talking, not hearing the other. No one seemed to know what was happening. Jo felt unmoored, as if the ground they were on had broken away and was riding with the tide. More and more students were getting to their feet. Words poured out, unplanned, blurting, interrupting. They were saying things about self-righteousness and pride. The song leader used the microphone to get everyone's attention, and things became more orderly. They spoke one by one.

A girl said she had been going her own heedless way, unaware of people's true needs, and a boy said he had lost the love of Christ for souls and had forced the Gospel on them anyway; and another boy said he had been wearing the air of a spiritual person, but he had never learned to live for God alone.

When one stopped the next began immediately. It was hard to catch all the words. ". . . reproach on His name . . . unworthy of His love." They spoke softly or on the verge of tears.

Jo was still feeling distaste for what Clyde had done, and it was carrying over to the others. She felt critical of these students for publicizing their personal problems. She thought they ought to keep their private sins to themselves. Yet the room was packed, absolutely packed, with a power of some kind, that she wanted to be part of, wholeheartedly and without reservation. "And so I've . . . failed Him," someone was saying. More stood, more all the time.

The Dean had taken the microphone. "When He breaks us, He heals us," he said. Soup, two rows ahead, began to cry. Others were crying, too. But not Jo. Of all the times when she had fought tears at this school, she'd gladly feel like crying now, and there was nothing there. She was empty—vacated. Far across the room a boy prayed, his voice hitting the word "sin . . . sin."

Where was Karen? There were so many people standing it was hard to see across the room. Now Louise was speaking: ". . . wanting my own way, not willing to trust." Was everyone going to say something? Jo wondered. She felt conspicuous sitting while so many stood.

The surprise was gone now, and they were responding to one another's speeches without reticence. "Amen," they were saying, and "God bless you." There was no self-consciousness at all. They flowed into each other, while she sat like a sealed unit. She raised her head to see Pecky on the platform. What did he think of this? Surely he hadn't meant it to happen. But he was certainly not objecting. Every person in the place was in accord except herself. With all that was wrong with her, how could she be without the impetus to get to her feet? She was an outsider, an unbelonger, and she could see that unless you were part of what was going on here it was impossible to understand it.

"As I look into this stony heart of mine," said a boy, "if there's any sin I see above another, it's coldness. I resist this show of emotion."

Thank goodness, there was someone else. But he had *confessed* it. He cared enough to state it. "Your need is the door to His presence," a teacher said. She ought to be touched by that. She was, with her head. But all she *felt* was—she thought she would like a cup of coffee. It frightened her that she could think of coffee. So at least she was feeling fright. Not really, not as much as her head told her she ought to. Her buttocks were going to sleep.

Ruby was speaking. Oh not trooly, Ruby! She said it. "This is trooly a precious moment."

They were singing again. Someone had started it spontaneously. "Have Thine own way, Lord, have Thine own way. Thou art the Potter, I am the clay."

Bells rang, and no one left. Classes were forgotten. Jo stared at the notes she had taken of Pecky's talk, remembering the warmth and assent she had felt writing them. Now that was gone. There was just her silly handwriting with the round circles for dots and periods, a thing she had started when she was thirteen. " 'O Lord, thou hast searched me, and known me,' " someone quoted, " '. . . thou understandest my thought from afar off.' " Psalm 139. How could she not respond to that poetry? " 'Thou has beset me behind and before, and laid thine hand upon me. . . . Whither shall I go from thy spirit? Or whither shall I flee from thy presence? . . . if I make my bed in hell, behold, thou art there.' "

There were periods of silence now, sometimes broken by a song or a prayer. It didn't seem to matter much. Nothing could be wrong. A verse of Scripture from the right and a song from the left. "Help me the slow of heart to move, with some clear winning word of love," humming where they didn't know the words.

At noon the meeting was dismissed, but it was not over. They filed out slowly with snatches of songs rising here and there from different parts of the room. At lunch the singing went on at the tables. The mood was festive. Jo could see Karen and Beverly several tables away, singing as heartily as anyone. She did herself. It would have been impossible not to, and one thing she was sure of, no one must guess the true state of her heart.

All afternoon there were groups gathering on campus praying and talking. That night Louise and Beverly went to a prayer meeting on the third floor. They had invited Jo and Karen to go with them. Karen said, "What? Pray again? All that self-examination?" Was she serious? It was hard to tell. Louise laughed and said, "Coming, Jo?" and Jo went, thinking she might find the incentive to pray or talk. Instead she fell asleep in minutes, and when she awoke she slipped out the door while the others were on their knees. She learned in the morning that the meeting had lasted all night and that throughout the school there had been many prayer meetings and bull sessions.

Jewel said, "We'll see in a while how deep this is. His real work is slow and steady." She had not attended the dormitory meetings either.

"If it takes me through exams, I'll know it's real," Baldy joked, in the Pastry Shop that afternoon.

Because all at once the term was over. Finals were only three days away. Jo was as relieved as if vacation had already begun.

The noise level changed, not softer or louder, but different. People read as they stood in lines, and studied cards propped against saltshakers in the dining room. "Be sure to have the outline of the Pentateuch down pat and know the early names for God," Louise advised, standing on her head in the hall—to get the blood into her brain, she said. It was a tip from Charlie.

Lights-out was extended until midnight, when flashlights took over. Karen plugged away diligently, and Jo did her best, did well, in fact, glad to throw herself into this unquestionably necessary exercise. The breakdown of an outline absorbed her entirely. Roman numerals, A,B,C, uppercase, lower, 1,2,3, parentheses. She had never been so thorough. Her numbness, like the fear, slipped into the background, as if aspirined. If you took aspirin, was the headache still there unfelt? After exams she absolutely must get to the bottom of her trouble. Right now she had the names of God to deal with. El, Elah, Elohim, Jehovah. The Self-Existent One, self-revealing. Jehovah-Jireh, Jehovah-Rapha, Nissi, Shammah, Shalom. El. Strong One. "Names in O.T. very important," said her notes. "To know a name was to know the person." El Shaddai. Shadd meant breast. The name meant He-who-nurtures-me-like-a-woman. Two-sided truth again. For a moment something in that beckoned to her imagination. Then it was gone.

She went to her first exam wide awake. The objective questions were a cinch. She raced through them, pleased with herself. At the first essay she came to a dead stop. "In no more than two hundred words discuss Joseph as dreamer."

The question was not hard. She worked it out in her mind, but when she picked up her pen the first sentence had slipped away. She shut the blue book while she thought again. She doodled, filling all the hollow spaces in the mimeographed questions, the b's and d's and o's. She opened the blue book and stared at her penmanship. She was going to have to change it soon. It was from the same era in which she and Gloria had applied three coats of red polish to their stubby fingernails and chewed charcoal gum to make their teeth white.

They had written goofy poems for each other.

Gloria glows.
Her name keeps me warm
When the wind blows.

Jo's my favorite,
That's the truth,
I love her hair,
Her eyes,
Her tooth.

Gloria now had a baby, Mother had written a while back. She had met a soldier at the U.S.O. in Framingham and followed him to his post in San Antonio, Texas, where they were finally married. "She was in her seventh month before she left," said Mother. "The boy didn't want to get married."

Someone was writing on the blackboard next door, like sleet against a window. There was ice on the lower edges of the windows, and there was a new itching along the edges of Jo's throat. In a few minutes she took her blue book to the front of the room and left, the exam more than half uncompleted.

That afternoon she and Karen drew the curtains and slept, then studied again until 3:00 A.M., this time for Doctrine.

In three days everyone was silly. Soup's mouth was never still. At night she bartered her way into the room with crackers and peanut butter and scattered crumbs on Jo's bed. She muttered meaningless things into her books. "Hey nonnynonny and a ha-cha-cha." Whatever time they went to bed, Soup was up early, gargling at the sinks—"Aa-ee-eye-oh-you"—her movement of the vowels, Louise called it.

One afternoon she began to sing loudly in the kitchen.

I've got the joy,
Joy, joy, joy
Down in my heart!
WHERE?
Down in my heart!
WHERE?
Down in my heart! . . .

She shouted her way through all four stanzas. I've got the love of Jesus, love of Jesus. I've got the peace that passes understanding. She was joined on the last stanza by Beverly and Louise.

And if the devil
Doesn't like it
He can sit on a tack!

They were off into half a dozen Sunday school choruses, three-part harmony, adding flourishes and frills.

I may never march
In the infantry,
Ride in the cavalry,
Shoot the artillery,
I may never zoom over Germany,
But I'm in the Lord's arm*ee!*

They were marching out there, stamping their feet and shooting and zooming. Jo opened the door, and all three saluted her. Jewel's door opened, and they marched down the hall to their rooms. "Off we go, into the wild blue yonder!" sang Soup.

She sang that the rest of the afternoon and evening, hummed it, thrummed it like a Jew's harp, hissed it through her little teeth. Early that night she was an uninvited guest in their room again, eating candy bars and rattling paper. "Doopy-doop," she sang softly to the same tune, "doopity-doo-doo-doo-doo!"

"Oh, Soup, spare us!" Jo cried.

Even Karen said, "Heela teeden!" But it was Jo Soup answered. "Okay, I thought it was a nice song. It ought to be one of your favorites, I would think."

Jo turned back to her notes. She knew Soup would not let the subject drop.

"Isn't it?" she asked from the bed. "G.I. Jo? Isn't that a favorite of yours? With a brother in the Army Air Corps?"

Jo didn't answer.

"Heard from him lately? Hmmm? How is he?"

"My brother is fine."

Soup let a moment go by, then started in again. "Know what I say? I say you haven't got a brother at all. I say that boy in the picture there, that charmer, is your—uh—secret lover. That's it. You can't fool the Campbell kid." She laughed and went on babbling happily. "Jo has a secret lover. Lover-dover. . . . Ignoring me, aren't you? Really angry? Hmmm? Seething? Victorious Christians don't get angry, Jo, you know. This ought to ride right over you, never touch you. . . . Or didn't you get the second blessing yet? I haven't seen you crying, so maybe not. Don't you know tears are a sign God has touched your heart? 'A broken and contrite heart, O God, Thou wilt not despise.' When you get the second blessing, you either cry or speak in tongues. Speaking in tongues is out around here. We don't do it at Calvary because, because—oh, yes, God speaks to us in this dispensation through His Word instead. Did I get that right? Hmmm. No need to get too noisy, lose control. We don't like spectacularism, the noisy kind. So we cry. Softly. Not boo-hoo. I haven't seen you cry, Jo, I haven't seen you cry, Swede."

"Swedes are reserved, Soup," said Karen evenly. "We hold it all in. Didn't you know that?"

"Oh? What are you hiding, Eckstrom?"

"All sorts of evil secrets."

"See, Karen doesn't get mad," Soup said to Jo. "You should learn not to get so angry, Shrimp. You're touchy lately."

"A few of us around here have to study, Soup," said Karen.

"Oh . . . . That's a hint, isn't it? I know a hint when I hear one. Okay, study, study. 'Knowledge puffeth up,' says Paul. Right, Jo, old sock, old kid, old shoe? . . . Jo, I am speaking to you!"

In half a second she had tipped back Jo's chair, pulled her off it, and slung her over her shoulder. She whirled around the room.

Jo beat her on the back. "Cut it out, Soup! Put me down. I don't like to be carried!"

She saw her own face in the mirror, upside down. It was very red, and her hair hung in a tangle. She grabbed a handful of Soup's flesh just above the waist and squeezed hard. She knew it hurt her. Soup lowered her onto the bed, pretending not to mind. "Oh, ruffled feathers, little one," Soup said, and left the room almost immediately, her face turned away.

In a little while Jo took her towel and soap dish, as if to go to the bathroom, and headed for Soup's room. She had just had a huge revelation, possibly the key to whatever was wrong with her. It was time to get things straightened out with Soup.

"I'm sorry, Jo," Soup said, as she let her in. "I was awful. I was just coming to tell you. I crack up during exams." She was wiping her eyes. "We weren't very Christlike, were we?"

"It's my fault," said Jo. "The whole problem is . . . I've never liked you the way I should, Soup."

"Oh." Soup's eyes were startled, then hurt. "Well, Shrimp, is this a confession?"

"I'm sorry about it. That's the whole point. I came to tell you that."

"Okay, okay. I'm naive. I thought you did like me. I thought we were friends." Soup pulled toilet paper off a roll by her bed and blew her nose. "Have you said everything?" she asked, coldly now.

"What do you mean?" asked Jo. Things were not turning out as she had thought they might. She had expected Soup to be more forgiving and glad it was out in the open. The whole idea had been to throw light into this shadowy corner, expose it, and start again.

"I know what you meant to do," said Soup. "Make sure there's nothing standing between you and the Lord, right?" She was lurching around the room. "What's the matter with us?" she asked. "We're supposed to go by the New Testament and we don't. They washed feet in the New Testament. They greeted each other with a kiss. Christ touched people, do you realize that?"

What was she getting at? "Soup—."

"Well, what are you standing there for? Do you want me to pray with you about getting Christian love for me?"

"Soup, don't. I just thought it was right to tell you. I made a mistake, I think. I've been trying to sort things out, and I'm not doing very well at it."

"Have you gotten everything off your chest—or off your heart, as we put it here? . . . Are you sure? Because I've been called up to the Superintendent's office. Yes, in the middle of the revival, mind you, there were some complaints about me."

She began to pick up her room, diving here and there. She slapped books together on the desk and snatched clothes off the floor. Jo had never seen her in this spirit. She watched her ball up a skirt and throw it hard into the closet. "It seems there's been some question about my sexual tendencies. You know, do I like little girls better than little boys. I was told—." She stopped and buried her face in a sweater.

"I don't know anything about that, Soup."

"It wasn't you then."

"Absolutely not."

"All right. Then it wasn't anybody on this floor. Except maybe—. Oh, forget it. It's just . . . I mean, Jo, *me*, of all people. Doesn't everybody know about me? I'm so normal it hurts! I'd give my right foot for the right guy—and my left foot for the left guy . . . Oh, not funny. Name any part of this gorgeous body, you can have it. Oops! No, not you. . . . My trouble *is*, I want a *man*. . . . Don't you? Tell the truth."

"Of course, someday."

"Sure, sure. In the Lord's good time, huh?" Soup was dusting her bureau with the sweater. She sprayed Brilliantine on the bureau and rubbed over it as if it were furniture oil. Jo stood by the desk and watched her. She felt wretched. She wanted to crawl out the door.

"I'm not a patient person, Shrimp. I'm not like Ruth and others around her. I can't go tooting off cheerfully to the foreign field alone. Oh, I'll go. I'll do it, don't worry. Won't I do anything for Him? He knows it's true. But not so victoriously."

"Maybe in Mexico—." Jo stopped and shrugged, sorry she had started it.

Soup picked it up instantly. "Down there in Mexico some guy won't care what I look like, right? Forget it. You can't marry the natives. Mission boards don't like that at all."

She shook out a blanket with a snap. "Most of the time I don't like myself, and I intend to improve with the Lord's help, but I want to say, I see kids around here who are concerned about themselves. I mean, they are very careless about regular devotions, and they sleep in the back pews during chapel, and they are stuck on themselves and sometimes catty. But God blesses them too. There's the sticker. And He *uses* them. They even win souls. How about that? And I tell you what I think. I think God doesn't just love us in *spite* of ourselves, I think He loves us *for* ourselves, and I don't care if that's not good theology!"

Soup had just made her bed. "My stars!" she cried. "I just made my bed!"

"Soup, I'm awfully—."

"No, Jo, listen. You know what He told His thick-headed disciples." She came over to the desk and wrote in the dust with her finger: "70 x 7."

Jo shook her head, puzzled.

" 'Lord, how many times shall I forgive my brother?' they asked Him. I mean, it isn't even a question."

"I didn't realize it would hurt you. That wasn't what I meant to do."

"Who's hurt? It feels good to rant and rave once in a while, that's all. And besides, my hemorrhoids have been kicking up."

Jo went to the door. She paused there, thinking she might say, "Soup . . . about my brother." But she didn't.

"You ought to come more often," said Soup. "I'd get my room really clean."

Harold Hall was closed for the Christmas holidays. Jo and Jewel, who was also staying at school, moved into the women's quarters in Van Housen. Karen's father would come to pick them up on Christmas morning to spend the day at Oak Park. Ruth and Ruby went home, and Soup and Beverly went to Long Island with Louise.

The rooms in Van Housen were neat, buff-colored rectangles. Jo was assigned to the third floor, the room of a December graduate. Everything was new, the slick bathrooms down the hall with your pick of tub or shower, and the easy access to the dining room. Jewel was several doors away. She had a job in one of the business offices. About fifty students were remaining at the school during the two-week vacation.

Jo's first job was to empty and wash every salt and pepper shaker and sugar bowl in the dining room, then refill them and return them to the tables. There were two hundred of each. She collected them on trays, which she stacked at one of the big steel sinks. First she buried them in warm sudsy water, then a scalding rinse, and turned them upside down to dry in racks. The hot water made her feel peaceful and her hands got very clean.

The plan was that at 2:00 each day she would work on her overdue papers. She hated to leave the brightness of the kitchen. Upstairs her floor was deserted for the day, except for two sisters who kept to themselves. They did everything together. They each had a double name: Esther-Fay and Carol-Sue. They each wore a Sunday school perfect-attendance pin on their jacket lapels, the bars for each year hanging in clusters like a military decoration. Jo had the feeling the floor belonged to them and she was trespassing.

The library was a better place to be. She worked hard there for an hour or so on an Ethics paper, gathering material. She already had too much. The required length of the paper was five pages. She had enough for twenty and had only nicked the subject. Her title was "Hell and Its Relation to the Problem of Evil." She had known from the start the topic was too broad, but whenever she tried to narrow it down it seemed to get more complicated. Was hell an evil? It could hardly be called a good. If God, as First Cause, had created everything, wasn't He responsible for hell? Even now, empty of feeling as she was, she was anxious about it. "If in our own love we could not send our worst enemies to an eternity in hell, then . . . ." Then what? Grace without judgment was meaningless, she had heard. But Christ bore the judgment. But if an individual could not *accept* that fact . . . .

By 4:30 she was too sleepy to work, and the voice of the student librarian needled her. He was trying to whisper over there at the desk, and it didn't work. His voice chirped all afternoon.

She shut her books and went for a walk before dinner. The snow had become ugly. Remnants of it along the curbing were black right to the bottom. She broke open a clump with her heel to see. The late low sun was blinding and provided no warmth.

At night she kept the light on and Karen's radio tuned low to an all-night station playing popular music. Once she heard a dance band at Glen Island Casino, and once at Frank Dailey's Meadowbrook. Loring had listened to these programs sometimes. Music and voices kept her from falling deeply asleep, where the dream waited. At 6:00 A.M. the news roused her. The fighting in Belgium was bitter. U.S. forces were staggering under the "German winter offensive." The weather was terrible—fog, snow, mud.

On the second day, Jo saw Clyde in the dining room. She hadn't known he was here. She had seen almost nothing of him since his speech in chapel, and she was not glad to see him now. His face was larger, she thought. Or maybe he had gotten a haircut.

As she opened her books in the library later, he walked in and dropped a piece of yellow notepaper in front of her: "You have lost the joy, haven't you. Ichabod! I can tell by your face."

That evening Jewel said, "You look tired, Jo. You look all played out." They were talking in Jewel's room.

"I must do something about my face," said Jo. Then she asked what Ichabod meant. "The glory of the Lord has departed," said Jewel. "Why do you want to know that?"

So Jo told her about the emptiness. Just that part. Jewel was unalarmed. "You're in good company," she said. "I've seen that in just about every biography I've read of Christian leaders. Hang on. When we're faithless, He abideth faithful."

"But I don't want to be faithless. I feel like a washout."

"I know. But sometimes He hides His face in order to show us that we have nothing worthwhile in ourselves." She'd had to wait ten years, Jewel said, before she was able to come to school. "When I was younger there was this woman who used to come around to the hollers on a mule. She was a preacher, a 'good talkin' woman,' our people said. I knew I had to learn to teach like that, and when I was eighteen I was ready to come to Bible School right then. But first my mama got sick and then my daddy. My mama had low blood. She just faded away. My daddy had arthritis and heart trouble. I stayed and tended them and buried them both before the Lord let me come to school."

Scoo-el. It was a nice word in Jewel's voice. Her accent came and went, the way it always did, as if she could not quite control it. She wore an upper bridge fastened on with little wires and she still wore her cotton housedresses, even in this weather. But those were not unattractive qualities. If she came riding to your house on a mule, you would let her in and listen to what she had to say.

"At first I thought I'd die with impatience. Talk about low periods. I did a terrible thing once. My daddy was hanging on and on, and I had to do everything for him, even clean his hind parts, and one day I went into the woods where nobody could hear me and I yelled, 'Why don't you die, you old coot? Why don't you die?' Then I went back and saw how he was suffering. I was very good at feeling sorry for myself, and the Lord fixed it so every time I felt bad for myself I had to think about those old folk. In a while it didn't matter any more where I was. A whole world was turning inside me, and every day was a kind of adventure."

Jo felt honored that Jewel would tell her this. She had never heard her talk about herself before. "I don't want to be crude, Jo," she went on, "but I learned to clean up my Daddy's hind parts for Jesus. Does that sound absolutely cracked? I think it's in the bathroom parts of our lives that we test His love the most." She stopped and studied Jo for a moment. "Oh, Jo, you look so forlorn. Give Him the problem. Just pick it up and give it to Him."

"I have. Many times. It's like giving a hole in the ground to the sky."

"So? He can make something out of nothing. He's done it before."

Jo laughed. She felt better in Jewel's presence. But back in her room nothing had changed. She turned on the radio for company and got war news again. Onrushing enemy columns . . . spearheads unchecked. Germany claimed to have taken 25,000 prisoners.

The day before Christmas there was a package from home and a card from Yooney. The card had ten dollars in it. "Don't do anything I wouldn't do. Ha! Love from Looney Yooney." Good old Yooney. Her handwriting was vague, as if she could not take seriously this business of writing with the wrong hand and meant to switch soon. In the package were flannel pajamas, bath powder, and a green pullover and skirt to match. Jo went to the phone immediately and placed a person-to-person call to her parents at Cannons' number. The circuits were busy. Of course. Every serviceman in the country must be calling home. She tried again that evening and received a return call in half an hour.

It was a casual chat, first with Daddy, who said nothing about his letter. He talked about an air raid practice the night before. He was a warden. Mother said, "You've got a cold, haven't you?"

"It's nothing," said Jo. She told them she missed them. It was all she dared to say. None of them said anything about Loring.

She could hear Mrs. Cannon talking in the background. "She wants to know if Gary has called you yet from Great Lakes Naval Station," said Mother. Jo said, "Tell her no. Why should he?"

He phoned that evening in the middle of a carol sing around the lounge tree. Someone handed Jo a slip of paper from the switchboard: "Call operator 64." She knew it was Gary because when the operator told him how much to put in the slot, he said, "Holy Moses." She heard the change go in, then the operator said, "Go ahead," and he said, "Thanks, baby."

"Hello?" said Jo, her voice failing.

"Is that really you?" he asked.

"It's me," said Jo.

"Speak up! It doesn't sound like you."

"I have a cold," Jo said, making her voice as croaky as possible. "How are you?" She didn't know what to say to him. Surely Mrs. Cannon put him up to this. She wished she hadn't.

"I'm fine. What are you doing at a Bible School anyway?" His voice had the same old buzz, a Mack truck in first gear, Loring used to say.

"Getting an education," Jo answered. "Couldn't you get home either?" She hoped there would be no dead spots in the conversation.

"Somebody has to stay here and run this place," he said. "They're tightening up on everything lately, with all that business in Belgium."

"Oh, really?" She had to do better than that.

"They did agree to give me liberty tomorrow. I thought we might spend part of Christmas together. Can I meet you?"

"Oh." Now she knew Mrs. Cannon was behind it. She was a schemer.

"Well, I have plans to go to my roommate's house. She lives in Oak Park."

"I see. . . . Too bad. I should have called before."

It was not really Karen's house that stood in the way. It was fright and Mrs. Cannon.

"To tell you the truth," Gary went on in his funny truck voice, "I was really scared to call you. That's why I put it off."

"Why were you scared?"

"It's been a long time. You may have grown up."

"Of course I haven't. That's silly. Listen, I can change those plans. When would you like to meet?"

"Don't do that."

"It's perfectly all right. I can go there again sometime. It's not far away. They'll understand." Maybe.

So they made arrangements. He would have to catch a train around 4:00 to report back on duty, so he would arrive at 11:00 and they could go to dinner. When Jo hung up, she left a sweaty handprint on the telephone.

Other students went caroling through the neighborhood, then had popcorn and cocoa in the dining room. Jo didn't join them. She had a million things to do. Her coat needed to be pressed, and her suede pumps would have to be brushed, and her fingernails were a mess. She did the hardest thing first. She called Karen.

"But why didn't you say for him to come here with you?" Karen asked. "You know he'd have been welcome." In fact, she went on to add, they were having two or three other servicemen for dinner. Everybody in the world was having servicemen for dinner, didn't Jo know that? She sounded almost exasperated. "You should see the food in this house," she said, "and Mormor will be disappointed. She wanted to feed you."

"I'm really sorry," Jo said.

"You could still change your mind and bring him."

Jo tried to picture that—herself and Gary, Karen and her family, Jewel, the other servicemen, all together. The combination of people and factors were utterly impossible, a fantastic mix of past and present. She said no and apologized again.

Jewel had to have an explanation too. Jo wrote her a note and left it in her room, then washed her hair and soaked in the tub. She could wear the new clothes from home. She steamed her nose with a hot washcloth and applied a thick layer of Vaseline on her red moustache. The green skirt was too long. She turned up the hem. When she had finished everything and went to bed, her heart was racing. Gary had never seen her at any time except in the woods with Loring, in the summer. How would she seem to him in the winter, in the city, bundled in clothing and alone?

He would be twenty-two now. The only picture she could get of him was in cut-off dungarees, climbing a tree. He and Loring had called themselves the "Bloomer Girls" that summer. They talked with sibilance the whole two months and posed mincingly for her camera with their hairy legs.

"What's our fetish this year, chum?" Gary always asked Loring, on arrival.

There was the summer of the dirty-word collection. Their whispers and guffaws were maddening. "Oh, that one is corking!" Gary would chortle, imitating Mrs. Cannon.

"Tell me!" begged Jo.

"Never mind. You're just a little girl."

"I know more than you think." She knew nothing.

They set up boys' quarters in the tent or the tree house. She invaded their territory, forced her way in and got the worst of things. A warm milk fight, milking Cannons' cows. She went home sticky and stiff from her hair to her shoes. They squirted it right from the cows' teats.

They made rules. She could stay with them if she kept a measured distance of six feet. She accepted that. Whatever they did was exciting. They sat in the pasture and made squawking noises blowing grass between their hands. The cows moved painfully around them in the late afternoon, dragging their swollen bags, like Mrs. Legue, Jo's fourth-grade teacher, who carried her huge breasts as if they were sore and she might bump them. Once, in a troublesome spirit, they stuck green apples on switches and flung the apples at the herd. The cows stampeded out across the field, their sides heaving and their full bags swinging, a dozen Mrs. Legues on the run. Mr. Cannon scolded them, his own voice lowing like a cow's.

Sometimes the three of them went to a matinee in Framingham. The boys refused to let Jo sit with them, and when it was over they left the theater ahead of her. She rushed out, blinking in the pale real world, to find them gone. They would leap at her with bloodcurdling yells from a doorway or an alley.

Jo was up at daylight on Christmas morning. She was sure she had not slept, but it didn't matter. The Vaseline had improved the nose situation, and after ten minutes of brushing, her hair sprang off the brush into soft curls around her neck. She studied her eyebrows, wondering if she ought to pluck them, and decided not to. Gary wouldn't know her without these eyebrows.

Eggs and sausages and muffins were served at breakfast, while Christmas music played over the PA system. Jo ate very little. She finished her coffee, then went back upstairs to fool with her hair some more. Loring had once sent her a silver chain with the Army Air Corps insignia hanging from it under a little bubble of glass. It looked nice against the green sweater.

At ten minutes before 11:00 she entered the lounge, already in her coat, and sat by the tree, then moved to a chair in a nondescript corner. Three boys played chopsticks on the piano, turning it into a concerto. It sounded marvelous, but the noise made her nervous. She didn't know when she had ever been so jumpy. Her hands were pressed together tight, and her jaw was set so hard it hurt. She would never be able to rise from the chair.

Someone down the hall said, "Right in there. That's the lounge." A buzzy male voice answered, "Thanks," and Jo was out in the hall, running to meet his outstretched hands. He was much taller than she remembered him. He picked her up and spun her around until one of her pumps flew off.

"God, you've shrunk," he said. "And you've got more freckles."

"I see your nose has grown," she answered. His face was older and thinner. She wanted to stare at him.

He put his head down and sniffed her hair. "Ahhh—just as I thought. New England!"

"That's Breck Shampoo," said Jo. He laughed as if it were really funny. She remembered that about him now. She had forgotten how good he could make you feel.

"This is a pretty nice place," he said. He seemed surprised.

"Want a tour?"

It was a strange reality, to walk the corridors of C.B.I. with Gary, up the stairs where she had sat in the shadows with Clyde. Was this happening? She kept glancing at him. He had taken off his pea jacket. He looked trim and hipless. She wanted to tell him how great he looked, but she had never said that to a boy before. Instead she said, "Look at you in your uniform." Blouse to mid-hip, T-shirt showing just a little at the neck, dark silk neckerchief tied in a square knot the way they used to do their Scout ties. A cluster of lightning streaks was sewn to his sleeve.

"What does that mean?" she asked.

"Radio," he said, and shrugged. His mouth turned down at the corners, not sulky, but as if he were deliberately trying not to laugh. If he let it go, it would spring up. She had always liked his mouth.

Much of the campus was locked. Through the windows of doors they saw blackboards, scrubbed clean, the circles and arrows and bits of Scripture gone.

"It's really a school," he said.

"What did you think?"

"I don't know. A big church?"

The varnished tabletops shone faintly in the unlighted library. Outside they crossed the courtyard, and Jo pointed out the Music Building. She thought she saw Clyde's face at a second-story window. Then it was gone, a ghost. Gary was asking her something. What about her folks? What were they doing today? They were eating Christmas dinner at her aunt's with relatives from Maine, she told him, leading the way through the arch and down to the auditorium through the tunnel. Inside the auditorium he was impressed with the size.

"What's that big map at the back for?"

"Oh, that's to show where Calvary alumni are working." She didn't say mission field.

They paused at the corner of Putney Street to peer into the display windows of the bookstore.

"Is every book in there about God?" asked Gary. "What religion is this, anyway?"

"It's just plain Christianity," said Jo.

"You're really wrapped up in this, aren't you?" he said. "When did it start?"

"Two and a half years ago."

If he had asked her *how* it started she would not have avoided the question. Now, in the seconds that she paused, to go on seemed inappropriate. If he asked further, she'd answer him, she told herself. She didn't know much about what Gary thought. She supposed Mrs. Cannon had given him some fragments of information in the mail, sifted through her own views. Gary had never gone to church anywhere, Jo knew that much. "We're supposed to be Catholics, but we're not," he said once, several years ago.

"Do you like the Navy?" she asked him.

"It's been a pretty soft life, as wars go. Very dull sometimes. I can't complain."

He'd been in Virginia a year or so, at Newport News, and to sea four times, he told her. He had not seen any important action.

"But now I don't know. I expect they'll ship us out again soon."

They decided they were hungry enough to head for the restaurant. Gary had in mind a small place near the lake down below the Public Library. It was called Lakeview Something. Some guys had told him about it. Jo said that sounded good.

"What would you think of walking there?" he asked. "I've had this yen to walk along Lake Shore Drive. It's not exactly the weather for it, but I may not have another chance."

"Why not?" said Jo.

She tied on her kerchief, and they started. She hoped her nose would not run. It was very cold and cloudy, and the wind was brisk.

218

"If we walk fast enough we won't freeze," Gary said. The collar of his jacket was up. She was proud to be walking with him. She became aware of the sound of his step on the sidewalk. She had forgotten that too. Step, scuffle, step. He dragged the heel of his right foot ever so slightly. She had heard it millions of times—beside her, ahead, behind. She liked the way he moved, head forward, swinging a little from side to side, a dumb, funny walk. On the concrete her own quick heels and his clicked together, on the way to the lake, not Garfield Pond, but one of the biggest lakes in the world.

He caught her glancing at him.

"I can't believe this," she said, laughing.

Loring's step was missing from the orchestration. He walked with a little spring, up on his toes, his head alert, on guard. The three of them must have been a funny sight from behind—she bustling, trying to keep up, and they with their spring and scuffle.

They were talking about Chicago. Gary had been in a few times, mostly to movies. He didn't really like it. He preferred the East.

Once he turned to her and buzzed, "*Bible* School?" and gave her a push on the shoulder. "What do you do all day? Fast and take vows of silence?"

"Me? Not likely," Jo said.

It grew distinctly windier as they approached the lake, and as they crossed Lake Shore Drive it drove against them, almost stopped them in mid-street. The lake was gray and there was fog on the horizon, but its size was still apparent and Jo was astounded, though she said nothing. She didn't want Gary to guess she was seeing it for the first time. It was an ocean. Ice floes undulated within the breakwater. Further north, breakers three or four feet high beat against the frozen spume. Gary pointed out fragments of blue sky above them where the sun was a faint blurred circle behind the overcast. It was too cold to linger, so they headed south, bucking the wind. "Take my arm," said Gary.

In a few minutes the sun struck through, and they both said, "Oh!" The lake was beautiful. Everything was green, blue, white. White light reflected from the glass and concrete of the buildings on the other side of the street. It bounced off icicles and crusted snow, threw itself against the passing cars and fell back around them in broken arcs of color.

Gary started to sing, loudly, in his awful voice. "Deck the halls with boughs of holly!" he belted into the wind, fitting the rhythm to their steps. "Fa-la-la-la-la-la-la-la-la-la!" Jo joined him, croaky, as loud as she could. They sang and sang, first stanzas of every carol they could walk to, emptying their voices into the mixture of wind and sun. "Joyful, all ye nations ri-ise!"

"Merry Christmas!" Gary yelled across the street to a furred lady out with her dog. He waved his hat at her, and she waved back.

"Merry Christmas!" Jo shouted at a passing car. Then they were shouting and waving at all the cars. The cars tooted back. "Good King Whatsisname looks down!" sang Gary, pointing to the sky. They sang da-da-da where they didn't know the words. The wind swung around behind them. They were not really walking. They were held aloft by some marvelous compound of elements from off the lake.

In a while they were tired and much too cold. They left Lake Shore Drive and got onto Michigan Avenue, where the buildings protected them. "We'll get a bus," said Gary. But no bus came. Finally he hailed a taxi, and they arrived in a few minutes at the restaurant, to find it closed for the day.

"What a fiasco," Gary said. "I should have called them. I never thought about reservations or anything."

"I don't care," said Jo. They walked back across Michigan Avenue and found a tinsel-draped diner on a side street. "Let's go in there," she said. She ached with cold now.

It was a dreadful-looking place. Sections of its chrome siding had dropped off. Inside it was wonderfully warm and steamy and smelled of coffee. "Harry and Fern Welcomes You All," said a sign at the back of the counter. The walls were lined with mirrors. Jo caught a glimpse of her own face as she entered the door. Her cheeks were red. She liked the way she looked.

"Hi there," said the waitress. "Was Santa Claus good to you?"

There were no other customers. They had their choice of ten booths. They made a big thing of sitting where the view was best of a dirty gas station across the street.

There was another sign over the grill: "I'm not a fast cook. I'm not a slow cook. I'm a half-fast cook."

"What'll you have?" asked the waitress. Fern? She wore a mass of tiny ringlets across the top of her forehead.

"How's the war?" Gary asked her.

"I'm definitely losing," she said, and laughed hard.

Gary said, "Have you heard a newscast lately?"

"It was just on," she said. "We've stopped the offensive. That's what they said."

"Christ, it's about time," said Gary.

"Our planes did it."

"That's the stuff."

"But Glenn Miller is missing."

"No kidding!"

"Right. He was flying to Paris from London. Nobody knows yet what happened. Want to start with soup? We've got vegetable."

Turkey croquettes was the Christmas dinner special. They decided to take a chance on them. They weren't bad except that there was no turkey in them, and one of Jo's had a wad of paper in it. It looked like a folded-up note from Clyde. He will go to any length, she thought. That struck her funny, and she began to giggle. For a minute she couldn't stop. Her eyes ran and her breath came in noisy gasps. Gary thought she was only laughing at finding paper in her food. She knew he must think her reaction was extreme. But he laughed along with her, and in a minute, blowing her nose, she got control.

"I wonder where Glenn Miller is," she said, to prove she was all right.

Other than that they were quiet while they ate. Several men came in and sat at the counter. You could hear a radio going in the kitchen and

Fern singing along as she washed glasses. She wisecracked with the men. Jo and Gary grinned at each other. "Your nose is red," said Gary.

When they had finished eating he took out a package of Chesterfields and offered her one. It occurred to her then that he really didn't know much about her, or her him. No doubt he drank too, and picked up girls in bars. He was a stranger over there across the table. Then she put that out of her mind. He smiled at her as he smoked. Black hairs showed at his wrists below the blue cuff. "Tell me everything about yourself," he said. "I want to feel I've known you forever." It was Loring's old joke.

"Well," Jo answered slowly, "I swallowed a furry caterpillar when I was eight months old." Gary had heard that a hundred times. Mother was always telling it to somebody. It went along with "I don't think Jo is afraid of anything."

"I bet you were an awful pest," Gary said. He was playing with his napkin. He rolled it and stuck it in his ear, peered at her through it like a telescope, and made a moustache out of it.

"I bet you were an incorrigible show-off," Jo said. "I bet you still are."

"I can still sound like Vaughan Monroe if I stand on a chair," he said. Then he stood up on the bench and let it roll, his mouth wide open. " 'Racing with the moon'!"

"That's good!" Fern called from the kitchen.

"I can sound like Helen Forrest if I spread my arms," Jo said.

"Let's hear you."

"Not today. I have a cold."

"What a nuisance you are," said Gary, sitting down.

"Listen, who else would have thought you were so witty?" Jo answered.

She had never gotten tired of their awful repetition. "It's quite beyond my ken," Gary said all one summer. "Doan get bersonal," Loring answered.

"Boy, did I—." She stopped. She was going to say, "Boy, did I love you guys," but she decided against it.

Gary was smoking his napkin, a fat white cigar.

"How much do you know?" Jo asked suddenly.

It surprised him, she saw in his eyes. She surprised herself. She had been sure she would wait to see if he raised the subject himself, and if he didn't neither would she. Now she saw it was up to her and that he wanted to talk about it very much.

"Whatever my folks got from the Cannons they passed on to me," he said. "You must have seen the note I sent your folks in July. I'm not very good at that sort of thing. Then I heard there was a survivor who wrote to you. One of the gunners, right? They were over the Adriatic when the planes collided. What the hell caused that to happen?"

"Nobody's sure," Jo said. "The ball turret gunner—Alec Burke, that's his name—says their plane must have lost altitude or speed in formation. They were transferring gas just before, whatever that means."

"Did that cause it?"

"He said that was routine. He didn't know anything was wrong until he heard a crash and looked back and there was a hole where the tail gunner had been. The plane went into a spin, and there was another explosion." She was intrigued at the calmness with which she was telling this. "Burke was alone on a piece of metal when he came to. That's what the letter said—sailing through the air."

She had never been able to imagine it. Parts of the plane falling, crew members trapped inside or tumbling out. How would it have been, really? What happens when a plane blows up? Does it break apart? Loring would be in the nose over the bombardier in the tiny compartment he had written about, sitting at his chart table. "Got my own swivel chair and my own starboard window," he said. The nose would separate from the rest of the ship perhaps. Did he look out his little window and see what was happening, that he and his chart table were on their own, going down? If you could see it piece by piece, what would it be like?

"That guy must have had his chute on," Gary said. "The gunner."

"Yes, he did. He said he opened it and bailed out of the metal and landed in the water. His Mae West was full of holes, so he swam until an oxygen bottle floated to him, and he hung on to that. He wasn't hurt.

"Did he see anything?"

"A wing and one engine."

It was like a story she had rehearsed, all the sentences worked out.

"In a couple of hours they got him. A seaplane came. They towed him aboard with a rope because of the sharks. He said there were no other survivors."

Gary frowned. "Didn't that spotter plane rescue anybody else?"

"No."

"He was sure . . . no others?"

"He saw parts of bodies floating in the water." Her head said it, as simply as that. She was operating in two layers. The upper part talked and said anything that had to be said while the lower part, from the neck down, was shut off. The upper part could talk about parts of bodies, legs, arms, intestines, floating in the water. It was nothing.

She said to Gary, "If there was one survivor, why couldn't there be two?"

Gary was looking at her intently across the table.

"When someone is missing," he said, "what you want to do is go look for him."

"Yes," said Jo, "that's exactly right."

He reached for her hand and began to stroke the back of it with his fingers. Her head, that upper part of her, watched him.

"Once I was lost," she said, "when I was six years old. Not really lost. Mother didn't know where I was. I'd made a new friend in school that day, and I went to her house after school without going home first. I didn't think I'd stay long, you see. But Mother was worried, and she sent Loring to look for me. He must have looked a long time—an hour or two—because it was getting dark when I finally started home and saw him ahead of me on Prospect Road. He was walking slowly, with his head down. And like a ninny, I didn't know what was wrong and I sneaked up behind him and yelled 'Boo!' and he burst into tears."

She couldn't believe she was doing this. The story was flowing out of the upper part of her without a thought. Gary was listening, unembarrassed, as if telling stories was part of the day's schedule.

Jo went on. "He must have been very humiliated. He was nine then. And that evening he took me out behind the privy and said he was going to initiate me into his new club. Whatever he did, he said, I was not to cry or make a noise. Then he slapped me on the cheek—not too hard—and hugged me, just a little. Then he slapped me harder, and hugged me harder. He did it seven or eight times, one cheek, then the other. I don't think I even peeped, though it really hurt. I never questioned it. I just wanted to pass the test so he'd be proud of me. Only I remember I kept thinking how nice it would be if it were all one long hug. When we went inside, Mother wanted to know why my cheeks were so red, and I said I'd been pinching them to make a dimple. . . . I don't think Loring would mind if I told you about that."

"Of course not," said Gary. In a minute he said, "We talked about enlisting together once, did you know? But he didn't want the Navy. He said he wanted to fly, but your folks wanted him to finish school and go in as a medic. So he was going to do that. I've often wondered how come he decided to quit school and enlist."

"I guess he just changed his mind," said Jo. One story was enough. He was gone in his green car like the greenie croquet ball he had once shot into the woods. Holy Christ, my sister is a holy roller! He had never driven like that before, the car door slamming, tires screeching on the road. The next day he enlisted.

"I guess he just wanted to fly," she added. "After he got his wings, he still could have chosen ground work, but he didn't."

Gary nodded. He said, "Let's get some pie and coffee."

There were five kinds of pie, so they ordered one piece of each and split them in half. When they were through it was after 2:00.

"If there's time, let's walk back," Jo suggested. She felt like running. Her legs were restless and jumpy.

While Gary paid the bill, she slipped outside and hid in a doorway. He went several feet in the other direction before he came back and walked past her slowly, not looking. She leaped out at him with a yell, and he grabbed her hand and ran with her at full speed, until her shoe fell off.

"Stop! Stop!" she gasped. They had left the shoe half a block behind. Gary ran back to get it. The sun was still out, though weak and indifferent and westward already. The wind cut across them. It drew tears from their eyes and froze the insides of their nostrils.

"Keep moving!" yelled Gary. "Don't stand still!"

He leapfrogged a hydrant. Jo did it too. Her coat caught, and she wet her pants a little and wondered if they would freeze. They trotted backwards, skipped sideways, met the wind with their heads down, until they arrived finally at Van Housen Hall and leaned against the building a minute, red-faced and out of breath. To the north the sky was a pale winter amber. A squadron of planes flew against it, very high up, tiny, black, and silent.

"Would you like to come into the lounge and get warm?" asked Jo.

"No, I have only a minute or two. Let's stay out here," he said.

She was shivering hard. He pulled her into the archway out of the wind and unbuttoned his pea jacket and wrapped her up next to him inside it. Her head was buried against the scratchy sailor wool of his blouse. It was lovely and warm in there. I feel warm to him too, she thought, amazed that there was still heat in their bodies and they were sharing it. Someone walked by behind them. She didn't care. The whole world could go by. She slipped her arms around him and pressed her face against his chest. He smelled faintly of cigarettes and sweat. His dog tags made a hard lump under her cheek. She could hear his heart pounding.

"You must be feeling mine in the solar plexus," she said, smiling up at him. He laughed and bent his face down. That close, he had three eyes. "Jo . . . Jo," said Gary. He kissed her. They swayed together gently, locked in.

"I've always loved you," Jo whispered. "Did you know that?"

"Yes."

She wanted to touch him everywhere, all over, run her hands down the scratchy wool, touch the lightning on his sleeve, and down, down across his firm rump, and never, never let him go. She kissed him again. He moved as if to pull himself away. She held on.

226

He lifted his head. "Good-bye," he said. "Thanks for a wonderful Christmas."

She couldn't let go of him. The wool of his blouse was clenched in her hands. He reached behind and unclasped her fingers gently.

"I have to go, Jo. I'm sorry." He said he would try to write or call before shipping out.

"I hate this war," sighed Jo. "I hate this horrible, terrible war."

Jewel came back in the evening loaded down with goodies from Karen's house. "Smorgasbord," she said. "I've never had it before. There was never so much food in all this world."

There was a sample of everything for Jo. "I don't remember all the funny names," said Jewel, "but eat it before it goes bad."

Jo could hardly eat. She sampled the different kinds of fish, jellied veal, a tiny meatball. They held a conversation, she and Jewel. She heard herself talking, doing a convincing job of saying yes, I had a good time, and isn't that nice and imagine. She watched herself get ready for bed several hours later, pull up the blankets, and lie there all night with her eyes open. No real thinking, just a rehearsal, over the day, words, glances, touch. In the morning she would face whatever she had to.

She did her work in the kitchen and went to the library in the afternoon, where she sat for three hours and did nothing. She had expected to think today, but her mind was still swollen and tender.

"Have you heard the news?" several people asked her. There was talk everywhere of the war. Things were the worst ever. Allied losses in Europe were phenomenal. A Christmas Day battle, going on yesterday, even at the moment when they thought the news was good. The word "salient" hissed statically throughout a newscast at dinner. Jo had never heard the word before.

That evening she sat in her room and said, Think, think. What she thought of was the possibility of calling Gary on the telephone. To talk to him or be with him was the only reality that seemed imaginable to her. Anything else was unnatural and wrong. But she was sure that this was not the thing to do. He had not offered his phone number or suggested she call. It would be Jo the pesty kid tracking him down.

At 10:00 she was still sitting on her bed in the same position. She had not done one moment of controlled thinking. She slipped off her shoes and got into bed with her clothes on. Did she lie awake another whole night? Or did she dream she was awake? If she did, it was the only dream she had. The light was on. At some point she looked at the clock. It was 4:00 A.M. and it seemed as if only an hour had gone by. Hours later she looked at it again, and it was only 4:15.

At 7:00 Jo got out of bed in the same clothes and went to work. It was the middle of the morning before she realized she hadn't brushed her teeth or combed her hair. The radio in the kitchen crackled and buzzed. The war news was worse than ever.

With her hands in hot water, she was able to think at last. She had said that she loved him, but Gary had not said that to her. Was his affection an outgrowth of something else, old times, sorrow, or maybe even pity? Or a mixture of feelings too hard to separate, none of which added up to what she really wanted them to be? Who had done the kissing really? Had she made a terrible fool of herself?

Early in the afternoon she was in bed again, fighting. She imagined the phone call, how it would go, several versions. No, it was wrong. It was not really what she wanted. She wanted him to call *her*, or better, to come back. Just come, be in the corridor as she rounded the stairs from the dining room tonight, his hands held out. "I had to come, you understand?" he'd whisper.

"Oh, of course, of course I do," she'd murmur into his coat. "I knew you would. I always knew you'd come back!"

Oh Lord, she said, praying to the buff-colored rectangle of room, but praying anyway. Why can't it be? Send him back to me. Send him back, send him back.

Maybe she slept. A tap at the door sprang her from the bed. One of the twin sisters was there, in her blazer with the Sunday school medals. A young man was waiting to see Jo in the lounge, she said with a little smile.

"Oh!" said Jo. "Of course!" and realized how strange that must sound. "Oh yes . . . thank you. I'll go right down. Oh tell him. . . . Never mind. It's all right. I'll go right down. Okay? I mean thank you."

Oh God, it was happening. God, you've done it, you've done it. He's come back! Of course, of course. She'd known it all along, hadn't she? What was the matter with her? How could she have doubted this way all these weeks? Doubted ever, anything?

She flew down the stairs, shouting inwardly, "Oh, thank you, thank you, thank you!" and ran into the lounge. It was empty. She hesitated, glanced back out into the hall, then into the room again. "Is anyone here?" she asked.

Clyde stepped out from behind the Christmas tree. Her responses came in powerful overlapping waves. She turned to run.

"Wait!" he said. "I have to talk to you." He caught the sleeve of her blouse, pinching her skin. "I have to talk to you." His eyes were bloodshot, and his breath was bad. Jo pulled herself free and backed toward the door.

"Don't go," he begged.

"I can't talk," said Jo. The sentence seemed longer than she had air for.

"I'm in love with you," he blurted miserably.

"Oh, my gosh," said Jo. She shook her head. "You're not."

"Not?"

"You can't be. That's stupid."

"But I am, I know I am!"

"It's hogwash!" cried Jo. She was in the doorway, backing. "It's a stupid thing for you to think!"

He started toward her again, then stopped and looked wildly around the room, as if for a witness to her absurdity. He started to speak. Words knocked against his lips. "Do you think I *like* it? I want to be rid of you. . . . Wait, don't go!" He shut his eyes. Dry foam had gathered at the corners of his mouth like bits of cotton. "You be*long* to me. The Lord has shown me that!"

"You're crazy," said Jo.

He moved in closer to her, in the doorway. "You're defying God and you know it, don't you?" he said. "I'm giving you your last chance."

"Oh, get away from me!" whispered Jo, into his face. "I hope I never see you again! Ever! Not ever! Do you hear? . . . Do you understand?"

His posture altered. One shoulder dropped down and his head pitched to the side. His nostrils went pink and dilated. She ran for the stairs, her knees slipping and buckling.

"We are losing this war!" Clyde shouted after her. His voice broke. "In case you don't know! . . . Can you live with that fact for the rest of your life?"

Jewel was not in her room. Jo called her name down the hall, then raced for the business offices. No one knew where she had gone. She was not working today. For half an hour Jo searched, asking everywhere. A girl said she had seen her going into Harold Hall.

She was there, scrubbing her room, all alone in the unheated building. Her furniture was out in the kitchen; somehow she had dragged it there. She was on the floor washing the woodwork. Her hair was in a long braid. She did not seem particularly pleased to see Jo. "Oh, hey there," she said without a smile, and returned to her work. Jo watched a minute, uncertain, then turned away.

Jewel said, "You got a worry?"

"It's all right."

"What's wrong?"

"I guess I ought not to bother you."

"Are you in love?"

"What?" Love or hate? I have declared my love and spit out my hate. She couldn't form a reply.

"Is it the sailor, Jo?"

"Bad things are happening."

Jewel dipped her rag in the bucket and wrung it out. "Is he a Christian?"

"We didn't talk about it."

"Ah."

"We were together for four hours, and we never discussed it."

"It never came up?"

"Oh, it did, in a way. It could have. He'd have talked about it quite willingly, I think."

"But chances are he'd have brought it up himself if he were a Christian too," said Jewel, inching her way along on her knees. "My goodness, he comes to see you at Cal and he has *some* idea how you feel."

"The point is, *I* didn't say anything. Don't you see? It was me. I didn't want to talk about it. I don't care if he's a Christian or not."

"Oh, la," said Jewel into the bucket. "That's the issue. I see.... How do you feel about that now?"

"Rotten."

Jewel got to her feet, both hands down flat first, the good foot on the floor, then the bad one. "Well, you've prayed about it, of course."

"I knew you'd ask that! . . . No! Not really. I don't want to pray about it, if you want the truth."

"Well, don't get snappy. *You* came to *me*."

"I wish I hadn't." She hated this image of herself, running to someone for help. "I shouldn't be bothering you. . . . Can we forget it? I'll just leave."

"You seem to make everything so hard, Jo."

Jo walked out into the kitchen and leaned on Jewel's dresser. There was a hairbrush on top of it and two elastic bands with brown hairs caught in them. In the edge of the mirror a card said, "How beautiful upon the mountains are the feet of him that brings good tidings."

"I can't tell you what to do," said Jewel, coming from her room. "No one can, except the Lord, and for some reason you can't ask Him. Maybe your love for this sailor is filling a vacuum."

"Don't call him 'this sailor,' please."

Jewel sat on the bed in the middle of the kitchen. She was rubbing both knees.

Jo said, "I have to make a decision. It can't go on like this."

"If you're really asking me, I think you've got some pretty clear signs. You're unhappy about it. You've got no peace. You don't want to pray. Could you say this boy has driven you any closer to Christ? Where does the Lord fit into all this?"

Jo turned her back on Jewel and walked to the sinks. The old prayer request list was still hanging there, spotted by water. The prayers that had been answered were checked. Ruth's brother, a "nominal Christian," had given his life to Christ. Beverly's money for pipe organ lessons had come through. Louise had been admitted to the home of one of her street children. "Soup's prostitute," one request read. Not checked. "Jo's family." Not checked.

"Maybe it would help to study on it," said Jewel. "Just suppose you and this young man are really in love. You'd marry. What would it mean? What about the Lord's work? What about being unequally yoked? Have you thought it through?"

Jo had no desire to cooperate with Jewel. Her questions seemed irrelevant. In spite of that, the kitchen became the kitchen of a real house. There were children in the yard, and Gary would be home for dinner. A neighbor was at the table, over there where Jewel sat, having a cup of coffee.

Something was badly wrong with the picture. Despair hung in the corners of this room. It was not the children or Gary or the neighbor, not particularly, nor the potatoes Jo was peeling at the sink with quick tiny motions like her mother's. It was what she, Jo, was telling the neighbor— that she had planned to go to the mission field once, believe it or not, and oh yes (a little laugh) she had even started Bible School. How about that?

"Well, Jo, I'm sure you were very sincere," said the neighbor. "But you got over it. Thank goodness."

Over it? Jo could see who it was now.

"I didn't think you'd stick it out," said Gloria. "It was just a phase, a stage in your adolescence. Right?"

Jo shook her head, appalled at such an easy conclusion.

"You were defying your parents. That's natural." She was not Gloria. She was Mrs. Cannon.

"That isn't true," answered Jo. "It was much more than that."

"A dream. We all give up a dream or two along the way," said Mrs. Gloria Cannon.

"A dream!" Jo protested. "You can't just reduce it like that." She was overwhelmed with the need to make the correction.

"Your intelligence won the day," said the neighbor. She set down her cup and got up briskly. She was sure she had it all figured out, and she knew nothing.

"There's a poem I learned once," Jewel was saying. "If I remember it right . . . 'God has His best things for the few who dare to stand the test. He has His second best for those who spurn the best.' "

Jo gave her a nod. She moved toward her own room.

"Wait a minute, Jo."

"Yes?"

"Don't be hasty. Wait on Him. I don't know how to say this. I . . . sense something about you. You fight too hard maybe. It's in your walk—Oh, I don't know. Everything has to be so all or nothing. Sometimes you remind me of Clyde MacQuade."

Jo was stunned. "How can you say a thing like that?"

"Never mind, Jo. Maybe I'm wrong. I'm sorry."

Jo entered her room and shut the door firmly. The room was strange and cold. She put on her desk light and found a sheet of stationery. She understood exactly what had to be done.

> Dear Gary: This may turn out to be the most puzzling letter you ever get. My life belongs to Christ. That means more to me than anything in the world. How I feel about you is damaging that commitment, so I must cut it off right now. Our true relationship is in the past—a lovely memory and that's all. Keep me in your mind, now and in the future, as your pesty little sister.
>
> Jo.

She sealed the envelope and stamped it. Gary's address was on the back of her father's letter where her mother had written it in October. She had torn it up. Where had she put the pieces? She had taken them out of her pocket and put them in the desk drawer at some point. She pawed through the drawer and finally, exasperated, pulled out the whole drawer and dumped its contents on the end of the bed. The torn pieces of paper were all mixed in with the pencils and paper clips and returned quizzes and Clyde's notes. There was the Zipper's tract with the dark scrawl in the margin—"fuck you holy daughter of God." She had not thought of it in a long time. The insult of it came to her freshly, and his eyes outside the glass door, so close and so far.

She put the scraps of address together and copied it onto the envelope. She hesitated. Should she write to Clyde too? "I didn't mean to be cruel . . . ." But what would he make out of that? What good would it do? She left the room and without speaking further to Jewel, who was still on the bed in the kitchen, went out and dropped the letter to Gary in a mailbox. It was the hardest thing she had yet done in her life, and she felt no better at all.

At the door to Van Housen she stopped and went back to Harold Hall. Jewel was right where she had left her.

"I'm going to scrub my room," said Jo.

Jewel smiled. "I'm glad you came back. I thought you would. I ought to explain to you why I was . . . I haven't been doing so well myself, Jo. I had a disappointment just before Christmas. Can I tell you? I got turned down by an Appalachian home mission board. The one I wanted. . . . Oh, it's the Lord closing one door, that's all. It's no big thing. But the *reason* they gave—they said I couldn't live the rough life of a rural missionary with this leg. They know I grew up there. I walked those hills. It's so silly. I'm no weakling. And they think I can't take it?"

"It's a mistake," said Jo. "Why would they give up on you so easily?"

"They have enough failures, they said, with normal applicants. They used that word. Look, I know how you feel right now, but do you think . . . . Could you see your way clear to pray with me about this?"

Jo recoiled at the request. This was not what she wanted to do. Not at all. She couldn't, in fact, not possibly—but she saw she must try, pretend, for Jewel's sake.

They knelt by Jewel's bed in the kitchen. Jewel prayed first, slipping into hill tones. "Lord, I am tired of this leg and all the fretting it has caused me. Lord, I want to either get shed of it, or I want power over its bondage. Oh Lord, it's time for something to be done about this. Once and for all, Lord, once and for all!"

She stopped. For what seemed a very long time she said nothing more, and Jo had just decided she was through and was gathering up the words that she herself would be expected to say, when Jewel exclaimed, "Oh, my lands, I've got it backside to!"

Jo opened her eyes to see what she meant—her dress, or even her leg. Jewel's eyes were closed. She was still praying.

"Lord, I have got this dumb leg. I know it's not going to get any better. No one is going to fix it, and it's going to trouble me every day of my life. But *You* gave it to me. You made it, and You must have known what You were doing. So if it's there, it's there. I can't be bothered making a stew about it any more. It's Your leg, and I give it back to You. It's Your worry from here on in. In Jesus' wonderful name! Amen."

For a moment Jo longed intensely for a crippled leg. So concrete, an undeniable and comprehensible problem, something specific to surrender to God. It seemed like such a simple answer to everything: Here, Lord, is my *leg*. If all problems could become so solid—if she herself could say, Here, Lord, is my *hand* which will not span an octave, here is my *ankle* which turns in the street, here is my *cold* that will not go away. Here, take my silly woolgathering *brain*—take my whole *body*, take it, for life or for death.

Not death.

She rejected that. She did not want to die. Under no circumstances. She was absolutely unwilling to die. This body insisted on life; it wanted to keep going, this clownlike machine, just as it was. She wanted *this* body to go on forever and ever. She counted it dear, all its fleshly members. Not heaven or the resurrection life. She was not willing to die, not for Christ nor anyone.

The recognition brought a flood of relief. Here it was at last, the area of surrender she had been missing all along. She had tried everything else and nothing had worked. Now here was the key to the whole problem. It was perfectly obvious. She had been holding out on God all this time, clinging to this clump of grass that was her earthly life.

There was only one way to deal with it, and it had to be done immediately. She was not sure whether she spoke out loud or not. Whatever, it was only a matter of seconds. She told God she would die for Him, if He wanted her to. Any time, any way. She abandoned herself, consciously and willfully, that instant, to death.

They stood, she and Jewel, and faced each other. Jewel was smiling, gently at first, then something inside her grew and grew like a big sunflower.

"He did it!" she cried. "It's all over!" She grabbed Jo and danced around the kitchen with her, between the furniture. Jo thought for a minute her leg had been straightened, but there it was, shooting out to the side as crooked as ever.

"I don't care, don't you see?" sang Jewel. "Not any more! I'm really free!"

She let out a whoop and leaped onto the bed and began to jump up and down like an overjoyed child, flying into the air, unmindful of her leg, while she shouted, "Praise God! Praise God! Praise God!"

Sorrow engulfed Jo. She began to cry, right there in front of Jewel, entirely unable to control it. Jewel, alarmed and unbelieving, seemed to stop jumping in mid-air. Her face froze into a kind of injury as she watched. "Jo . . . ," she whispered, "what can be the matter?"

Jo shook her head. She didn't want Jewel to touch her. It would be over in a minute. She made a gesture with her hand, backing into the hall, leaving Jewel there on the disheveled bed staring after her. She fled down the hall to the bathroom, bolted the door and splashed water on her face. The crying would not stop. It seemed to come in giant waves, starting at her feet and breaking against the back of her head.

She flushed the toilet to drown out the noise. Finally she opened the cold water tap in the tub with a rush and undressed and climbed in, only to discover as she sat down that she hadn't taken off her girdle and stockings. What was more, it was her oldest girdle, limp and gray, and the sight of the water rising steadily around her, over the garter she had sewn on with green thread, over the stretched-out elastic, the gray turning grayer as it got wet, flooded her with rage. She felt herself slipping under and reached for something to grab and hold. Christ stood above her in the River Jordan. She struggled for another image. Rock! Anchor! Lion! Lamb! She pictured Him on the cross. He was there. He was a man. He was dead.

An unspeakable assurance was filling the tub, as chilling as the water and with the same driving force. Jesus was dead. There was no Christ. No God, no Holy Spirit. Everything said it. The water said it. Her girdle said it. It echoed off the white porcelain. She began to bang her head against the edge of the tub to knock out the thought. The tub rang like a belabored bell.

Far in the background Jewel was calling and pounding on the door. "Jo! Let me in! Please!"

The water was up to Jo's neck. She was lost in the big tub. She let her head drop back. The bathroom was awash with green. Water stung her nose. She came up gasping.

"Jo! I'm sorry! What did I do? I shouldn't have done it. Let me in. . . . I'm going after help. Right now."

Jo turned off the tap. The crying had stopped.

"I'm okay!" she called.

"Are you coming out?"

"If you go away."

There was no answer.

"Go away, and I'll come out," Jo repeated. Her voice was unsteady. She took a deep breath. "I'm perfectly all right." She said it again. "I'm perfectly all right."

She heard Jewel's uneven step receding down the hall to the elevator. The cage door clanked open and shut. Jo scrambled out of the tub and dried herself with her slip, then dashed to her room and dumped the contents of her laundry bag on the floor. She found underwear and a blouse in the pile, and before she could be overcome by the fact that she was utterly alone, she dressed and left the building.

She was encased in a shadow, shut off from everyone. She knew that at supper. It was the only way she could explain it.

"I am fine," she reassured Jewel. "You won't tell anyone, will you?"

"Of course not."

"I'm fine. You'll see."

That night she walked for hours, avoiding the bed. Then she sat, propped on pillows. Sleep, if she slept, was like thin ice over her head. She broke up through it, rousing suddenly. Throughout the night, noises from the street rose with remarkable distinctness, and she responded with new understanding. Streetcars threw convulsions, sirens wept. Other sounds triggered waking dreams, concoctions of real and unreal. Clyde peered in the window, tapping on the glass, wearing Loring's hat and going completely bald before her eyes. It was only the wind. It had begun to sleet. In the morning she found blood on her pillow. She had scratched her face.

She got out of bed in a daze. Night and day consciousness overlapped. The shadow was still there.

No one must know. She found she could operate as if nothing were wrong at all. She could pretend to eat though she had no desire for food. She could talk without thinking. She had a conversation with a girl who was planning to be a missionary to the Jews of French Morocco.

"I didn't know there were any Jews in French Morocco," Jo heard herself say. This girl was studying Hebrew and Yiddish, Jewish customs and Messianic prophecy. Later she would take French at Northwestern. She was very excited about it.

"What about you?" she asked Jo. "Do you have a definite call?"

Jo told her she had been thinking about Afghanistan.

"Then you'll have language study too," the girl said. "And you'll need a thorough knowledge of Islam."

Later that evening Jo came close to giving up her secret. She and Jewel were in the lounge, Jewel studying and Jo pretending to, when a group of students came breezing back from the Pacific Garden Mission. They sat on the floor and talked enthusiastically until 10:00, repeating the stories they had just heard from the lips of transformed alcoholics. Jo sat with Jewel and listened. The stories were remarkable and convincing. She was moved. Tears pressed at the back of her eyes. "Oh, help me, somebody," she almost said.

The week went quickly. There was no time, really. Nights she dreamed while awake. Days she was awake in a dream. It was all the same. Asleep or awake there was a roaring in her ears. Her lips were chapped, and her cheeks were hot. She cooled them on the windowpane in her room in Van Housen. The neighborhood as she saw it from there was distressing. A young mother, trailed by four small children, walked below her. The fourth child had something the matter with him. He wavered and stumbled as he walked and could not keep up. He called for his mother to wait, but she kept right on going almost a block ahead of him. The child began to cry, and the woman ran back and shook him terribly by the arm. "Oh, don't, don't," groaned Jo, three stories above. For a second she thought, like a habit, "That woman needs Christ," and imagined the change it would make in their lives. She went out, preferring to be down there at street level.

She shivered on Chicago Avenue and wondered why she had put on her coat. What difference did it make, on or off? Habit again. Arms into sleeves. Button, keep warm.

A squadron of planes rumbled above the cloud blanket. She felt them in the sidewalk. She would finish dying soon. It was only a question of how. It could happen so fast. A car careening up on the sidewalk. The wonder was that cars stayed in the street at all. There was no safe place to stand or go.

North Clark. She had walked here with Beverly the night the Portuguese sailors whistled and teased them. Back then she would never have dreamed of walking here alone. Now it made no difference. She joined the traffic of people whose lives held dreadful secrets, trudging without interest past the bars and hangouts. In one window an effeminate Jesus floated in clouds of purple satin—a spiritualist's parlor. A woman in the doorway of a tavern made sucking noises at her. Her hair was in a sticky updo and her stockings were rolled around garters to her ankles. Our lives are equally ludicrous, thought Jo. Inside, dark figures moved against the red glow of a jukebox. White slavery crossed her mind, bringing a kind of relief. She wished it would happen. Such a monstrous evil left no questions to be answered.

Her legs were very tired, and she went back to the school.

In her room a low murmuring voice greeted her. She had left the radio on. It was on every minute now, day and night. Music tinkled faintly. Newscasts cut in. The war was out there darkly. Things were bad again. The news was on in the kitchen too. "Our boys," people said in prayers at mealtimes. "Boys." The word was a heartbreak. Sometimes she thought she heard the news in the atmosphere, without a radio, a man's voice urgently reading. They were killing at this moment. "Hand-to-hand fighting in the woods of . . . ." Hand to hand. She found herself stopped partway up the stairs from the dining room, her hand tight on the railing.

Something would happen soon. She watched for it at night. She longed for sleep. Her eyes would fall out. But the dream was always there, just behind a thin curtain. One slip and it would overtake her.

At some point in the week Miss Mackey stopped her in the hall outside Darby Chapel. "Jo, I thought I ought to tell you." She looked very serious. "This is confidential. Clyde has been sent home. I thought you deserved to know."

Miss Mackey was wearing a brown pillbox. She seemed subdued.

"I see," said Jo.

"He's had a lot of counseling lately, but he'd gotten very far behind in his work and was not feeling well. He's very upset about the war, as we all have been, of course. We thought it best he see his own doctor."

"Sure."

"Pray for him, won't you, gal?" Miss Mackey paused to take a breath. She gave Jo her penetrating look and seemed to lose her train of thought. "Jo?"

"Yes."

"Have you had a good vacation?"

"Oh, yes."

"Fine. Come and see me any time you need to."

"I will."

"Bye-bye now."

Vacation was over. Jo and Jewel moved back to Harold Hall. Karen sailed in from the suburbs with white angora mittens and boxes of food. The room was a mess. The contents of Jo's desk drawer was still at the foot of her bed and the dirty clothes in a pile on the floor.

"What happened here?" asked Karen. "It looks like a hurricane struck." She opened the window.

"Sorry about the mess," Jo said. "I've been working on papers and things."

"Did you turn them in?"

"One anyway. I guess I'll get a passing grade. . . . How was your vacation?"

"Good. Did you get some rest and have some fun? You look tired."

"It's just my cold."

Everybody was back, shouting and hugging each other. Soup had great news. Beverly and Roger Honey had written to each other every day during vacation. They were thick as pea soup, a perfect couple.

It snowed. How it snowed. All night, and still coming down hard in the morning. In opening chapel they sang "Whiter Than Snow." The singing was wonderful. Jo had forgotten about the singing in chapel. It was like a sock in the stomach. They sang "Immanuel's Land" again. Then a boy sang a tenor solo: "I've discovered the way of gladness, I've discovered the way of song!" Jo thought, I'll go on, I'll pretend, I won't give up. It was easier when the visiting speaker led in prayer. He was the pastor of a big church in California where they had to hold three services on Sunday morning to accommodate the crowds. He had a deep ringing voice, and he brayed the word "gre-e-eat" in his prayer—great God, great land of ours, great church, great task. His message was boring. The girl beside Jo took notes avidly. The subject was Jonah. Jonah's Directive,

Jonah's Disobedience, Jonah's Deliverance. The girl's notes grew in a triumph of D's.

That morning Jo registered for her new courses and bought new notebooks and texts. For a while she was almost lost in that. Like the singing, it brought the pull of the old enthusiasm, and she wanted to be lost in it. Then that faded, and she asked herself why she was doing this, hanging on and going through these motions. She ought to leave. But where would she go?

At lunch a boy with a camera moved about the dining room taking opening-day pictures for the new yearbook. He had brought four boys from the men's side over to Jo's table, which happened to have four empty places. The boys were kidding around, saying, "Please pass the *cheese*," and hogging the scene, when one of the men's proctors asked for attention over the microphone. The room grew silent.

"I have sober news," he said.

"Oh no," whispered the girl next to Jo. "The war."

"Our brother Clyde MacQuade has gone to be with the Lord."

Who? asked the girl. Who did he say? MacQuade, said a boy. He said MacQuade. You mean Clyde? Yes. What did he do? He *died*. Died? Oh no! Shh.

The proctor asked for quiet. "We have just had word from his home in Iowa that he passed away in a coma. We have no more details as yet. . . . Shall we look to God for a moment in this hour of sadness?" He prayed. He mentioned Clyde's zeal and fervor for the work of Christ. He recognized the joy that was his now, in the Savior's presence, but acknowledged the vacancy his absence would cause on earth. He told the students to think of Clyde as they continued their labors for God, and to go on with business as usual.

The meal resumed, quietly at first, then the level of noise grew to normal. The photographer took a minute to tinker with his camera. There were hushed discussions about Clyde at the table, but Jo didn't hear them. The photographer told them to pass the food to each other and "act normal." Flash! Flash! "Thanks, everybody," he said. "As you were." The boys went back to their side of the room, and Jo, benumbed, drank her milk.

After lunch she faced her unmade bed and sorted out the contents of the drawer at the foot of it. She collected the paper clips into a box and sharpened the pencils and threw away the Zipper's tract and Clyde's notes. The room smelled. She opened the windows and emptied her wastebasket and put on clean sheets. Still it smelled, foul, like the smell on Madison Street. She took her laundry bag to the basement to do later. When she came back the smell was still in the room. She brushed her teeth and washed at the sink (she could not bear to get into the tub) and changed her clothes. All she had clean was a pink blouse and her red plaid skirt. The blouse was unironed.

Karen found her sniffing her hairbrush. "What on earth are you doing?" she asked.

"It smells bad," said Jo.

"Wash it."

"I did."

Karen couldn't smell anything.

"It's in my hair too," Jo said.

"Let me see. . . . Nonsense. Your hair smells like shampoo. Oh, Jo, you're such a funny creature," Karen said. She gestured with her arms as if inviting a hug, but Jo stiffened and Karen seemed to notice. In that instant Jo decided she would tell her everything. But Karen's eyes were so clear and blue it was hard to begin, and then Karen was gone, like that, over to her own desk to set down a pile of new books.

That was my last chance, thought Jo. Whatever was coming would come soon. In a minute Karen left on an errand and Jo lay on her bed, waiting.

Dormitory sounds rose and fell. Louise and Beverly laughed at something. Then Jewel's voice blended happily with the sound of running water at the kitchen sinks. "Morning by morning new mercies I see," she sang, repeating the same words over for all the lines of the hymn. There would be a pause, and she would begin again, with her half-yodel, sloshing water and singing, "Morning by morning . . . ," just under the note.

Jo swung herself off the bed and pulled open the door. As Jewel looked up, she met her eye and slammed the door hard. Then she opened it and slammed it again.

There was silence on the floor, and someone said, "Wow." Jo charged out, passing the sinks where pink undies billowed in the suds, and ran to the library without her coat. She stayed there, too exhausted to see, until the room began to be vacated at dinnertime. "70 x 7," Soup had written in the dust. She would go back and apologize to Jewel. After that she saw no future.

It was still snowing and quite dark. When she got to the door downstairs in Van Housen, the shoveled walk was covered with a clean new coating and cars were cutting wavy ribbons along the street. It was windy. Frail white curtains draped and redraped under the streetlamps.

A group of students swung in from outside in a rush of laughter and cold air. A snowball sailed in after them and splattered on the post beside Jo. The group was just back from an assignment. They were carrying their Bibles, and girls wore their dressy hats with veils, and they were covered with snow. There was a flurry of subdued giggly excitement as they scurried to clean up the mess, and in the process several faces were washed. Then they broke up and went their ways and all that was left was a puddle of water on the floor at Jo's feet. She went out into the wind. She was so tired her legs wobbled.

There were three streetlights to pass under on her way to Harold. On the new snow their coronas assumed distinct and delicate shades of color. Something was lying in the third circle of the second light, almost not visible since it was also white, or nearly so. A piece of wrapping paper, Jo thought, but twisted so queerly, narrow and rounded and bent on one end, and with a ragged red edge across the top. She stopped and covered her eyes with her hand. It could not be, but what she was seeing was a human leg lying in the snow, as if it had been tossed from a passing car. She thought, this is the dream. But she knew it was not. She must go by it, that was what mattered, go by it and look at it squarely. Move. Look. It was a fringed woolen scarf, probably lost by one of the students she had just seen. But what remained in her mind as she entered the building and rode the creaking elevator to the fifth floor was a torn-off bleeding leg. She was terribly tired.

The floor was quiet, which was baffling. This was the time for pre-dinner noise and stampedes to the bathroom. Lights were on in three or four of the rooms, but the rooms were empty. No running water. Her own room was dark. She stood outside it looking down the hall. Where was Karen? Voices drifted faintly from somewhere. She walked toward them and stopped by Jewel's closed door.

Someone was praying, she could tell by the tone. She heard the words "her" and "she" repeated. It was Karen's voice. Jo was about to go away, feeling like an eavesdropper, when she heard her own name. Now Beverly's voice took over, her words blurred and earnest. Jo something. Jo. Then Soup. She was crying. Work in her heart, they were saying. Bring her back before it's too late. Deliver her. Jo stood outside the door. Her name reached her again and again. Jewel. Louise. They were all in there, praying for her, and she was out here. Ruth: . . . from this backslidden condition. Ruby: Break the bonds of sin. Free her from the hands of Satan. Trooly, said Ruby.

Jo kicked open the door. The seven of them were kneeling there, crowded around Jewel's bed. Their heads flew back, eyes startled, sentences cut short. They were strangers. She glared at them, waiting for the right words to boil up inside her.

"Fuck you, holy virgins, fuck you, fuck you, fuck you, holy daughters of God!"

She heard, and couldn't believe it. Those words in this hallway? Had she said them? To these people? Her voice echoed. She had. Oh, Zipper! Unzip the skin and show the world your heart! She ran to her room and locked the door and dropped to her knees by her bed, not to pray, certainly not, but to give up at last.

Someone knocked gently, then louder. "Jo!" called Karen. "Can I come in?" Jewel's voice said, "Leave her be." There was a discussion, voices whispering, worrying, with Jewel's breaking through. "No, let her alone. She'll be all right. Give her time."

The whispers faded and Jo fell asleep, all the way, deep, deep so deep she did not even hear the dinner bell.

When she awoke in the dark room, she thought days had gone by. She felt weak, as if she had been sick—but good, as if she had broken a fever. The hands of Karen's clock said 6:25. She had only slept through dinner. In a while everyone would be on their way to Moorehouse for Evening Fellowship.

She remembered her outburst in the hallway. It seemed like something she had done long ago as a child. But it was not time that had passed. It was distance. She had gone very far. How many miles? No miles. Something had happened. She had dreamed the running dream, she knew that, but she had no memory of it.

She got up, stiff and warm, and moved to the window, drawn by the quality of light outside. It was the new snow, reflecting city lights, clinging to the rooftops and sidewalks, remarkably clean. Billows of white rose and fell with the wind.

Where had she been?

The scarf had been right there, under the streetlamp, where the rings of color softly merged. It was gone.

What had she done? She had been forced to look and had come back with a fact. It was already a familiar piece of property, something she owned and would never lose or get rid of. The thing that amazed her and that she wanted to probe was this: For all its horror, the fact did not frighten her. The shadow was gone, and the smell and the roaring in her ears.

Over the Adriatic, west of Trieste. Not west or north, but into what she had to see. She had run to the end of the running. Something had waited there, as she knew it would. It. He. Terror. Here I am, she had said, panting and sick with fright, I have come to find my brother, and gave herself up to the danger.

Not quite. It was not so clear as that. Or it shifted as she thought about it. She had said, "Oh, thank goodness, it's you!" It was Loring. But it was not. Remotely, without changing at all, it was someone else, and then someone else. Daddy? Gary? Certainly not. But yes. It was somehow all of them. Mother, Yooney—even Clyde. She struggled to grasp it, staring down at the white sidewalk, but it disintegrated under the weight of remembering. What remained was only the fact and a feeling. Whoever it was had loved her. It was like a hug, long and dangerous, close to disaster and absolutely safe.

It was only a dream. She thought she would go outside, to test the fact—whatever it was—out there, and because already her eyes were turning outward, away from herself. She put her coat on, wondering if she should leave a note for Karen. Saying what—I have gone to find my ems?

The air was cold and fresh-smelling. Jo headed north, alone on the street while the other girls sang safely in the auditorium. The wind gusted against her, coming from the lake. Snow sifted into her face, cold but not cold. The fact held steady. She saw it better now out here. There was more to it than she had thought. It ached brightly. Sorrow, I baptize you, friend and enemy. Newborn. Ancient of days. Was she making any sense? Having no sense, we are sensible. Sorrowful, we rejoice. She was, she saw now, sorrowful to the core of her bones. Loring was dead. She had known it a long time. It was not a dream at all, only what she had already known.

She turned right. Under the coating of snow, in the moonlight of the streetlamps, the crumbling steps of the houses looked good. The wind followed her, raced ahead and came back, giving her white clouds to walk through. It was an illusion, of course, that this dirty street should look so good. But it was also a fact. Boys across the way, small dark figures, yelled and pelted snowballs at her. She was an easy target. Up ahead a little whirlwind danced crazily, into the gutter, off and down the sidewalk, losing itself in its own motion.

Her future spread out along the straight street as sure as any day that had passed: sad, uncertain, changing, joyful, bungling, full of dirty laundry and mistaken impulses. Irresistible and perilous. It was a risk, all of it. Dark and light together. Oh, Loring, Loring, I loved you. Do. Always will. Loving, we tremble on the brink of disaster. But to pull back—that was extinction. How she saw that! It came like a warm wave, the wholeness of it. Warm and cold. Lion lamb. Two-sided truth. She stopped.

So, was it He, all along, there in the hug? *Was* it a dream, or was it too a thing she had already known? His love, the most perilous of all. Had He ever chosen a way to show it that was not wild with danger—wrestlings and knives and fire and crosses, catching the world by surprise again and again? Immanuel. El Shaddai. Brother, parent. My name is Jo, she thought, as if in answer. I am who I am. I believe/I do not! Yes and no, uttered with the same puff of breath. But that was all right. It was whole.

How could she know so much and still know nothing? There was such a lot to sort out. But there would be time for that. Right now she owned just one undeniable fact. Loring was dead. He was gone. She gasped for breath. Standing by the black fortress wall of the Newberry Library, she sobbed, giving the rising sound to the wail of the wind and the city and not caring who heard. Snow blew into her mouth.

Then she wiped her face with her hands. Dearborn stretched south-ward, long and straight, lost in whiteness and slow, probing headlights. Her mind went down it, free and easy. She could go anywhere. She could walk the streets of Chicago all night, or she could stop for a doughnut and a glass of milk. Hunger had returned, like an old friend. She could go home. She must and surely would. She could come back. Maybe. She could do anything, not because she wanted to, but because she could.

Down Dearborn, whirling and dancing and sliding. She spread her arms for balance and she was Helen Forrest. " 'Here I go again! I hear those trumpets blow again!' " Her voice traveled, clear and loud. " 'Gonna give my all again! Takin' a chance on love!' "

Along Chicago Avenue, still singing. She was back, full circle. At the door of the auditorium she stopped. The girls were in there, all the Calvary girls, her friends. Maybe they had saved a seat for her. They would do that. She thought she might go in and sing, for a while, because she could. She was ready for people.

But there was no hurry. She waited under the peaked arch of the doorway, her hand on the knob. This moment was all that mattered, all she was required just now to give her life to. She must saturate her mind with it and never forget—that there was a time when she had been given the eyes to see and see. Because tomorrow she might only remember that there had been such a moment, a memory without involvement, as if it had happened to someone else.